A New Language, A New World

To Joan --
with gratitude
-- Nancy

Oct. 2010

A New Language,
A New World

Italian Immigrants in the
United States, 1890–1945

NANCY C. CARNEVALE

UNIVERSITY OF ILLINOIS PRESS

URBANA AND CHICAGO

Library of Congress Cataloging-in-Publication Data
Carnevale, Nancy C.,
A new language, a new world : Italian immigrants in
the United States, 1890–1945 / Nancy C. Carnevale.
p.   cm. — (Statue of Liberty–Ellis Island centennial series)
Includes bibliographical references and index.
ISBN 978-0-252-03403-9 (cloth : alk. paper)
1. Italian Americans—Social conditions—19th century.
2. Italian Americans—Social conditions—20th century.
3. Italian Americans—Languages.
4. Italian Americans—Ethnic identity.
5. Immigrants—United States—Social conditions—19th century.
6. Immigrants—United States—Social conditions—20th century.
7. Immigrants—United States—Language.
8. Sociolinguistics—United States—History
9. United States—Ethnic relations—History—19th century.
10. United States—Ethnic relations—History—20th century.
I. Title.
E184.18C29   2009
305.89451'073—dc22   2008037213

To my mother, Rosina Carnevale,
and in memory of my father, Ercole Carnevale

Contents

Acknowledgments

It's a pleasure to acknowledge the many people who have supported my work in various ways. I have to begin by thanking the nine Italian immigrant women I interviewed in the early 1990s who inspired this project, some of whom have passed on in the interim. I am grateful to them for their honesty, their trust, and their courage in sharing their stories with me.

I was fortunate to have the guidance of exceptional scholars while I was a graduate student at Rutgers University. Virginia Yans has been instrumental to the development and execution of this project and, indeed, to my career as an academic. I can't thank her enough. Joan W. Scott gave me a good deal to read and to think about as this study was taking shape. Samuel L. Baily and Ronald J. Grele offered insightful comments and encouragement.

I would like to acknowledge the History Department of Rutgers University, the International Migration Program of the Social Science Research Council with funds provided by the Andrew W. Mellon Foundation, the Rockefeller Foundation Humanities Institute sponsored by the Lower East Side Tenement Museum and UNITE!, and the National Endowment for the Humanities. All of them provided financial support essential to the completion of this book.

Archivists at the following institutions were enormously helpful: Balch Institute for Ethnic Studies; Center for Migration Studies; Gottesman Libraries at Teacher's College/Columbia University; Immigration History Research Center; Library of Congress; National Archives in College Park, Maryland, and Washington, D.C.; National Archives Regional Facility in New York City; New York City Municipal Archives; and New York Public Library.

Over the years, a number of people have read and commented on parts of the manuscript, related articles, and conference papers. Others have pointed out relevant materials or information. I am thankful for their help: Ronald H. Bayor, Andrew M. Canepa, Ron Cannatella, Kathleen Neils Conzen, Bénédicte Deschamps, Lawrence Di Stasi, Fred Gardaphé, Maria Galletta, David A. Gerber, Victor Green, Jennifer Guglielmo, Herman W. Haller, Matthew Frye Jacobson, Stefano Luconi, Jadwiga Pieper Mooney, Adele Oltman, Fraser Ottanelli, John Parascandola, Kathy Peiss, Matteo Pretelli, Gia Prima, David R. Roediger, Joseph Sciorra, Marian L. Smith, Mary Ann Trasciatti, Reed Ueda, Rudolph J. Vecoli, Peter Vellon, and Pasquale Verdicchio. Special thanks go to Donna Gabaccia, who has read the manuscript in different incarnations. Her suggestions and encouragement have been invaluable. I would also like to thank the anonymous readers at the University of Illinois Press for their comments. My colleagues at Montclair State University have been wonderfully supportive.

Some friends who double as colleagues deserve special mention. Edvige Giunta has been an astute editor and a great teacher to me. I thank her for the "voice" lessons and look forward to more. I am grateful to Mary Poole for her longtime support of this project and of me. Stacey Kinlock Sewell has been reading drafts of my chapters for far too long. I thank her for her generosity, her good sense, and her good humor. My thanks also to Suzanne Abedini, Diane Ippolito, and especially *comare/cugina* Anna Marie Toto for their many years of friendship, encouragement, and wisdom. Ivan Greenberg has seen me through the homestretch by reviewing chapters and offering sound advice and steadfast support.

To my brothers and their families, thanks for your love and support through everything. My young children, Matteo and Cristiana, tolerated the many hours I spent away from them working. I hope that in the process they learned something about the value of meaningful work and that, down the line, these pages will give them a greater understanding of where they come from. I have dedicated this book to my parents whose own histories led me to write this one.

A New Language, A New World

Introduction

It seems as if the drama of the immigrant centers in *language*.
—Leonard Covello

The first time I traveled with my family to Italy to see the village and the people that my parents had left behind when they emigrated in the 1950s, I was eleven years old. It was 1973. My older brother was a teenager and my younger brothers were eight and nine. My parents, not yet forty, were still in their prime, though my father had been ill. The family thought it would do him good to spend some time breathing his native air; the *paesani* in the United States were always touting the superiority of the air in Italy over the paltry stuff we breathed in America. The trip required him to take a lengthy break from his job running the family restaurant in New Jersey. Although he was the co-owner, he worked long hours, seven days a week. We lived modestly; the trip felt like an extravagance. This was the first visit my parents made to their hometown of Pettoranello since they had married in 1955. "Pettran," as we called it, is situated in the Apennine Mountains in the south-central region of Molise. By the time we visited, no more than a few hundred people were living there, down from close to one thousand in the 1950s: the town had been nearly bled dry through emigration. During that visit, I came to understand why so many of them had left even though they retained a deep nostalgia for their hometown.

On our month-long visit, we stayed with my maternal grandparents except for the week or so we spent touring Italy. Their old farmhouse sat alone, alongside a single-lane road in the valley beneath the mountain with the village of Pettoranello atop it. Their house was fitted with a toilet and sinks in anticipation of the running water long since promised that still had not arrived. Once, we visited an elderly widow with no one in America to support her. We sat on the few rustic chairs of wood and straw that were standing on a dirt floor. When my father gave her some dollars before we left, she wept with gratitude and shame. My mother had often tried to describe to my brothers and me the poverty she and the other *paesan*i had known in Italy, but we were always skeptical of what sounded to us like outlandish stories of hardship and deprivation, growing up as we were in a land of leisure and plenty. On this trip, she maintained an air of self-satisfaction, as if she had finally been vindicated.

One day, in the piazza up in the village, I watched my parents standing on the steps of the church wearing their colorful, suburban American sportswear as they were engulfed by a sea of old women in black dresses and kerchiefs, all of whom seemed to have the same shrunken and bent frames. The women were calling to them, using the diminutive forms of my parents' names, as if they were still the young children the women had known long ago. My mother, Rosina, became Rosinell'; my father, Ercole—Hercules—was demoted to Ercolucc'. I had never heard my parents referred to in this way in the United States. It was as if, through these old women, I was discovering another part of my parents: the people they used to be, before they left that place. The women's use of the childish versions of my parents' names recalled an entire world that predated me, both because I had not been born and because their lives had been lived in a place so far from the world I inhabited, not just in space, but in time. Yet, there I was, an American-born girl of the latter part of the twentieth century, witnessing and understanding this scene that, through the figures, the voices, and the words of the old women, seemed invested with ancient and powerful meaning.

Language figured largely on that trip. Among the many observations I made during that visit was that even though my father spoke the same language—the Pettoranese dialect—as our *paesani* in the United States, when he was among Italians elsewhere, such as when we went to a restaurant in one of the Italian cities we visited, he spoke something else. The language he used outside of Pettoranello sounded different, more pleasant, delicate, even refined. My mother's brother, who lived with my grandparents and was traveling with us throughout Italy, commented admiringly to me on how careful my father was never to let slip a word of dialect or English in those situations. As I would later learn, my father's ability to speak Italian was limited because he had not gone past the equivalent of the eighth grade in Italy. Although he had promise as a student, school was an unthinkable luxury in the terrible aftermath of the war. My father never used that elegant language with any of the *paesani* in America except during some formal, public occasion such as making a toast at a wedding or a baptism. It was on this trip that I first understood that there was more than one kind of Italian language, but that only one of them was "correct" or "pure."

On that same trip to Italy, my mother developed a peculiar form of aphasia; she seemed to forget a number of words in her dialect. Her speech was littered with many more English and Italianized English words than she normally used at home in the States, where she mainly spoke dialect.

She would speak these words in an offhand way, never bothering to explain their meanings, as if speaking them was second nature to her. So I learned something from her about the singular value that at least some immigrants attributed to the English language. Words—language—could elevate or debase a person. My brothers and I, while in Italy, spoke English to my parents as we always did. When speaking to our relatives, we wielded the dialect as best we could. My father continued speaking to us in English, and my mother spoke to us in her usual mixture of dialect along with the occasional English and Italianized English thrown in. My parents spoke to each other in dialect, adding yet another piece to our linguistic puzzle.

At the time, I took the linguistic complexities of our family life in America for granted, even if I was beginning to develop some self-consciousness about it when we were in public, outside of our ethnic enclave, among "the Americans." Nevertheless, the burgeoning awareness I developed on that trip, of the role context plays in what language people use, and of the meanings language carries beyond the manifest content of the words spoken, stayed with me.

I would have occasion to make more observations and develop many feelings about the languages I grew up with, but those early experiences form the roots of this book. Although they do not appear here, this study grew directly out of interviews I conducted for a women's history seminar in the graduate history program at Rutgers with Pettoranese immigrant women living in Princeton, New Jersey, where I was born and raised. Although the interviews were open-ended, language was a prominent theme, explicitly or implicitly, in all of them.

In researching the topic, I was surprised to see how little of the complexity and intensity of the immigrant experience of language was represented in the historical literature on immigration. The subject has received scant scholarly attention beyond the bounds of language maintenance and language shift as they relate to cultural persistence or assimilation. As even the brief examples I have presented above suggest, there is clearly more to say. I wanted to hear from the immigrants themselves and from their children, and I wanted them to be heard. How did they understand language—dialect, standard Italian, English, their own distinctive fusion of languages?

Subjective accounts written by immigrants and the second generation offer some insight into language, echoing Leonard Covello's observation on the salience of language for the immigrant. In her memoir, *Lost in Translation*, Eva Hoffman suggests the cultural dislocation involved in substituting her native Polish with the English of Canada, her adopted homeland: "The words I learn now don't stand for things in the same unquestioned way they did in my native tongue." She uses the example of the word "river" that is in Polish, "a vital sound, energized with the essence of riverhood" but becomes an empty signifier in English, "a word without an aura. It has no accumulated associations for me. . . . It does not evoke."[1] The adopted language has no resonance for the immigrant speaker and appears to lack depth. The loss or transformation of meanings that some experience in a new language can affect interpersonal relationships. As Joseph Tusiani, the bilingual poet, put it: *"Dal giorno in cui il figlio dice 'Mother' per 'mamma' e 'sky' per 'cielo', fra madre e figlio c'è già una separazione spirituale che lo studioso di linguistica non può catalogare."* (From the day when a son says "mother" for *"mamma"* and "sky" for *"cielo,"* between mother and son there is already a spiritual separation that the student of linguistics cannot catalog.)[2]

The separation between people, even within the same family, may find literal expression. In *Hunger of Memory*, Richard Rodriguez writes that, when he was growing up, his world was divided by language; Spanish was the intimate language of home and family life, and English came to embody the public world of individual achievement and its attendant isolation. Rodriguez writes movingly of his inability to bridge those two worlds or the two languages that constructed them. Once he mastered English, he could not return to Spanish or the family it represented. As he explains, "a powerful guilt blocked my spoken words . . . I'd know the words I wanted to say, but I couldn't manage to say them. I would try to speak, but everything I said seemed to me horribly anglicized."[3] Hoffman articulates the potential losses and gains involved in adopting another language best when she writes: "This language is beginning to invent another me."[4]

Language is not only important to immigrants and those who study them. It continues to be a flashpoint for controversy over immigration. In the recent past, the United States has witnessed public outrage over a Spanish language version of "The Star Spangled Banner." Various attempts to reform immigration laws at the federal level have included provisions to make English the national language and English-language proficiency a requirement for obtaining permanent resident status.[5] In the current era of multiculturalism and political correctness, when explicit expressions of racial prejudice have become taboo, immigrant languages can function as a kind of stand-in for different immigrant groups that are perceived in racial terms. This seems to be the case today with the Spanish language and Mexican migrants in particular.[6] In turn, the ability to speak standard English, preferably without any trace of a foreign accent, continues to be a recognized way of establishing an American identity.[7] This understanding of how language operates in relation to immigrants in this country helps account for the recurring flare-ups around bilingual education and the English-Only Movement, both of which were particularly explosive issues at the height of the large wave of Spanish-speaking migrants in the 1980s.[8]

Nor is language a new concern. Language has been a matter of national interest from the very beginnings of the Republic. Early Americans such as John Adams and Noah Webster believed that language held a central place in the creation of the country and the formation of a national identity. By creating a distinctively American language, they thought that Americans could more readily distinguish themselves from the British in establishing a new nation. Although not widely debated at the time, there was post-Revolutionary talk of creating an entirely new language or adopting an existing language such as Hebrew, Greek, or French to further distance Americans from the British. Webster's near fanatic devotion to perpetuating a standardized spoken and written form of American English was an expression of this desire for linguistic distinctiveness. Like John Adams, who wanted to establish a national language academy to enshrine English as the national language, Webster believed he was laying the linguistic groundwork for a new national identity.[9]

Early America's concern with establishing and perpetuating an American form of English belied the new nation's linguistic diversity. Even though Americans continue to exhibit a form of amnesia regarding the multilingual origins of their country, according to the 1790 census, one in four Americans did not speak English as a first language, independent of Native Americans who had hundreds of different languages and African slaves who arrived with their own diverse languages. Advertisements for runaway indentured servants and slaves provide some sense of just how many languages were commonly spoken. According to ads placed between 1725 and 1775, the runaways spoke a variety of languages including Dutch, French, Welsh, and Irish. In perhaps the most striking example of the tenuous sway of English in early America, German was the first language of as many as two-thirds of Pennsylvanians.[10] As literary scholars have recently noted, a large multilingual literature produced in America exists that has not been acknowledged nor included in the literary canon. Yet, with the exception of Spanish, language does not form a significant part of the current understanding of multiculturalism.[11]

Despite the centrality of language to the history of immigration as well as to the larger narrative of American history, it continues to be discussed by immigration historians, with few exceptions, as little more than a dimension of straight-line assimilation into English mono-lingualism.[12] The continued paucity of work on language and immigrants by immigration historians is particularly curious because language has been a major field of inquiry across disciplines, including history, for some time now.[13] Recent trends in immigration history cry out for greater attention to the role of language in immigrant life. The focus on ethnic identity in immigration studies has not led to a substantial historical study on the relationship between language and ethnic identity even though there is a large interdisciplinary body of literature on the subject.[14] Similarly, the interest in immigrant subjectivity has not extended to language although its critical role in the formation of subjectivity is a given.[15]

How can we account for the relative absence of historical inquiry into language in American immigrant life? It is no accident that language has been the purview of sociolinguists and linguistic anthropologists dealing with contemporary immigrant groups. Historians have been at a clear disadvantage in studying language when their subjects are, more often than not, long dead and gone, leaving behind few written records. Other barriers may have limited inquiry in this area. On a practical level, American immigration historians may not have had the language skills needed for such an inquiry. Nor can we rule out an unconscious ethnocentrism that privileges English over immigrant languages, obscuring the importance of examining the linguistic histories of non-English speakers in greater depth. On a psychological level, the subject may hit too close to home for those immigration historians, who, like myself, are second-generation ethnics. I discuss my own linguistic history and how it has influenced my scholarship elsewhere.[16]

The present moment, however, both in terms of historical paradigms as well as cultural politics, may be more suited to an examination of language than was the case in the past. Today, immigration historians discuss migration in terms of transnationalism, diaspora, and globalization. They recognize ethnicity as a social construction that is enacted and reproduced through cultural practices rather than a fixed element that can be lost, diluted, or maintained. Multiculturalism, including the acceptance of the United States as a multilingual nation, is a widely shared ideal. In this context, the possibility of conceptualizing language outside of the bounds of the assimilation model is greatly enhanced. The relaxation of disciplinary boundaries in recent years also bodes well for inquiry into the subject. Colonial historians, for example, are more likely to recognize the immigrant dimension of early America. There is increasing overlap between immigration studies and cultural studies that is expanding both subjects and sources. For their part, immigration historians have been looking outside of the narrow confines of the ethnic enclave that forms the basis of the traditional community study.[17] Nor has the need for studies of language beyond those that are keyed to assimilation gone entirely unnoticed among immigration historians. Rudolph Vecoli, for example, has noted that "linguistic assimilation has not been a 'normal' process of Anglicization, but a turbulent, sometimes violent, history of cultural and political conflict."[18]

Through a historical examination of Italians and their children from the Age of Migration through the Second World War, I hope to broaden and deepen our understanding of the meaning of language in immigrant life and in American society. This is not a study of language per se, but rather of its social, cultural, political, and personal significance over time.[19] It looks at the encounters that occurred through language between Italian immigrants and the dominant society as well as within the immigrant/ ethnic group itself. It asks how language issues play out within immigrant communities as well as between immigrant and host societies. To what extent has American government and society influenced the construction of ethnic identity through its language policies and attitudes? How does the historical moment condition the linguistic experience of immigrants? What is the role of country or region of origin, gender, and generation? What is the meaning of language—English and immigrant languages— in American life and how has it changed over time? What is the relationship between language and ethnic identity? I explore these questions and others through an examination of diverse sites and sources that allow access to different aspects of language for Italian immigrants and ethnics as well as for native-born Americans. Building on the existing sociolinguistic and sociological literature on language and ethnicity, this study incorporates insights from work on language in the humanities and social sciences, most of which is not directly related to immigrants, in fields such as linguistic anthropology and cultural studies. Reading this literature into the historical record allows for a reconfiguration of the field of inquiry into immigrant understandings of language—their own as well as English—and America's linguistic history.

One of my central concerns is how power and control are exercised through language, a predominant theme in the anthropological and related literature. Work on the "ethnography of speaking" has emphasized social inequalities between speakers, whether in colonial relations or in bureaucratic settings, such as job interviews, that are reflected in and constituted through language.[20] Immigrants encountered the dominant culture through official representatives at many points in their sojourn in the United States, from the moment of arrival onward. These contacts involved inequalities of power that were negotiated through language. I explore some of these encounters using Ellis Island and the courts as examples. Relations of power within immigrant groups were also exercised through language, with certain elements of the population able to exert control over others through their knowledge of English or standard Italian. I take on this subject through an examination of the comic songs performed by the variety theater performer Eduardo Migliaccio (aka Farfariello).

However, the impact of linguistic inequality extends well beyond relations between individuals. Because it is through the control of language that access to resources is limited and institutional power maintained, language is, in Bourdieu's terms, a form of "symbolic capital" that can create social and economic capital. Through "symbolic domination," the dominant language comes to appear inherently superior when it is legitimatized through the state and in particular through the educational system. Linguistic minorities and the working class internalize this belief to the point where the superiority of the dominant language becomes unquestionable.[21] Such an understanding helps explain the extraordinary rates of language loss in the United States that justify the description of the country as a graveyard of languages.[22] Moreover, it helps to account for the potentially serious economic and social consequences of linguistic subordination.[23]

The concept of *language ideologies* developed by linguistic anthropologists suggests a more dynamic conception of how language operates in society. Language ideologies, broadly defined as the meanings and values attached to a given language, do not necessarily determine lived social relations in a unidirectional manner. Linguistic practices "on the ground" inform ideologies. Language ideologies then are formed in a social context marked by power differentials and inequalities that have real consequences for language use.[24] These understandings of the ideological functioning of language inform this study. Other disciplines provide their own insights into language as it relates to American immigrant life. For example, performance studies suggest the ways that subordinate groups can subvert totalizing language ideologies by playing with nonstandard forms of oral language in "in-group" settings. The critical insights into how language reproduces gendered relations of power and gendered identities and how language can be used to rework them are also relevant.[25]

Work in sociolinguistics and the sociology of language has dealt most explicitly with language and immigrants and, specifically, the relationship between language and ethnic identity. Beginning with his seminal study, *Language Loyalty in the United States* (1966), Joshua Fishman has been the leading figure in this area. Fishman has found (and other sociolinguists would agree) that language and ethnic identity are strongly linked, "whether indexically, implementationally, or symbolically," but not all ethnic groups in the United States or elsewhere experience the link between language and ethnic identity in the same ways. Social circumstances condition the degree to which ethnic groups connect the two. Works that provide substantial historical context, such as Einar Haugen's early full-length study of bilingualism among Norwegian Americans, also suggest the danger of making generalizations and the need for historically grounded studies of language and immigrants.[26]

On a subjective level, native speakers of minority languages often consider language as an "essential or inborn (therefore 'essentialist') characteristic of 'the people'" that is constitutive of both the individual and the larger group culture.[27] However, sociolinguists have also found that the ethnic language is not essential to the transmission or maintenance of ethnic identity and culture. Even if not actively used, language has been found to serve a symbolic function in transmitting ethnicity.[28] Although mine is not a study of language maintenance, language shift, language policy, or bilingualism—the traditional concerns of sociolinguists—I look at some of these issues to get at the various meanings attached to language or the language politics of a particular historical moment. For example, my discussion of the identity politics evident in the overlapping language maintenance efforts of both Italian American leaders and the Italian fascist government in 1930s and '40s New York City illustrates the different interpretations of Italian American identity in relation to language usage. Rather than establish any model, the Italian case in America illustrates the instability of the relationship between language and ethnic identity and its dependence on historical context.

Although this study largely deals with language in American immigrant life as a social phenomenon, I am interested in how the individual experiences language—the degree to which language informs a personal conception of ethnic identity as well as issues related to immigrant consciousness and thought. The psychological implications of living in another language is a subject that has not been explored to the degree one would expect given the number of immigrants and exiles among the great psychoanalysts. Indeed, it may have been precisely the resonance that the subject held for many of the early prominent psychoanalysts who were themselves European multilinguals that prevented them from addressing the topic.[29] Freud, who analyzed patients in French and English in addition to his native German, was cognizant of the role of language in individual psychology. Even though he did not treat the subject in any sustained way, as this excerpt from an unpublished letter reveals, he was well aware of the costs of abandoning one's native language: "Perhaps you missed out the one point which the emigrant experiences so particularly painfully. It is—one can only say: the loss of the language in which one lived and thought and which one will never be able to replace with another, for all one's efforts at empathy."[30] A systematic exploration of the psychology of language is beyond the scope of my project, but it is an underlying concern that surfaces, for example, in my discussion of immigrant and second-generation writings.

By expanding the study of language and immigrants beyond the role of English in the process of Americanization, I do not mean to abandon the issue of assimilation in American life. Our understanding of assimilation can be informed and refined through a consideration of language and immigrants within a broader context. Earlier conceptions of assimilation assumed that immigrants and their children were subsumed by a monolithic, homogeneous Anglicized culture. Although this model has been substantially reformulated over the years, the implicit conception of language in immigrant life remains largely unchanged.[31] Specifically, sociologists have posited a model of generational linguistic change as part of the assimilation process: the first generation uses the native language almost exclusively with only a rudimentary knowledge of English, and the second generation is bilingual to various degrees, with at least the ability to understand and perhaps even to speak the language of their parents. This group experiences a complete language shift to English by the time they reach adulthood, although private usage of the native tongue in the household of origin may persist. By the third generation, the immigrant language is lost. Interest in the language on the part of the third generation may resurface only as part of an attempt to construct a symbolic ethnic identity. This model has been used to explain the fate of European languages in America from the wave of "new immigrants" at the turn of the twentieth century as well as the linguistic experience of more recent immigrant groups including Spanish-speaking and Asian-language groups. Sociologists and sociolinguists attribute the relatively rapid and complete shift to English to the economic and social advantages that accrue to English speakers, along with the pervasive association of English with the dominant American culture. The clearly elevated status that English enjoys above all other languages is also significant.[32]

Recent studies of language and immigrants are refining the generational model and challenging the common equation of language shift with straight-line assimilation and language maintenance with the retention of ethnic identity. Other factors condition outcomes regarding language maintenance and language shift in addition to generation, such as the family's socioeconomic status, parental values, and the specifics of parental nationality. Nor does the model hold across the board; there are differences in language shift and language maintenance between national and linguistic groups.[33] Data based on interviews with second-generation youth indicate that lack of facility in the language of the immigrant generation is not necessarily a marker of cultural assimilation. Even in the absence of knowledge of the parental language, the second generation can identify with its national (e.g., Mexican American) or pan-national (e.g., Hispanic or Latino) group of origin. The way youths in one study self-identified was found to have more to do with perceived discrimination or limitations to opportunities for social and economic mobility than with whether or not they speak the language of their parents.[34] Nor is language fluency coterminus with a native sensibility or understanding of a given culture. Second-generation youth with limited fluency in the parental language can nevertheless have a direct knowledge of and identification with that culture. However, in some cases, language may be a more salient feature of ethnic identity than color, contrary to the American presumption that race trumps all other categories of identity.[35] This historical study supports the notion that multiple configurations are possible in the relationship between language and immigrant/ethnic identity and much depends on the historical specifics of each situation.

The generational model of language change obscures other points. As my chapter on Farfariello illustrates, first-generation Italian immigrants spoke a creolized dialect that consisted of a fusion and elaboration of standard Italian, Italian dialects, English, and Italianized English words. This idiom was often more commonly used among the first generation than dialect alone and certainly more than was English. Additionally, language learning took place in an inter- and intraethnic context. Immigrants were not only exposed to English for the first time, but to other immigrant languages as well, including, in the Italian case, different regional dialects and standard Italian.[36]

The phenomenon of code-switching—the use of two or more languages in the same linguistic event—further complicates the generational model of linguistic assimilation. Code-switching is used to assert a specific identity, to signal in-group status, or to position oneself in a particular way with relation to the addressee. Second-generation ethnic Americans are most likely to have the ability to use elements of both English and the language of their parents, even if they are not fluent in the latter. Sometimes it is an imperfect knowledge of the parental language that requires code-switching to English to express concepts that may be unique to the American context but that the speaker cannot otherwise convey. In some cases, it is precisely those with a mastery of both languages who integrate them with the greatest verbal dexterity. In the case of the first generation, who may have limited fluency in English, code-switching allows them to claim some knowledge of and the attendant status associated with the dominant language. Code-switching is both a reflection and a performance of the hybrid identities of immigrants and ethnics.[37]

As the example of code-switching suggests, the process of forging a new identity in America involved more than simply becoming subsumed by an all-pervasive American language and identity. Immigrants and ethnics created entirely new identities in part through language. It should come as no surprise then that language was a major site of struggle. For example, my analysis of the efforts of Italian American leaders to teach standard Italian to largely working-class second-generation children reveals that English was not the only language used to Americanize ethnics. In keeping with recent scholarship, my work also confirms the transnational character of Italian migration. Returning to my example here, second-generation youth in New York City felt the pull of Fascist Italy no less than that of Americanizing leaders within their own community as they negotiated their identities in America.[38]

Language then is a dynamic issue that cannot be completely accounted for through a single model. For example, in certain language communities today with high concentrations of foreign language speakers who are also relatively isolated, the immigrant language can be maintained for several generations. Spanish speakers in the Los Angeles area, who number over three million, are an example of one such group.[39] This suggests a different linguistic trajectory than the generational model of language shift, one with implications for how these groups construct their identities. As part of a historical approach to language and immigrants, this study examines key points in the history of Italian immigrants and language in the United States, such as the Americanization movement of the early twentieth century and the Second World War. By highlighting such pivotal moments, I call attention to the ways in which historical circumstances condition linguistic experience.

A brief consideration of Yiddish and the Italian dialects that were brought to America at roughly the same time highlights the need for a historical approach to the subject of language and immigrants. Although the languages that eastern European Jews and southern Italians brought with them were blended with English, there are important differences in the histories and particularly in the reception of these immigrant idioms by Americans. Yiddish incorporated English in various ways, but for reasons unique to the Yiddish language, American English borrowed from it as well. This level of reciprocity did not occur with Italian. As a result, Yiddish has attained a degree of acceptance through familiarity, at least in major urban centers with large Jewish populations, such as New York. Even so, Yiddishisms long ago acquired a comical status that reflects a devaluation of the language and its speakers.[40]

The blending of Yiddish and English did not happen unconsciously; the Jewish community actively debated the changes to the language as they were occurring, demonstrating an appreciation of the relationship between language and culture that was not evident in the Italian case. Indeed, Yiddish was by definition a diaspora language that served to unite disparate groups of Jewish immigrants. Even when it was not the spoken language of the community, Yiddish "preserved the quintessence of the memories and perceptions of a people aware of its history, its 'chosen,' extrahistorical status, and its Diaspora predicament."[41] It stood in marked contrast to the fractured versions of Italian brought to the United States by immigrants that reflected, "the endemic division in the old country between the language of a small elite and that of the masses."[42] The different trajectories of these immigrant languages and the meanings attached to them by both immigrants and the host society reflect in part the premigration histories of each group. Although this is not a comparative study, I do occasionally draw comparisons between Italians and other groups.

The book also engages ongoing debates among historians regarding the construction of ethnic identity. Since the 1960s, the traditional assimilationist position has been under siege by immigration scholars who began focusing on the persistence of ethnicity and later on the construction or "invention" of ethnic identity.[43] The latter position argues that ethnicity is chosen and formed by the ethnic group itself in negotiations within the immigrant group and between immigrants and the host society. Rather than persist over time, ethnic identities are continually renegotiated and reenacted. The role of language in the construction and perpetuation of ethnic identity has not, however, been sufficiently considered. Nor do immigrants choose identities unfettered by their environment. As this case study demonstrates, immigrants and ethnics negotiated identities within an often-coercive American society, and that negotiation is both evident in and carried out through linguistic practices.

In addition to the issue of assimilation, the book encompasses several other areas of interest to historians. Recent work has drawn attention to popular confusion over the racial positioning of eastern and southern Europeans in the early years of the twentieth century.[44] This study builds on the existing scholarship, illustrating the role that language played in those years in the perception of race and national belonging. According to studies on the evaluation of foreign accents by social psychologists and sociologists, the relationship between language and race has contemporary significance as well. This work demonstrates that nonnative American English speakers are evaluated according to the listener's attitudes toward the perceived group, region, or country to which the speaker is presumed to belong. The attributions given to speakers of high- or low-status accents in turn influence attitudes and behaviors toward linguistically distinct speakers and can contribute to the formation of raced identities.[45]

By examining language, we can also better understand the diversity of immigrant life within a given diaspora population. Emigrants in the Italian diaspora had different linguistic histories. Italians who immigrated to Argentina, for example, entered a very different linguistic context than their American counterparts. The nature of the immigration—northern Italians with higher rates of literacy than the largely illiterate or semiliterate southerners who poured into the United States, the similarities between Spanish and Italian, the relative ease with which Italians were able to integrate into Argentinean economic and social life compared to the American case, all contributed to a different history with language.[46]

Finally, a study of language can illuminate the role of gender in immigrant communities, as well as the symbolic and functional roles of women within the immigrant family in negotiating American life. Linguists and sociolinguists have found marked differences between the speech of men and women, with implications for differences in the ways women construct ethnic identities for themselves and their families. For example, studies of lower class women indicate that women are often assigned or assume the dual functions of elevating themselves through use of the standard language as well as maintaining the traditional forms of the culture including local dialects. My chapter on Italian American immigrant theater treats the gendered meanings the immigrants attached to the languages they used and encountered as well as the linguistic roles women were expected to play for the community.[47]

The Italian migration to the United States is particularly apt for a case study of language and immigrants. The breadth and magnitude of this migration that extended into the 1970s when Italians constituted the second largest linguistic minority in the United States—second only to Spanish speakers— provides an excellent opportunity to examine language and immigrants over time.[48] Southern Italians were initially perceived as darkerskinned at a time when eugenics, Social Darwinism, and nativism pervaded American society. The Italian example then allows for an examination of the relationship between language and the construction of racial identities in America. Southern Italians overall also had lower rates of English language fluency than other immigrant groups, and their lack of facility with English figured prominently into popular stereotypes.[49] There is also evidence that language may be a particularly important ethnic marker to Italians.[50] In addition, as a European immigrant group whose existence carried over into the era of bilingualism, a study of language and Italian immigrants lays the groundwork for future comparisons between the linguistic experience of older immigrant groups with that of more recent non–English-speaking groups. These features of Italian immigration make this a case study with potentially broad implications.

The book is divided into two parts. Part 1 provides the context for understanding the linguistic history of Italian Americans. The first chapter is an overview of the politics of language in Italy and illustrates the divisions within Italian society—between the North and the South understood in racialized terms and between upper and lower classes—that occurred in part along linguistic lines. Language has long been a loaded issue in Italy, one that followed the immigrants to the United States where they not only encountered English, but other Italian dialects. "The Italian Languages in Italy and in America" considers how Italians used their languages in the New World, including the immigrant idiom developed by the first generation.

The second chapter presents the American context that the immigrants encountered upon arrival. It begins with a brief history of language in America that included virulent linguistic xenophobia along with periods of greater tolerance. During the Age of Migration, except for a few voices to the contrary, immigrant languages were devalued and the transformative powers of the English language were exalted. This chapter considers how

American conceptions of immigrant languages and the perceived limited ability of southern Italians to learn English reinforced the prevailing popular uncertainty regarding their racial identity. This discussion is situated within a consideration of the Americanization campaigns of the period, the 1917 Literacy Test, and the educational practices of the New York City Board of Education. My analysis reveals the importance placed on knowledge of the English language as a criterion for full membership in a racially constructed American society.

Part 2 examines language among Italian immigrants and ethnics within specific contexts and at particular historical moments. The four chapters are organized thematically, and the meaning of language varies accordingly; each source allows for an exploration of a different facet of language. Chapter 3, organized around the theme of translation, examines three sites: Ellis Island, the courtroom, and the English and Italian writings of first- and second-generation Italian Americans. The chapter explores the immigrant perspective on translation in the literal sense of the consequences of having to rely on translation from one language to another as well as the figurative translation of the self through the encounter with another language, raising the question of the relationship between language and identity. Chapter 4 analyzes the lyrics of comic songs written in the Italian immigrant idiom and performed by Farfariello. These song lyrics expressed problems of immigrant life as problems of communication, often between the sexes, and over the issue of Americanization, suggesting the centrality and complexity of language in the immigrant imagination. The identity politics of language maintenance forms the subject of chapter 5. During the interwar years, New York City's Italian American leaders and Italy's fascist government presented competing notions of Italian American identity through their language maintenance programs. While leading Italian American figures, notably Leonard Covello, attempted to make Americans out of the second generation by first creating a fictitious, pan-Italian identity through the teaching of standard Italian, the Italian government language maintenance efforts encouraged a fervent identification with Italian fascism.

The last chapter in part 2 considers the conflicted meanings that Italian took on during the war years when Italian Americans were regarded with suspicion once Italy entered the war. While the Federal Bureau of Investigation scrutinized Italian American individuals and organizations that used the Italian language, such knowledge became a means of proving national loyalty for Italian Americans chosen to serve in separate Italian divisions of the Office of Strategic Services (OSS). The popular Italian American performer

Louis Prima, who achieved fame with novelty songs that incorporated Italian and Italian American expressions, represented a limited assertion of *italianità* within this ambiguous environment. The chapter argues that, by the end of the war, Italian Americans had achieved a new level of acceptance in American society, but at the cost of a constrained expression of ethnic identity, including the erosion of Italian language usage. The epilogue reflects on the current linguistic landscape in America.

Each chapter examines language and Italian immigrants in a different context and draws attention to different issues. As a whole, this study illustrates the process of creating (and recreating) an ethnic identity in the United States, a process that is carried out through language and is reflected in struggles over language. By looking at language from the perspectives of both the immigrant and the dominant cultures, often in interaction with each other, I draw attention to the sometimes coercive context within which immigrants have negotiated identities. The book expands our understanding of linguistic transformations in America and what they mean for ethnic identity along with the whole process of assimilation. Moreover, by focusing on language, this study provides insights into the subjective experience of immigrant life. As a case study providing a partial portrait of one immigrant group's linguistic history, it seeks to contribute to our understanding of the meanings attached to language and immigrants in American life.

Although some might find it odd to see Benjamin Franklin and other quintessentially American characters sharing these pages with Farfariello and Rosa Cassettari, the immigrant storyteller, the juxtaposition of these figures is not only valid, but essential to one of my underlying concerns: to integrate the history of immigration with the larger narrative of American history. The story of Italians forms only one piece of America's larger linguistic history, a history that has been integral to American conceptions of nation, race, and ethnicity. A focus on language in the ways that I propose holds the possibility of incorporating immigrants into the national history without erasing them by positioning them within the totalizing narrative of assimilation.[51]

PART ONE

ONE

The Italian Languages in Italy and America

> A language is a dialect that has an army and a navy and an air force;
> that is the only difference really from a linguistic point of view.
> —Gianrenzo Clivio, sociolinguist

Italian immigrants who came to America during the era of mass migration brought with them a long and complicated linguistic history that would inform their experiences of language in the New World. Language was a central preoccupation of the literate classes that predated the establishment of the Italian state by several centuries. As the title of this chapter suggests, there was no single Italian language in Italy or in America. The Italian peninsula was and is home to numerous dialects. What came to be known as Italian is the Florentine dialect that eventually achieved the status of a language. For centuries prior to the de facto establishment of a national language and the slow process of its diffusion, the number and distinctiveness of the dialects spoken throughout Italy made it difficult and sometimes impossible for people from different areas to communicate. The lengthy period of debate beginning in the sixteenth century on the need to establish a common language along with the problems created by the profusion of dialects—*la questione della lingua*—emblazoned the subject of language onto the Italian national consciousness.

Italy's language question was further complicated by matters of class and race. Because standard Italian was known for centuries to only a small, elite segment of Italian society, the issue of language was infused with a powerful class dimension. A deep North-South divide has long pitted a more developed North against a socially and economically lagging South; northerners, along with some southern intellectuals, believed southerners were inherently inferior to northerners. This longstanding split lent the southern dialects an added racial stigma. The association of standard Italian with the educated elite and of the southern dialects with a racially lesser people exercised a stranglehold on the linguistic imagination of the immigrants. Southern Italians arrived in America with an acute awareness of their linguistic inferiority that only compounded their struggles with language acquisition in their adopted land. The predominantly southern Italian immigrants, possessing command of only their local dialects, found themselves isolated not only from Americans, but also often from their fellow Italians. They compensated by developing their own idiom, an Italo-American dialect, that enabled them to communicate with other Italians while forming and expressing a new identity.

Language and Nation in Italian History

Italy was late to the join the ranks of European states, achieving unification through the political and military struggle known as the *Risorgimento* only in 1861. The political, cultural, and economic fragmentation that characterized the area for centuries prior to unification was mirrored by the plethora of dialects spoken throughout the peninsula. During the rule of the Roman Empire, a variety of peoples from both Indo-European and non–Indo-European linguistic groups coexisted. The Romans were tolerant of other languages and the various ethnolinguistic groups remained culturally and linguistically independent of Rome. That Roman elites along with some slaves were bilingual in Latin and Greek both reflected and supported the linguistic diversity of the Roman Empire.[1]

Other political and natural features of the Italian peninsula contributed to its exceptional linguistic diversity. Exercising its influence from Rome, the Catholic Church reinforced existing political and related ethnolinguistic divisions on the Italian peninsula at various times. In 323, the Council of Nicea favored the continuation of Roman administrative partitioning that invested power locally. The lack of a political center for so many years contributed to the linguistic diversity of the area. Later, with the Council of Tours in 813, the church sanctioned the use of local idioms by priests to communicate with the lay public, further contributing to the spread of vulgar forms of Latin, the precursors of the Italian dialects. In the ongoing absence of a centralized government, there was no entity to impose a standardized language, nor did other institutions or traditions exist that might have led to the rise of a dominant language such as elementary level schooling or an emphasis (as in Protestant countries) on reading the bible and other sacred texts. The rise in the late Middle Ages of powerful city-states accorded prestige to the speech of each one, thus accentuating language differences between rival political and cultural centers. Geography too played its part. The natural barriers within Italy resulted in the isolation of individual communities, contributing to the development of numerous and distinct languages. At the same time, its accessibility by sea and through mountain passes made Italy an inviting target for invaders who introduced their own linguistic influences beginning with the fall of the Roman Empire.[2]

It was not until the fourteenth century that the roots of what would become modern Italian were established in Florence. The literary flourishing of vernacular works, notably by the legendary triumvirate of Petrarch, Boccaccio, and Dante, created the basis for a written *lingua franca*, if only for Italian elites. Dante, who self-consciously determined to write his *Divinia Commedia* in Florentine to help establish it as a common vernacular, was particularly influential. Even though fourteenth-century Florentine eventually became the basis for the standard language, the debate on which language to use as a common medium for communication did not begin in earnest until the 1500s, prior to which most administrative and legal documents, as well as literary and scholarly works continued to be written in Latin. The sixteenth-century majority view, represented by the Venetian humanist scholar and poet Pietro Bembo, gave preference to fourteenth-century written Florentine as opposed to then contemporary Florentine. He and others believed that literary language should not resemble everyday speech. The Florentine dialect was chosen because it was better understood than other dialects and was closer to Latin, making it comprehensible to at least the elite classes throughout Italy. The economic dominance that Florence enjoyed from the fourteenth through the sixteenth centuries also helped solidify its position as the linguistic capital of what would become Italy.[3] Already by the end of the sixteenth century, Florentine had become the language of Rome, the largest and most cosmopolitan of the Italian cities of the time. Yet throughout the rest of Italy, Italian was little known. As late as the period of unification, only between 2.5 and 12 percent of the newly established nation's entire population knew Italian.[4]

The absence of a common language at the time of unification and the continued use of the dialects meant that the *questione della lingua* would become central to the new nation.[5] Italy's intellectuals hotly debated the issue of language in the early years of the *Risorgimento*. Author Alessandro Manzoni stimulated these debates when he turned the focus away from the written fourteenth-century Florentine used by Italy's elites to the Florentine language as it was spoken in his day. Manzoni argued that *uso* (usage) should take precedence above all and, given the historical association of the Italian language with Florence, contemporary Florentine was best suited to become the national language, uprooting the *malerba dialettale* (dialect weeds). His novel, *I promessi sposi*, was written in nineteenth-century Florentine and served as "a kind of linguistic gospel" during the era of unification.[6]

The opposing view was represented by Graziadio Isaia Ascoli, a language scholar who contended that from a purely historical perspective, Italy already had a national language in the written fourteenth-century Florentine and it would be artificial to impose any other language or version of the original. Nor was the eradication of dialects in favor of the national language necessary or desirable. Ascoli and others maintained that the dialects were part of the nation's cultural heritage and could coexist with a national language.[7] By the 1880s, Manzoni's detractors had won. The language of Dante effectively became the language of state and civil society, although the Italian language was never enshrined in law, and historically, Italy has exhibited a tolerance of linguistic minorities that was formalized with the 1948 constitution.[8]

Yet Italy's language question did not end with the designation of a standard language. The vast majority of the population continued to use their dialects and remained unable to speak Italian, as the Florentine dialect came to be known, although some had a passive knowledge of the language. Outside of Rome and Tuscany, even the well-educated continued to use elements of dialect along with local pronunciations.[9] This situation ensured that the issue of language would continue to be a national preoccupation for years to come.

Over time, the social, economic, and political changes wrought by unification contributed to the spread of Italian and the weakening of the dialects. Building on the introduction of limited free primary education in 1859, the Coppino Act of 1877, which mandated elementary school education for children over the age of nine, helped to diffuse the language, albeit slowly and unevenly. Industrialization led to the rapid growth of cities that drew immigrants from all over Italy. The need for people from diverse areas to communicate encouraged the use of Italian. The creation of a national bureaucracy and a standing army further encouraged the abandonment of dialects in favor of the national language. The expansion of the press and the growth and availability of theater and other forms of mass entertainment that later included television and radio further eroded dialect use in favor of Italian.[10]

Although internal migration facilitated the diffusion of Italian, the vast emigration of Italians during the Age of Migration slowed its spread. Ironically, the emigration of those who were least likely to know the language—poor, young, illiterate men, and especially southerners—slowed the diffusion of Italian by removing the emigrants from Italian society before they had the opportunity to learn the standard language and contribute to its spread. In other ways, however, emigration stimulated the spread of Italian. The remittances men sent home to their families helped revitalize rural areas, especially in the South. Schools benefited from this economic stimulation, resulting in more children learning Italian. In addition, the numerous returning immigrants from the United States, having experienced firsthand the hardships of illiteracy while away from home, came back to Italy with a newfound sense of the importance of education. Enrollment in adult and elementary schools boomed in the early 1900s as the emigrants returned to Italy to establish themselves with money earned abroad or to sojourn temporarily in their homelands before emigrating again in search of work. In Sicily, for example, elementary school enrollment rose from 54.5 percent around 1901 to 73.5 percent just five years later, and female enrollment in both Sicilian elementary and adult schools rose significantly as women were faced with new responsibilities and opportunities in the wake of male migration. The areas that saw the greatest numbers of emigrants—including most southern provinces—saw the greatest reductions in the rates of illiteracy. The United States' continual threat to impose a literacy test on immigrants, beginning in the 1880s, spurred the Italian government to offer literacy classes that were attended by potential emigrants.[11] Although knowledge of the standard language in and of itself invariably contributed to the decline in the use of dialects, the schools were self-consciously engaged in eradicating dialect usage despite voices of opposition. Even if the schools were supposed to promote the use of Italian at the expense of the dialects, in practice, teachers still tended to use their own dialects in the classroom. This situation prompted Manzoni's proposal to send teachers from Tuscany throughout Italy.[12]

Even though unification created the conditions for the diffusion of Italian, there were many obstacles. By one estimate, at the time of unification, fully 31 million of the newly formed nation's 35 million inhabitants did not know the national language.[13] Even with the implementation of compulsory elementary education and the formal attempt to teach Italian, most people did not acquire Italian unless they went beyond the elementary level, an uncommon practice at the time given the grinding poverty with which most

Italian families had to contend. A mere 4 percent of the population attained postelementary education in 1911 and even as late as 1931, only 15 percent of the population had a high school education. The schools were underfinanced for years and the absence of an overarching bureaucratic entity to oversee and implement the diffusion of Italian ensured that the process would be slow and inconsistent.[14] Indeed, Italian only became a mother tongue to large numbers of Italians beginning with those born after 1950. Even today, despite the widespread diffusion of the standard language, many Italians are bilingual with fluency in both their local dialects and Italian.[15]

Language continued to be high on the national agenda well into the twentieth century. During the Fascist era, language figured prominently in both the internal and external fascist goals and programs from the 1920s until Mussolini's fall in 1943. The imposition of a national language—fourteenth-century Florentine with a Roman pronunciation—was crucial to the Fascist project of fostering nationalistic fervor. To this end, the government promulgated a mythologized linguistic history that claimed a direct link between Latin, the language of ancient Rome that Mussolini idealized, and Dante's written Florentine. In her study of linguistic policies under Fascism, Gabriella Klein notes three forms of linguistic interventions within Italy during the reign of Fascism. First, in an effort to standardize the language, the government attempted to do away with the use of dialect or regionalisms of any kind, particularly in the schools. Second, language was linked to nationalism as evidenced by efforts to linguistically assimilate ethnic minorities within Italy and a generalized hostility toward minority languages. Finally, a kind of linguistic xenophobia erupted. An example was the government policy of dubbing foreign films into Italian so that Italians would not be exposed to any outside languages, an unfortunate practice that continues to this day. Even the names of non-Italian actors were Italianized. Fred Astaire, for example, was known to Italians as Federico Astorio. For all of Mussolini's efforts, however, dialect usage did not decline significantly.[16]

Initially, the Fascist repudiation of the dialects was shared by the Italian Left, with some notable exceptions. Antonio Gramsci, a linguist by training and a southerner who was born and raised in Sardinia, appreciated the need for a standard language. He believed that dialect speakers, who had little or no knowledge of the standard language, necessarily held parochial worldviews and so were limited in their ability to understand ideas that originated in a language of the larger world. Moreover, the lack of a common language facilitated the exploitation of the northern proletariat and southern peasants who the elites of both areas were able to set against each other. Despite his belief in the need for a common language, he rejected the Manzonian idea of superimposing an essentially foreign language onto dialect speakers. In the Italian case, the standard language based on the Florentine dialect also reinforced the dominance of the industrial North over the less developed South. Rather than forcing the use of a literary Florentine that was shaped by and that expressed a particular lived experience that is unknowable to those outside of that linguistic domain, Gramsci believed in the possibility of forming a new "normative grammar" in the interplay between existing languages (dialects) within Italy. In this way, a common language would emerge directly from the people, though it is not clear how he proposed to overcome the considerable barriers to such linguistic intermixing in Italy.[17]

In later years, the Italian Left would come to celebrate the cultural diversity represented by the dialects. The history of Fascist opposition to dialect usage has given a leftist tint to the idea of celebrating Italy's diverse dialects since Mussolini's fall, particularly in northern cities. Leftist filmmaker Pier Paolo Pasolini, for example, wrote poetry in the Friulian dialect. However, the positive reappraisal of the dialects has largely been limited to the North; in the South, dialects remain stigmatized to the extent that parents discourage their children from speaking them. Beginning in the late 1980s, however, some southern Italian rappers began reclaiming the dialects in an act of cultural assertion.[18]

Language and Race in the Italian South

During the period of unification, Italy was not alone in its preoccupation with language or in its association of language with race. In the eighteenth century, language was linked with nationhood. This idea reverberated in intellectual circles throughout Europe, but was most forcefully articulated by Johann Gottfried von Herder. The notion that language defined a people and formed the basis for an "imagined community" exerted a strong influence on nineteenth-century European nationalist movements, including the Italian *Risorgimento*.[19] Language was a topic of purely scholarly concern as well. A heightened interest in language is evident in nineteenth-century philological studies of ancient or obscure languages, and particularly in the search for a common linguistic origin. Implicit (and often explicit) in the Romantic and philological views of language was an evaluation of languages—and the people who spoke them—as civilized or uncivilized. Language became a reflection of the level of development of nations or "races" as they were commonly referred to in the nineteenth century.[20]

The *Risorgimento* may have unified the country politically, but in the minds of Italians and non-Italians alike, Italy was divided into North and South to the detriment of the latter. The evaluations of the southern dialects must be seen in this context. The idea of the Italian South and all things southern as "other" to the rest of Italy was substantially formed in the aftermath of the *Risorgimento*. The stereotypes of the South that had been generated by northern and some southern intellectuals as well as by foreigners in the decades leading up to unification were subsequently solidified and essentialized. Ironically, the country was split in half only after it had been politically unified. The perceived economic, political, and social "backwardness" of the South, its patriarchal culture, and its association with organized crime were collectively designated "the Southern question" or more ominously, "the Southern problem." Northern and southern Italian intellectuals scoured the region to document the social conditions they encountered for a largely northern audience. In the positivist tradition, these *meridionalisti* believed that accurate information would help the new government better address the very real problems of the region, including poverty, illiteracy, and brigandage. Although many of the *meridionalisti* were sympathetic to the situations and the people they found, they inadvertently created the foundation for a stereotype of the southerner as indolent, criminally minded, and incapable of social or political organization; in short, intellectually and morally inferior. Their interpretation of the South was juxtaposed against a North that excelled in every category. This view of the South was not limited to Italians, nor was the South's difference articulated in relation to northern Italy alone. Europeans outside of Italy participated in a discourse that pitted southern Italy with near savage traits against a civilized, rational Europe. Indeed, according to nineteenth-century European observers, the South occupied a liminal position between Europe and Africa, with the obvious accompanying racial overtones. As Augusten Creuzé de Lesser, a French traveler and administrator under Napoleon, commented on his tour of Italy between 1801 and 1802: "Europe ends at Naples and ends there quite badly. Calabria, Sicily, all the rest belongs to Africa."[21]

The burgeoning field of criminal anthropology (also known as positivist criminology), led by Cesare Lombroso and later disciples such as Enrico Ferri and Alfredo Niceforo, bolstered popular notions of southern inferiority by lending the weight of scientific authority to the southern mythology. These authors posited an essentialist image of the southerner as racially distinctive, more prone to criminal behavior, and inherently inferior to the Italians of the North, although the classifications used by Lombroso and others demonstrated great inconsistencies, sometimes even within the same works of individual authors. In keeping with broader Social Darwinist currents of the time, they viewed criminal deviancy in racial terms. Cranial measurement and physical traits such as skin color along with visible biological abnormalities were considered indicative of moral and psychological failings that could predict the likelihood of criminal behavior. Language and other cultural features provided for Lombroso further evidence of regressive characteristics that signaled a retarded evolutionary development. He notes in his 1862 writings, which were based on a three-month stay in Calabria, that the local dialects, like the behaviors and folklore of large segments of the Calabrian population, were manifestations of atavistic traits.[22]

In general, southerners were considered more prone to violent crimes or, as Ferri described them in a lecture given in Naples in 1901, "the crimes due to hot blood and muscle" as opposed to crimes against property that characterized the North. He attributed this division in part to "racial character." Similarly, Ferri accounted for the difference in levels of violent crime among the southern provinces to the various racial influences at work in each: "Graecian blood" in Catania, Messina, and Syracuse contributed to the industriousness of these populations, but the "Saracen" strain in the western and southern provinces of Sicily were responsible for the prevalence of violent crimes in those areas.[23]

Niceforo went the furthest of the criminal anthropologists of his day in asserting distinct racial differences between northern and southern Italians. He proposed, for example, that southerners, due to their lack of discipline and intelligence, required "energetic and at times dictatorial action," in contrast with the people of the North who were fit for liberty. The following assessment of the South by Niceforo was typical. He claimed that there were really "two Italies." In contrast to the "more fresh, and more modern" North, "the Italy of the South shows a moral and social structure reminiscent of primitive and even quasibarbarian times, a civilization quite inferior." *L'Italia barbara contemporanea* (Contemporary Barbarian Italy), the title of a study of southern Italy, encapsulates his assessment of the South and southerners. Ironically, Niceforo, like others who perpetuated these stereotypes, was himself a southerner.[24]

Although these authors acknowledged the role of environment to varying degrees, overall, they portrayed the behavior of southerners as a function of heredity. The inconsistencies in their arguments were overlooked because such thinking was a hallmark of Social Darwinist–inspired theories in other fields. There is little that we would recognize today as scientific in the work of Lombroso and his followers, and indeed, some social scientists at the time roundly condemned their findings. Nevertheless, they gave a scientific veneer to the pervasive stereotypes of the South. Even though their work was aimed at professionals in the field of criminology, Lombroso and his followers presented popularized forms of their work to a broad audience through lectures and articles. Their influence extended to America where nativists combined the "scientific" understandings of southern Italian deviancy with American racialist ideologies to justify restrictionist legislation.[25]

Even though the racial theories that informed the thought of Lombroso, Ferri, and Niceforo have long been discredited, the stereotypes of the South rooted in the North-South binary have persisted along with the related negative evaluation of southern dialects. Undercurrents of the traditional understanding of the South can still be found in influential post–World War II scholarship.[26] Recently, however, scholars have challenged the traditional interpretation of the South. Stereotypical images contributed to the construction of an "otherized" South by the northern and southern middle and upper classes that was posited in contrast to the Italian nation, which was synonymous with the North. As John Dickie argues, the South served an important role in nation building at the "textual level."[27] Other work has called attention to the fiction of the South as a homogenous entity that is made obvious by the shifting geographical space it occupied. Depending on the time of observation and the perspective of the observer, the South has been variously defined as "the Kingdom of the Two Sicilies," or Sicily alone; in some cases, it has included Rome and Tuscany, but in others, they are excluded.[28] The diversity of economies provides another indication of the slippage between myth and reality. The peasant tenant farmers on the *latifondi* or great estates in Sicily that the famous *meridionalisti* Sidney Sonnino and Leopoldo Franchetti observed in the 1870s, for example, were held up as representative of the southern economy, when in fact a variety of tenancy forms existed along with lands that were farmed by peasant landlords themselves. The economic, social, and political backwardness of the southern peasant has been recast in the new literature as a set of rational responses to existing social and physical conditions. The origins of the southern mythology have been located in what, according to the title of one study, is a form of "orientalism in one country."[29]

This new scholarship aside, the North-South split in Italy retains its hold on Italian political and social life, as evidenced by the 1990s rise of Umberto Bossi and his *Lega nord* (Northern League). The league sought to sever ties with a South associated with corruption and high welfare subsidies that it sees as a drag on the industrious North. The increasing numbers of nonwhite immigrants in the South in recent years reinforces the otherness of both these new immigrants and southerners through the intersection of race and language. The generic use of *Marocchino* (Moroccan) to refer to nonwhite immigrants has been replaced by *vu' cumprá* (do you want to buy?), a reference to the immigrants' use of southern speech forms.[30]

The Dialects of Italy

The southern dialects have historically been devalued independently of their association with a racialized South. Such derogatory views date back at least to Dante, who commented unfavorably on the suitability of a southern dialect, with its "heavy and rough [*rozza*] pronunciation" as a common vernacular language.[31] These dialects have been doubly stigmatized: for their lack of aesthetic appeal as well as for their association with southerners. Southerners, in turn, were marked by their dialects.

The localism of preunification Italian life precluded extensive contact between northerners and southerners. With unification, however, northerners and southerners, as well as their languages, came into greater contact. In the aftermath of the *Risorgimento*, the North quickly assumed political and economic dominance of the new nation. Beginning in the 1920s and accelerating at midcentury, thousands of southerners flocked to the developing northern cities in search of work. Southerners were easily identified by their use of dialects that were the subject of mockery in the North, especially in Piedmont. Their accents alone were enough to betray them, and this situation was not limited to the early years of the twentieth century. In an interview from the 1980s, a Calabrian woman was asked whether when she traveled in the North of Italy northerners could determine her regional origins from the way she spoke. She replied, "Yes, quickly, they knew from my accent . . . quickly, even if I spoke Italian they always could tell that the accent was from Calabria." That, as late as 1961, almost 68 percent of Italy's illiterate population was from the South has solidified the association between southern dialects and ignorance, poverty, illiteracy, and a general lack of sophistication.[32]

This negative evaluation of southern dialects is embedded within a generalized devaluation of dialect usage. As one linguist has noted, "many Italians regard the prescribed, literary standard as 'correct,' 'superior,' and as a kind of paragon in terms of which other varieties may be judged inferior."[33] This prevailing sentiment has coexisted with an appreciation of the greater authenticity and even beauty of the dialects and their importance in Italy's literary history within intellectual and artistic circles. Overall, however, dialect usage and particularly southern dialect usage has been a mark of the uneducated lower classes and a "symbol of backwardness."[34] An anecdote related by a contemporary historian reveals that southerners are well aware of the connotations of dialect usage. When the historian asked three Piedmontese if he could record them speaking in their native dialect, they willingly obliged. When he made the same request of the members of a theater company from Salerno in the region of Campania that performed in dialect, they hesitated and seemed embarrassed by the prospect of being heard speaking dialect in this more formal context. One of the performers explained, "We are a subject people."[35]

Beyond the negative association of dialect usage with southerners, an understanding of the formal features and usage of the Italian dialects is necessary for a fuller understanding of the linguistic history of Italian immigrants. Linguists divide the Italian dialects into three major groups: the *settentrionale* or Gallo-Italic dialects spoken north of what linguists have designated the Spezia-Rimini line, the central or Tuscan dialects, and the *meridionale* or southern dialects. The Sardinian dialect and Ladino (also known as Judeo-Spanish, which is spoken by some Italian Jews) are considered distinct from the other dialects.[36] The dialects can vary markedly from each other and from Italian itself. They are not merely regional variations of standard Italian, but "sister" languages that evolved from Latin. The difference between some dialects spoken within Italy can be as great as that between Italian and another Romance language, and each region has its own linguistic history.[37] The experience of being unable to communicate with one's compatriots has historically been commonplace in Italy. It was Manzoni's inability to communicate with Italians outside of his native Milan that inspired his lifelong goal of establishing a common national language.[38]

The following examples illustrate the often profound differences between Italian dialects. Generally speaking, the greater the geographical distance between different dialect speakers, the more likely they are to have difficulty communicating, although there can be sharp differences in pronunciation even between adjacent towns, especially in the mountainous regions. Consequently, the dialects of the South often diverge most profoundly from standard Italian that originated in Florence even though northern dialects can vary greatly from Italian as well. If we compare the various dialect words for the Italian *bambini*, for example, we see that in Piedmont, the term for "children" is *cit* or *fiolin*; in Campania, it is *criature*; in the Sardinia dialect, speakers use *pizzinnu* or *pipiu;* and in the Ligurian dialects it is *figgieu.* A comparison of dialect proverbs with their literal Italian translations further illustrates the considerable differences between many of the dialects and Italian:

El gà le man sbùxe. (Venetian)
Ha le mani bucate. (Italian)
(He has holes in his hands.)

'U mangiari senza vivari è tronàri senza chiovari. (Calabrese)
Mangiare senza bere è come il tuono senza la pioggia. (Italian)
(Eating without drinking is like thunder without rain.)

Cu' s'ammuccia soccu fa, e signu chi mali fa. (Sicilian)
Chi nasconde quello che fa, vuol dire che male fa. (Italian)
(Whoever hides what he is doing is doing something bad.)

A gatta pe' gghji' 'e pressa, facette 'e figlie cecate. (Neapolitan)
La gatta per fare presto fece i figli ciechi. (Italian)
(In order to finish quickly, the cat makes blind children [kittens].)

Dialects are typically used in particular settings. A survey and analysis of the linguistic practices of Italian Americans in New York during the 1980s provides information on the value Italian immigrants traditionally placed on dialects. Most respondents described the dialect as a language for use in the home with family and other intimates. The association of the language with home and family may account for the finding that women were more likely to hold a favorable view of the dialect than were men.[39] Even today when standard (or, more accurately, popular) Italian dominates public life, anywhere between 43 and 60 percent of Italians still speak dialect within the home and occasionally within wider contexts in addition to using standard Italian; 23 percent do not speak standard Italian at all. Southerners are still overrepresented (along with the elderly and those living in remote regions) among those with no knowledge of Italian and continued use of dialects, a likely result of the historic economic and social marginalization of the South.[40]

Because for so long the first language of most Italians was one of the dialects, they have traditionally been considered the means for expressing personal feelings. The emotionally expressive nature of the dialects has been favorably contrasted with the formality of the standard language.[41] In a 1926 article, the philologist Herbert Vaughn noted: "The Italian who moves to another city will never feel at home because he will find no one to whom he can unburden himself fully and openly in his own native tongue. Everything which he says will be given a tone of formality by the fact that it is translated into Italian."[42] In his discussion of Manzoni's recognition of the profound attachment of Italians to their dialects, the Italian linguist Francesco Bruni writes, "the loss or marginalization of the dialect . . . is a minimization of the personality, that can have serious consequences." The importance of the dialect to individual psychology is borne out by Freud's experience treating patients who spoke both German and dialect. He noted that they often reverted to dialect in their dreams or played with double meanings of the same words in German and dialect.[43]

The largely southern Italian immigrants who arrived in the United States in the era of mass migration were overwhelmingly dialect speakers. With little formal schooling or exposure to the world beyond their immediate environments, they were unable to speak Italian although some may have had a passive knowledge; that is, they were able to understand Italian (often with great difficulty) but not speak it, which suggests the great variation that existed in individual linguistic facility.[44] The history of North-South relations along with the greater difference between southern dialects and the standard gave the southern dialects a particularly devalued status in Italian society. Southern Italian immigrants internalized this evaluation of their dialects and brought it with them to America.

Italians and Their Languages in America

Italy's linguistic history ensured a problematic legacy for the southerners who emigrated *en masse* to America. A few additional points regarding that legacy are of particular relevance here. Italian is unusual in that, unlike other European languages, the language of the most powerful city did not come to dominate, as was the case with Parisian French and the English spoken in London. Rome, Naples, Milan, and Venice were all of greater importance than Florence in its day, culturally, politically, and militarily.[45] This relative lack of influence not only contributed to the difficulty of instituting Italian as the national language, it also made the standard language that much more remote to everyday Italians through its high culture association with Florence. The sheer number, diversity, and distinctiveness of the Italian dialects separated Italy from most other European nations.[46]

Italy was also unique in that the "common" language, commanded by only a fraction of the populace, was for centuries a dead language. Until the period of unification, with the exceptions of Rome and Tuscany where Italian was widely spoken, Italian was used primarily in its written form and so did not evolve through usage. It was spoken mainly on formal occasions such as funerals and political events that were dominated by the better educated. The limited way in which the language was used for so long lent it an artificial quality. It also explains why the ability to wield Italian required formal study even years after it became, in effect, the national language. Indeed, teaching standard Italian was long the focus of Italian schools, and well into the twentieth century, Italians at home and abroad equated education with mastery of the Italian language.[47]

Initially, language was not an issue of class; even King Vittorio Emanuele II used dialect when meeting with his ministers. In the years following unification, however, language took on marked class overtones as it became increasingly clear that the majority of Italians who were struggling for mere survival could not afford the luxury of sending their children to school to learn Italian. Language thus became a distinguishing feature of socioeconomic status along with region of origin, a loaded topic given Italy's North-South divide.[48]

The history of Italian and the Italian South accounts for some of the assumptions Italian immigrants brought with them to the United States regarding language. First, the immigrants believed that to speak the standard form of a language, whether Italian or English, one must be well-educated. Because education was the province of the well-to-do in Italy, immigrants assumed that standard language forms belonged to the better classes. Second, dialect usage was indicative of lower class status. Southern dialects carried the added onus of the South's historic, racialized inferiority. Because southerners were easily identified in Italy by their language use and were derided for it, they arrived in America with a sense of linguistic inferiority already in place. A final point is that in addition to their pronounced admiration for the Italian language, Italian immigrants brought with them a high regard for verbal dexterity. As Sydel Silverman notes in his anthropological study of an Italian village, "indulging in talk for its own sake" as a way to display "verbal expertise" was a hallmark of *civiltà* (civility), a central concept in Italian life. Men's public talk in particular, writes Silverman, "is developed as a skill, even an art, of discourse, argument, and verbal play."[49] The value Italians placed on the ability to speak well could only have compounded the immigrant's sense of inadequacy in the English language, a condition that has been compared with a form of castration.[50]

Upon arrival in the United States, Italian immigrants found themselves not only surrounded by English and other foreign language speakers whom they could not understand, but also by Italians from different regions who spoke a variety of dialects. Many of the immigrants chose to live among people from their own regions who spoke the same or similar dialects. In New York City, for example, tenement buildings and sometimes entire streets were organized by Italian region of origin or even by specific villages.[51] However, this did not obviate the need for a common language among Italian immigrants and a way to communicate with English language speakers whom the immigrants encountered primarily on the job. Although the national language of Italy would seem the obvious choice for communication between compatriots, the linguistic history of Italy made this all but impossible.

The linguistic situation of the immigrants on the West Coast differed from that on the East Coast. Northern Italians who constituted the bulk of immigrants to the West Coast had higher rates of literacy, thanks to greater educational opportunities in the North, and so were more likely to speak or at least understand Italian. In 1911, for example, the rate of illiteracy was highest in Calabria at 70 percent versus a low of 11 percent in Piedmont, followed by 17 percent in Liguria and 25 percent in the Veneto.[52] Because of the higher rates of literacy in Italian in northern Italy, it was not uncommon for Italians on the West Coast to be trilingual in Italian, a regional dialect, and English (or some variant of it), but on the East Coast this was much less common.[53]

Without a single language with which to communicate, Italians resorted to a hybrid language: a creole that combined elements of English, dialect—primarily Neapolitan—and Italian. This Italo-American dialect enabled the immigrants to function within the wider Italian community and, to a limited extent, within American society at large.[54] It was the language of the Italian immigrant, spoken not only in New York, but in Italian immigrant communities throughout the country, complete with regional variations. This linguistic phenomenon was first noted in 1860 on both coasts, and although it has died out as a large-scale phenomenon, it remains a feature of Italian American life in certain communities among some of the immigrants of both the pre- and post-1965 migrations.[55]

It would be inaccurate to assume any uniformity in the speech among the immigrants. The immigrant idiom was used to varying degrees. Some might speak their own local dialect with little interference from English or use only an occasional Italo-American word or phrase. Men, particularly those who worked in factories or other job sites that required greater involvement with non-Italians, were more likely to use the all-purpose immigrant idiom than women whose daily lives were generally circumscribed by the home and the neighborhood and thus could more easily communicate using their own dialects.[56] We can assume that the linguistic scene was even more complex than this based on Haller's study of Italian American languages in the 1980s in which he discovered, in addition to the creolized Italian American speech observed by others earlier in the century, "a linguistic spectrum ranging from the ancient and relatively uncontaminated dialect to a creolized type of Albanian-Italian with interference from Spanish, English, and Calabrese."[57] Although the linguistic influences were not necessarily the same for the pre- and post-1965 immigrants, it is likely that the earlier immigrants also evinced a range of linguistic usage even if the dominant idiom was the Italo-American dialect that contemporary observers noted. Even within this form of speech, Haller's study distinguished between "an Americanized version of a dialect or Standard Italian, considered *Italian-American proper*" and "an *Italianized* type of *English*" (italics in original). These two types of speech were further differentiated by "several transitional stages . . . as well as various levels of Standard Italian and English, together with several variations of bi- and trilingualism." Different speech contexts and speakers helped determine language usage.[58]

Because it developed within another context and it was based on northern dialects, the Californian version of the immigrant idiom differed from that spoken on the East Coast in terms of vocabulary. *Ranchio* (ranch) was commonplace among Italians on the West Coast but unknown on the East. Similarly, *livetta* referring to the elevated train was limited to the cities of the East Coast, although variations in usage existed even within the same geographical area depending on the region of origin in Italy. Idiomatic expressions developed in response to the local environment as well. Consider, for example, the expression *andarre a flabussce* that literally translates "to go to Flatbush" in Brooklyn (*Broccolino*), but was used as a euphemism for dying because Flatbush was home to a large Italian cemetery.[59]

Initially, this idiom was essentially Italian in terms of structure and pronunciation, but became more Americanized over time.[60] It included Italianized English loan words (*carro* for "car," *marchetta* for "market") as well as calques, that is English loan translations, such as *guarda bene* for "good-looking" (literally, "looks" as in "sees" good). In many cases, the immigrants required new words to represent new experiences or created new ones out of ignorance of the standard Italian equivalents. Even in cases where equivalents were certainly known, the ubiquity of certain English words—*stritto* (street), *boia* (boy)—ensured that they would be incorporated into the immigrant dialect.[61] Newly created verbs were, as one contemporary noted: "drafted for full service and made to run through all the genders, tenses, and declensions of Italian grammar, until it presents the very faintest image of its former self. Thus the word fight, which was first changed into *faiti*, can be seen in such unrecognizable forms as *faitare, faitato, faitava, faito, faitasse*, and many more."[62]

Because it was created by dialect speakers, the Italian American idiom reflected Italy's great linguistic variation. Dialect usage determined the endings of words along with their pronunciation. However, the variations in the language encompassed local as well as regional differences, because each town had its own dialect tradition. Thus, one Sicilian might use *abburdatu* for "boarder" but another would say *bburdatu*.[63] The influence of Neapolitan, the dialect that was the most readily understood by southerners throughout the peninsula, was evident in all versions of the Italo-American dialects, but especially that spoken in New York. Other immigrant languages also influenced the Italo-American dialect, notably Yiddish, which is evident in words such as *vorche* for "work" and *ticcia* for "teacher." *Buscellatore/buscellatrici* (tailor's trimmers) is reportedly of Yiddish origin. Irish pronunciation has also been noted.[64]

This idiom was remarkably adept. Certain pat phrases evolved or were borrowed from English that were easily learned and could be used in a variety of situations. Sociologist Michael La Sorte describes the phrase *azzorrait* (that's alright) as: "an all-purpose instrument of social intercourse. It was marvelously suited to the immigrant worker, who tended to be a man of few words and who was never quite sure whether he understood what was being said to him by an American. *Azzorrait* could mean yes; don't mention it; no harm has been done; good; very good; that's a good job; or have I done correctly? There was no limit to its usefulness. The expression accumulated other shadings of meaning, including: please do, help yourself; I don't care; suit yourself; no, I am not insulted; do a better job next time."[65] With this and a few other pat Italo-American phrases, the newly arrived immigrant could function in his limited world.

However, it would be a mistake to consider the Italo-American dialect a purely functional instrument; it was also an "insider's" language that reflected immigrant life and shaped it. It even provided some room for creative expression. Italo-American dialect lent itself quite readily to wordplay, all the more so because Italy had a long tradition of humor based on the country's great linguistic diversity and the comic possibilities inherent in communication between speakers of different dialects and Italian. The various versions of the word for "American," such as *'Merican, Merichen, Americane* could be, depending on the context, a play on the Italian and dialect words for "dog" (i.e., American dog) giving the word and the whole experience of America that it encapsulates a bitter twist. In general, however, the wordplay was more genial, poking fun at the immigrant's limitations with language and/ or the vicissitudes of American immigrant life.[66]

The Italo-American dialect was such a staple of immigrant life that it even made its way back to the Old Country. Examples abound of hybrid words that were and in some cases are still in use in Italy, particularly although not exclusively in the South. Returning immigrants sometimes found themselves unable to resume the use of their native dialects, a phenomenon that made them targets for ridicule while facilitating the entry of the immigrant idiom into the local dialects. Particularly troublesome for returning immigrants was their use of words that sounded like standard Italian words, but that had completely different meanings. So, for example, *fattoria*, which immigrants in America used for "factory," meant "farm" in standard Italian; *guai* was used for "why," but means "troubles" in Italian.[67]

The immigrant idiom enabled Italians to make their way through the maze of American life, but it was not a complete solution to the problem of language. The limited facility with English, common among first-generation immigrants in the era of mass migration and beyond, was often a source of embarrassment in dealings with the world outside of the neighborhood. In psychoanalytic terms, the lack of facility in a new language has been characterized as a form of infantilization; in learning to speak a new language, the adult is reduced to the status of a child. This linguistic infantilization paralleled the inversion of authority within the immigrant household. Italian parents relied heavily on their English-speaking children to help them navigate American society. Parents and children literally spoke different languages to each other, with children responding to their Italo-American/ dialect-speaking parents in English. The parents' inability to speak English and the child's incomplete mastery of dialect contributed to and reflected the generational divide.[68] Although this situation was not unique to Italian immigrants, the fact that southern Italians learned English at a lower rate than other immigrants meant that they were disproportionately affected by the communication issues common to most immigrants.[69]

Italians not only spoke and heard the Italian language and its variants within their communities throughout the United States, they also had a vital and diverse Italian language press consisting of dailies, weeklies, and periodicals. Between the beginnings of Italian immigration in 1850 and 1930, more than one thousand periodicals were published in the Italian language. Although most of these were weeklies and monthlies, many of which were short-lived, during the heyday of the Italian language press between 1900 and 1930, Italian language publications included about thirty dailies with circulations from several hundred into the thousands. Most Italian language periodicals originated in New York City, but they were published throughout the country wherever there were significant concentrations of Italians. Although some of these papers were organs for various religious, fraternal, or nationalist groups and still others represented political, mainly radical, movements, between 80 and 90 percent of the total circulation between 1880 and 1915 consisted of commercial papers that carried news from Italy.[70] In terms of the number of publications, the Italian language press had among the largest number of dailies and weeklies in the early decades of the twentieth century. With twelve dailies in 1910, it was second only to the German language dailies, a position it continued to hold in 1920 along with the Yiddish dailies, both of which numbered eleven. The Italian language weeklies were third behind Scandinavian weeklies and those written in German from 1910 to 1930, when the number of Italian language weeklies reached its high point with seventy-three. The large number of publications was indicative of the substantial divisions within the community. The Italian language press did not enjoy the highest levels of circulation; forty Italian language publications in 1910, for example, combined for a total circulation of 548,000, compared with twenty-three Yiddish publications that circulated to 808,000.[71]

The Italian immigrant idiom found its way into newspapers in the form of advertisements for jobs and products, and, over time, into articles. Italians perusing the *Bollettino della Sera's* February 7, 1917, edition would have seen advertisements for a *giobbista* (jobber), *pressatori* (pressers), and *operatori* (operators) of *mascine* (machines), among others.[72] The Italo-American dialect was so prevalent that at least one Italian newspaper was forced to abandon its practice of translating all advertisements into standard Italian when it became clear that poor response rates reflected the readerships' inability to decipher them.[73]

The Italian language press provided a buffer to immigrants overwhelmed by the English-speaking world around them. The longing for a familiar language could lead to a false sense of security that often worked against the immigrants, making them easy prey for unscrupulous businesses and cranks. As one New York doctor accused of placing false advertisements in foreign language newspapers said when questioned, "Immigrants found it hard to distrust anything presented to them in their own language."[74]

The psychological and emotional underpinning of the immigrant press was noted by Robert Park in his landmark study, *The Immigrant Press and Its Control*. Park recognized that in addition to the need to acquire information to facilitate the immigrant's adjustment to a new environment, he or she is also motivated to read the immigrant press by the "mere human desire for expression in his mother tongue." Although for most immigrant Italians, the actual mother tongue was an Italian dialect, standard Italian was still more familiar to them than English. The immigrant press, Park noted, continued to link immigrants with their past even once (and if) they eventually learned English: "Even if they learn the idiom of our language and it becomes for them a storehouse of new associations and memories, the earlier memories are bound up with the earlier language." He also notes "an intrinsic connection between the desire to preserve national identity and the written mother tongue," adding that many nationalist papers aimed to prevent assimilation rather than facilitate it.[75] Similarly, the use of the Italo-American dialect in Italian newspapers, rather than facilitating the Americanization process, underscored the complexity of immigrant identity.

Although Italian was the primary language for these publications (advertisements in the Italo-American dialect notwithstanding), English proper began to seep into them following World War I. The percentage of publications that contained articles in both Italian and English rose from 14 percent in 1910 to 18 percent in 1920 to over 30 percent by 1930, with some publications becoming fully bilingual. Overall, the number of articles written in English in Italian publications quadrupled between 1910 and 1930. Yet, for many first-generation Italian Americans, the Italian language press was more of an instrument for learning Italian than English.[76] Many of those immigrants characterized as illiterate in the United States might in any case more accurately be described as semiliterate, that is, capable through painstaking effort of making some sense of a newspaper article. In addition, the written word took on an importance in the New World that it had never had for the vast number of Italians at home, creating an audience of readers that did not exist prior to their emigration. Unbeknown to most of their readers, however, Italian language newspapers were a poor way to acquire a knowledge of standard Italian. Not infrequently, Italian American journalists were members of Italy's lower middle class, with little or no experience in journalism, who were determined to avoid lives of manual labor in America. Grammatical and syntactical errors abounded in their writings, reflecting the poor command that some had of the standard language.[77] The errors, combined with the injection of Italo-American dialect, raised the ire of any number of purists. The papers of the well-known journalist and playwright

Alessandro Sisca, also known as Riccardo Cordiferro, contain sharp rebukes to other journalists for their poor command of Italian. In a 1934 letter to a would-be journalist, Sisca writes, after noting some thirty errors in his correspondent's letter, "How is it possible to write in a language that one does not know perfectly? If there are newspapers that publish your stuff, that means that their editors know Italian the way I know Chinese."[78] Similarly, Adolfo Rossi, who became editor of New York City's influential *Il Progresso Italo Americano* in 1880, wrote in his autobiography that he found it impossible to find an Italian "who could write his own tongue with accuracy." Moreover, the lack of facility that most of the journalists had with English resulted in inaccurate translations of English language articles from the American press. The newspapers were thus unreliable both in terms of content as well as form.[79] Beside reading the Italian American press, the immigrants were exposed to various forms of Italian through the airwaves, primarily in the form of Italian language music programs.

Although most publications were written in or aspired to standard Italian, some reflected the regional distinctiveness of their audience in their language use. Some literary journals, notably *La Follia*, which Sisca edited for a number of years, published creative works, mainly poetry, written entirely in dialect. (Ironically, even though the lower classes generally accepted their languages as inferior and devalued in comparison with standard Italian, some members of the literary elite prized certain dialect poetry including southern dialects such as Sicilian and Neapolitan).[80]

Italian immigrants brought their Italian language heritage along with their specific dialects and combined them with American English to forge what contemporary Italian observers sometimes referred to as a *gergo* (slang) that was widely spoken and read in Italian communities throughout the nation. They arrived in America with their own notions of linguistic hierarchy based on the history of Italian in pre-and post-*Risorgimento* Italy along with their culturally conditioned understandings of the meanings attached to language. The language environment that the immigrants encountered in early twentieth-century America was colored by a virulent form of nativism. Fueled by the cultural and social anxieties left in the wake of the mass immigration of southern and eastern Europeans, nativism manifested itself in part through an intolerance of immigrant languages. At the same time, the English language became one of the preferred means of transforming the perception of immigrants. The movement to Americanize the new immigrants in the early decades of the twentieth century became, to a significant extent, a contest over the meaning and the place of language in American life.

TWO

Linguistic Boundaries in American History

> We want no more hyphenated Americans; no more German-Americans, Italian-Americans, or Polish-Americans. You *will* be Americanized, and that means to be Anglicized. And that means to speak English to the exclusion of any other language.
> —Theodore Roosevelt

Although the use of English is an unproblematic assumption in the telling of the nation's history, language has long been a contested subject. As the title of a study of Native American experience with language reminds us, English is "America's second tongue."[1] The importance of language in national life extends beyond communication alone; linguistic domination goes hand in hand with cultural and political domination. In America as elsewhere, language can be "a site of struggle over power, meaning, and representation."[2] However, groups outside of the mainstream have been included through language as well as excluded. Language has served as a kind of flexible boundary in America that is reconfigured as conceptions of the de facto national language and non-English languages change. These changing understandings of language largely reflect social, political, economic, and cultural anxieties regarding newcomers.

The history of language in America—English as well as other languages—is interwoven with the struggle to create a national identity. Given the racial dynamics of American history, this has been a raced identity, at different times implicitly or explicitly so. During the period of mass migration, a time of pronounced societal anxieties particularly around the issue of assimilation, the association between the nation and the English language, which was present from the revolutionary era on, was strengthened. The period was marked by linguistic xenophobia and a zealous linguistic nationalism. At the same time, English became the preferred means to facilitate the change in the perception of the racial status of southern and eastern European immigrants and their children.

English has not always held such a central place in American life. Unlike other nations, the United States has rarely imposed legislation related to language use. The most obvious example is the lack of a designated official or national language. Some legislation has indirectly affected language usage, notably the 1818 congressional ruling legislating that single nationalities could not create new homelands within the borders of the United States. This law had the effect of establishing English as the common language at the local as well as at the national level.[3] In the case of Native Americans and African slaves, the federal government took a more active—and punitive—approach to the suppression of non-English languages.

In the early years of contact between colonists and Native Americans, language itself initially carried no connotations of racial inferiority. It was not until the eighteenth century that European and American linguists linked what they considered the denigrated native languages with the presumed barbarism of Native Americans. Early British colonists did, however, believe that the English language was the only way to convert Native Americans to Christianity and thus redeem them from their "savage" state.[4] Missionary schools were established as early as the 1600s to "civilize" and convert indigenous peoples. Following the Civil War, as settlers were increasingly moving westward and encroaching on Native lands, the U.S. government instituted a formal "English-only" education reform movement. Boarding schools that kept Native American children isolated from their families and culture were premised on an English-only policy that was sometimes enforced through beatings. Schools run by sympathetic missionaries who taught the children in their own languages were threatened with loss of government funding. The emphasis on English as a civilizing influence coexisted with the belief that native languages—symbolic of Native American inferiority—should be allowed to die out. This policy dominated linguistic relations between whites and Native Americans until 1934 when the Indian Reorganization Act was passed, allowing for tribal self-government and the renewal of Native languages. The 1990 passage of the Native American Languages Act signaled the complete reversal of earlier policy; instead of promoting English to the detriment of native languages, the U.S. government assumed an active role in preserving Native American languages and culture.[5]

Historians have documented the struggle of slaves to become literate in English in the face of intense opposition by slaveholders. Less well known is that slaveholders jealously guarded their linguistic privilege and opposed efforts by slaves to acquire more than a rudimentary ability to speak English. Beginning with their capture, African language groups were separated by slave traders in an attempt to thwart any uprisings. Once in the New World, slave owners punished any who were caught speaking African languages: in at least a few cases, by removing their tongues.[6] As one scholar notes, "control over language use was an integral part of the system of racial domination that developed in and from slavery."[7] Ironically, the speech patterns of slaves and later free blacks profoundly influenced southern white speech.[8]

From the colonial period on into the early years of the newly formed nation, European languages coexisted easily with English. Indeed, the value of multilingualism was widely recognized. Printers, for example, benefitted from knowledge of a second language. Newspaper advertisements for private foreign language tutors and translators for a number of languages attest to the multilingual environment of the period and the general receptivity to foreign languages. Thomas Jefferson maintained a strong interest in foreign languages and was an advocate of learning French and Spanish. German and French armed forces were active during the American Revolution and later made their homes in the new nation while maintaining their original languages.[9]

Linguistic tolerance was linked in the minds of many American revolutionaries with the Revolution's egalitarian promise. Benjamin Rush, one of the signers of the Declaration of Independence and a member of the Continental Congress, believed that rather than suppress foreign languages and risk resistance from minority groups, other languages should be used to promote the newly formed government. Foreign language groups would learn English of their own accord. Rush and others also thought that maintaining the languages of Europeans was one inducement for them to immigrate to the United States. The tolerance of foreign languages exhibited by many early Americans reflected the view of language as a means of communication rather than the potent symbol of the nation that it would become in later years. This helps account for the failure of John Adams and others to establish a national academy of language, an idea that also smacked of the monarchism that Americans vehemently disavowed.[10] The decision against designating an official language is the clearest indicator of American tolerance for linguistic diversity. Nevertheless, early Americans did not envision the country as a permanently multilingual society, nor was the preeminence of English in the political, cultural, and social life of the nation ever seriously in question. Adams and Rush, among others, were secure in the knowledge that English would become the dominant language throughout not only America but also worldwide.[11]

Non-English languages, although generally tolerated in the colonial period, raised the ire of some prominent early Americans, presaging the linguistic xenophobia that would characterize the country in the era of mass migration. Benjamin Franklin, who had two failed ventures in German language publishing, became a bitter critic of the preponderance of German language usage. In a 1753 letter to a British member of Parliament, Franklin railed against the Germans in the New World who constituted "the most ignorant Stupid Sort of their own Nation." He lists a number of examples of the extensive use of written and spoken German including German language newspapers, legal documents, and street signs, and was no doubt equally infuriated, as we can assume others were, by the German language translations of the Constitution and the Articles of Confederation. He concludes his letter: "In short, unless the stream of their importation could be turned from this to other Colonies . . . they will soon so out number us, that all the advantages we have will not, in My Opinion, be able to preserve our language, and even our government will become precarious."[12] Despite the misgivings of Franklin and others, German in particular was accorded a high degree of recognition throughout the eighteenth and nineteenth centuries. In 1795, for example, the U.S. House of Representatives defeated by just one vote a measure that would have required German language versions of all federal laws enacted up until that time and from then on.[13]

Linguistic tolerance characterized early America, yet the English language and the new nation were intertwined in the minds of key figures in revolutionary America, and language remained a significant public preoccupation well into the nineteenth century. One form that this preoccupation took was the debate regarding which version of English to adopt. In the early national period, the question of whether Americans would speak their own brand of English or follow British usage was a politically charged one that was tied to the speed of social and political change. The more conservative, Federalist elements of society favored British English and opposed the coining of new words and other "Americanisms," as the linguistic innovations of the time were derisively called. Even Noah Webster, initially a staunch supporter of a distinctly American, popular language based on common usage, feared the excesses of democracy so vividly on display in revolutionary France that included the invention of new words. Attempts to reform and standardize American English in terms of grammar, spelling, pronunciation, and the use of newly created words reveal a broader desire for a more distinctive language that would not only reflect the new American citizenry but also help to create it.[14]

In the mid-nineteenth century, the concern with language took the form of handbooks of proper English such as Walton Burgess's popular 1856 work, *Five Hundred Mistakes of Daily Occurrence in Speaking, Pronouncing, and Writing the English Language, Corrected*, which was aimed at allaying the linguistic insecurities of the "undereducated 'man in the street' who did not want to be mistaken for a newcomer to America."[15] Although the interdependence between the English language and national belonging clearly predates the era of mass migration, the two were not yet indissolubly linked.

The nineteenth century was characterized by a marked tolerance of foreign languages that lasted until the era of mass migration. As the largest ethnolinguistic group aside from the British, Germans were the most visible beneficiaries of this foreign-language friendly environment. In 1835 and throughout the 1840s, further attempts at the federal level to have official documents printed in German failed, yet the fact that they were considered at all speaks favorably of American attitudes toward at least the German language. The last such effort was in 1862. From some time in the 1830s until the Civil War, banknotes printed in German were distributed by private banks in Pennsylvania and Ohio, home to large German populations. During the Civil War, entire military regiments were composed of German speakers.[16]

Perhaps the most notable example of linguistic tolerance in the nineteenth century can be found in the schools. For most of the nineteenth century, Germans were able to educate their children in private secular, Catholic, and Protestant schools where German either was the exclusive language of instruction or was used along with English. As late as 1886, some 180,000 students were enrolled in such schools in communities across the country wherever significant numbers of Germans lived. In the same year, an additional 150,500 students received instruction in German for at least some of their studies in public schools in areas with significant numbers of German language speakers. This openness to instruction in foreign languages began with the implementation of public schooling in the mid-nineteenth century when public schools started competing with private ethnic schools for immigrant students. Even large school districts in cities such as Cleveland, Milwaukee, and St. Louis offered instruction in the students' first language and/or in English. This surprising degree of acceptance was also facilitated by a greater appreciation for the advantages of foreign language knowledge. In 1870, for example, the U.S. Commissioner of Education stated that "the German language has actually become the second language of our Republic, and a knowledge of German is now considered essential to a finished education."[17]

Although some attempts were made midcentury to legislate that some subjects be taught in English, these measures were difficult to enforce in communities where the schools were run by non-English speakers. Beginning in the 1890s, however, more serious efforts to mandate English language instruction came in the form of state laws often directed at Germans. In Wisconsin, for example, the Bennett Law of 1890 was aimed in part at instituting mandatory instruction in English in certain subjects in all public and private schools. The law was quickly repealed one year later in response to protests by the German community, but not before it took its toll on German language schooling. A similar bill passed in Illinois the same year. The renewed legislative effort to implement English-only instruction in the public schools coincided with the beginnings of the immigration of southern and eastern Europeans. At about the same time, the public schools reached capacity levels in many of the nation's larger cities and so lost their motivation to appeal to immigrant sensibilities.[18]

Despite pressures to abandon German language instruction, the network of German language private and public schools remained fairly intact until it was decimated by the onslaught of anti-German sentiment during the First World War. Individual states passed laws prohibiting the use of German (and other languages) in the schools that varied in their severity, with Germans and other language groups in the Midwest faring the worst. Although the 1923 suit filed by German Lutherans against such laws in Nebraska, Iowa, and Ohio resulted in the *Meyer v. Nebraska* Supreme Court ruling that declared these laws unconstitutional, the ruling had little or no affect on popular sentiment toward foreign languages.[19]

The damage inflicted on foreign languages in the United States in the early years of the twentieth century went far beyond the schools. American entry into World War I and the related hysteria over national loyalties heightened nativist sentiment and gave rise to the ideal of "100% Americanism" that entailed the rejection of all things foreign. The use of immigrant languages in any form was a particular target of anti-immigrant activity. Local ordinances were enacted mandating the exclusive use of English in public. No group was more affected by the backlash against foreign languages in this period than German Americans. Although German immigration was eclipsed by the immigrants of the turn of the twentieth century, at the time of the war, Germans constituted a large, well-organized group and their language was widely spoken. With American entry into the war, the public use of German in any context was strongly discouraged by official actions as well as an overzealous public. Vigilantes painted the windows of the homes of German immigrants yellow or covered them with notices indicating that the inhabitants of the house spoke German or read German language newspapers. Public pressure led to changing the German names of towns, streets, and organizations. English equivalents for German words that had entered the lexicon became popular ("liberty cabbage" in place of sauerkraut, for example). The number of German-language periodicals declined dramatically, and librarians took German language books off the shelves of public libraries. German language books were publicly burned, and German was dropped from curricula in schools across the country, from the elementary to the college level, sometimes in response to student boycotts. Some localities issued formal laws prohibiting the use of German, but much of the decline in the language can be attributed to self-censorship within an era of pervasive and vociferous hostility.[20]

Issues surrounding the Spanish language are generally considered a recent phenomenon, but there is a long history of conflict as well as tolerance for the Spanish language in the United States. The 1848 Treaty of Guadalupe Hidalgo that formalized the annexation of land acquired through the Mexican American War was understood at the time to provide for the protection of the culture—including the language rights—of the native-born population, although scholars have cast doubt on this view. Spanish was widely used, despite the fact that the Anglos who had immigrated to the area held a disproportionate share of political power. In New Mexico, up until statehood was granted in 1912, the two languages coexisted, with Spanish sometimes superseding English in the administration of the territory. Court proceedings, legal documents, and official notices all employed both languages. In the early territorial phase, classes at most public schools were conducted entirely in Spanish, but others offered bilingual education with the smallest percentage reserved for English-only schools. Statehood was delayed until English speakers eventually outnumbered Spanish speakers. Once English speakers gained political ascendancy, Spanish lost its stature and began declining in public use. Still, the large numbers of Spanish speakers who remained in the new state ensured the continuation of the official language rights guaranteed by the state constitution on a "trial basis" that were renewed in 1931 and again in 1943.[21]

Language also figured into American imperialism. Upon acquiring Puerto Rico, for example, the island was anglicized into "Porto Rico," which remained its official name until 1932. By the early 1900s, the majority of the island's elementary schools were teaching in English even though only 3.6 percent of the public spoke it. The result was that most students quit school before entering the third grade. It was only in 1949, over the objection of President Truman, that Spanish was reinstituted in the schools.[22]

• • •

English has held a privileged if unofficial place in the mythology and workings of the nation. America's linguistic history has been a mix of tolerance and intolerance that has had the overall effect of militating against the use of non-English languages. Tolerance quickly gives way to intolerance under particular circumstances. As one scholar notes, "whenever speakers of varieties of English or other languages have been viewed as politically, socially, or economically threatening, their language has become a focus for arguments in favor of both restrictions of their use and imposition of Standard English."[23] During the Age of Migration, Americans felt that the newcomers posed just such threats. It is not surprising then that immigrant languages came to mark the undesirable new arrivals, and English was used to absorb those who had already entered. It was only in 1906 that, for the first time in the history of the nation, prospective citizens were required to pass an English test to become naturalized, albeit a nominal one. The implementation of this requirement for citizenship—along with the initial calls for a literacy test in the 1890s—signaled the formal beginning of the association of linguistic ability with full entry into American life.[24]

Language was also central to the confused discussions surrounding race that characterized the era. American preoccupation with race in the late nineteenth century and the early years of the twentieth century was fueled by the new arrivals, the vast numbers of largely southern and eastern Europeans who differed noticeably in appearance and customs from the northern European immigrants who preceded them and who did not appear to fit easily into existing racial categories. Between 1881 and 1920, over twenty million immigrants arrived in the United States. In 1907 alone, the high point of this migration stream, over one million people came to the United States.[25] Concentrated in urban centers, particularly New York City, where only one million of the city's six million residents in 1920 were white, native-born Protestants, the newcomers were highly visible.[26] As a significant body of scholarship argues to varying degrees, native-born Americans questioned the racial positioning of these immigrants. These views were supported and fueled by eugenics and racialist thought more generally. The overwhelmingly southern Italian immigrants who arrived in the United States formed one of the largest new immigrant populations, and they figured significantly in the racial preoccupations of the time. The racialist thinking that prompted the social scientist Edward A. Ross in 1914 to claim that southern Italians were in part "Negroid" and to note the potential for the "'Italian dusk'" to "'quench . . . the Celto-Teutonic flush . . . in the cheek of the native American'" was not limited to academics.[27]

As native-born Americans struggled with the question of how to define the newcomers, the term *race* took on varied and inconsistent definitions. As late as 1920, the noted sociologist and economist John Commons wrote in the introduction to the second edition of *Race and Immigrants in America* that he was using race in an "elastic sense" because it had still not been clearly defined. Race, according to Commons, continued to be determined by diverse criteria including color, language, "basis of supposed origin," and shape of the skull.[28] The imprecise definition of race helps to explain why, in early twentieth-century America, it was possible to grant someone legal status as a member of the Caucasian race for purposes of citizenship while still impugning his or her "whiteness." Although the courts almost always ruled in favor of the new immigrants, affirming their whiteness, popular doubt regarding their racial status persisted.[29] The confusion and misgivings over the racial positioning—including, at times, the color of southern Italians—were pervasive and had an impact on discussions regarding their ability to be fully assimilated and/or whether they should be kept out of the country through the imposition of restrictive immigration legislation. Even though southern Italians and other new immigrants had been extended the privileges of white status, in certain contexts, they were considered "probationary white[s]" at best.[30] That is, they were not consistently perceived as white (or at least, not as white as Americans of Anglo Saxon descent) and it is for this reason that I am concerned here with the popular *perception* of racial status that could at times include color rather than the status itself.[31]

Contemporary understandings of the relationship between language and race influenced the perception of the new arrivals, including southern Italians. Even though language and race were initially and most forcefully linked during the first half of the nineteenth century, lingering confusion over the relationship between the two persisted well into the twentieth century. Immigrant languages and the illiteracy of many of the new immigrants became markers of racial difference that included an assumption of intellectual inferiority. At the same time, literacy in any language, and in particular, the ability to speak English—the language of the exalted Anglo-Saxon (and later Nordic) race—connoted intelligence. Even though ignorance and intelligence were widely understood to be racial characteristics, it was also believed that intelligence could be transmitted by ways other than through bloodlines. The implementation of a literacy test for incoming immigrants and the emphasis on the use of English language instruction in the assimilation of the new immigrants reflected, in part, an assumption that knowledge of the nation's language would raise the level of intelligence, and thus enhance the racial standing of the immigrants.

Because the struggle to racially define southern and eastern European immigrants occurred within the context of intense Americanization efforts aimed at the large number of new arrivals, nationality and race became easily conflated.[32] That is, for some immigrant groups, Americanization implied a change in the perception of their racial positioning as much as it required a transfer of national allegiance. Knowledge of English or the perceived ability to learn it suggested by literacy in any language was indicative of the capacity of the new immigrants to begin this race-dependent Americanization process. In a period when nationality was explicitly raced, and language was implicated in racial status, the ability to speak English provided a means of transforming the perception of the newcomers, from racially distinct foreigners of various inferior "stocks" into intelligent, full-fledged white Americans. The contradictory and confused understandings of how immigrant languages, English, and literacy were connected to race are indicative of the degree to which racial ideologies were undergoing a profound reorganization at this time. The evident inconsistencies were resolved as the categories of white and nonwhite became fixed over time.[33] In addition to discussions surrounding the literacy test and the later Americanization campaigns, continued echoes of the association between race and language are distinguishable in the widespread concern with the proper use of English. The New York City public schools offer an example of a determined effort to protect the integrity of the English language and, by extension, of American society from the influx of the new immigrants and their children. This preoccupation with linguistic purity reflected the interest in racial purity of the time.

Language and Race

Language had long been implicated in race in American and European philological thought. The late eighteenth and early nineteenth centuries saw the emergence of the field of comparative philology that was concerned with the search for common linguistic origins. The discovery of similarities between Sanskrit and modern European languages along with Iranian and Indian languages led scholars to believe that there must be one common source for these Indo-European or Aryan tongues. In its heyday, comparative philology exerted a powerful influence across disciplines. Darwin, for example, used the philological analogy of a branching tree to describe the derivation of modern languages from one common root to illustrate his ideas on human descent.[34]

The influence of comparative philology on the natural sciences in particular went beyond the contribution of analogies. It provided the methodology for the emerging field of ethnology, the study of "uncivilized," dark-skinned, non-European peoples that sought to find the common origins of man in much the same way that linguists were looking for an original language family. Both philologists and ethnologists shared the belief that the search for an original language family would lead to the discovery of an original ancestral race. Through the 1850s and perhaps beyond, many ethnologists believed that by tracing the genealogy of the world's languages they could discover the various directions that humans took from common ancestors. Early practitioners of what would become modern anthropology relied heavily on language to draw distinctions between different peoples and helped shape later understandings of the relationship between language and race. To take one example, the monumental five-volume *Researches into the Physical History of Mankind*, by James C. Prichard and R. G. Latham that was published between 1813 and 1848, largely relied on language to determine racial kinship. As Stephen Alter notes regarding Prichard, Latham, and others, "this approach regarded language as a kind of natural trait, closely bound up with race, in the traditional, more flexible sense of that term."[35]

It was the search for language origins that led to the belief in a superior Aryan race. The research of early German philologists into Sanskrit, then believed to be the oldest extant language, led them to a mythology of an Aryan people who resembled Northern Europeans in terms of physical characteristics. These people were also considered innately freedom-loving and especially adept at self-government. By the mid-nineteenth century, the Teutonic peoples, including Anglo-Saxons, were widely viewed as the purest modern descendants of the Aryans, although the term would not gain currency until later in the century. The initial basis then for the notion of a superior people grew directly out of the relationship between language and race, a connection that Herder drew in the eighteenth century without any suggestion of hierarchy. As Reginald Horsman notes, by the 1840s, "the identity of race and language was taken for granted, and race was exalted as the basis of a nation."[36]

This conflation of race with language reached its apex at midcentury. As the nineteenth century wore on and physical anthropology assumed the dominant role in accounting for human variation, the connection between language and race eroded. Nevertheless, the idea that language, like other cultural traits, was linked with race continued to resurface in racialist thought inside and outside of academia.[37] Nineteenth-century ideas about race that confused biological and cultural traits including language persisted at least through the Progressive Era. Well into the twentieth century, many continued to perceive racial difference as what one scholar terms "a remarkable combination of fixed and fluid elements."[38]

There was a wide spectrum of racialist thought between the late nineteenth and early twentieth centuries. Some social scientists and racialist thinkers believed that cultural features such as language were fixed and immutable racial characteristics. Others distinguished between the affects of environment and biology. Nor was it uncommon to combine the two positions. Neo-Lamarckians, who constituted a sizeable portion of the scientific community up until the second decade of the twentieth century, yoked nature and nurture together by arguing that even acquired traits, such as language, could be transmitted genetically and the environment had the potential to transform the social and even physical features of a given group. So what we would now recognize as acquired cultural traits including language could be inherited and thus constituted a racial marker.[39] This formulation is evident in the work of the noted anthropologist Edward B. Tylor, who published in the second half of the nineteenth century. Even while denying a hereditary link between race and language, Tylor writes: "Although what a man's language really proves is not his parentage but his bringing-up, yet most children are in fact brought up by their own parents, and inherit their language as well as their features. So long as people of one race and speech live together in their own nation, their language will remain a race-mark common to all." Biology, or race, and culture were so intertwined that the distinctions we draw today between the two are artificial and anachronistic when imposed on the racialist thinking of the turn of the twentieth century. The fundamental concern of nineteenth-century racialist thinking, a category that extends beyond the bounds of scientific racism and that bled into the twentieth century, was "that race, understood as an indivisible essence that included not only biology but also culture, morality, and intelligence was a compellingly significant factor in history and society."[40]

An example of the continued association between language and race can be found in the late nineteenth-century interest in the Anglo-Saxon languages—Old and Middle English—as well as Modern English. By the 1890s, the study of Anglo-Saxon language and literature was enjoying a vogue in American universities with distinct racial overtones; the proof of Anglo-Saxon moral, intellectual, and political superiority was in its great literary works. Some academics even advocated teaching Anglo-Saxon language to elementary school children, again with a nod to racial superiority. Fascination with the Anglo-Saxon language was not new in America; colonial Americans, Jefferson in particular, were also interested in it, but in the late nineteenth century, the racial implications of Anglo-Saxon culture undergirded American popular interest in the language.[41]

The interest in Anglo-Saxons was short-lived. Still, even as the belief in an original Aryan race and its superior Anglo-Saxon descendants waned in the late nineteenth century, the language-race link was being subtly reconfigured and deployed. Prominent turn-of-the-century figures abandoned references to Anglo-Saxon descent in favor of a dominant English-speaking race. In an 1896 speech to Congress in support of a test of literacy, the Massachusetts senator and member of the Immigration Restriction League, Henry Cabot Lodge, asked rhetorically, "How, then has the English-speaking race, which to-day controls so large a part of the earth's surface, been formed?"[42] Lodge explained that a fusion of Germanic peoples, Saxons, and Normans over the course of centuries had resulted in "a new speech and a new race, with strong and well-defined qualities, both mental and moral."[43] This new intellectually and morally superior group of people was closely associated with democratic government. By the time of the Reformation, Lodge claimed, the "English-speaking people were ready to come forward and begin to play their part in a world where the despotism of the church had been broken, and where political despotism was about to enter on its great struggle against the forces of freedom."[44] It was members of this "stock," according to Lodge, who migrated to the colonies and formed the democratic republic of the United States.

In a bit of complicated logic, Lodge managed to include all of the older migration groups such as the Dutch and the French Huguenots under the rubric of the superior English-speaking peoples. Even the much-maligned Irish, "although of a different race stock originally," were by Lodge's time considered more acceptable because of their ability to speak English and their close association with English-speaking people who presumably civilized them.[45] Nevertheless, for Lodge and other restrictionists, language, like physical traits and culture, was "in the last analysis only the expression or the evidence of race."[46] The core of racial difference lay in the moral and intellectual character of a people that constituted "the soul of a race, and which represent the product of all its past, the inheritance of all its ancestors, and the motives of all its conduct."[47] In Lodge's day, intelligence and morality were considered by some to be raced traits that he and his ilk ascribed to the English-speaking peoples. The confused understanding of the relationship between culture and heredity resulted in language and race becoming more subtly entangled, so much so that it was difficult to tease the two apart.

The trajectory of the racialist thinking of Theodore Roosevelt provides another illustration of how the language-race link was perpetuated. In line with other nineteenth-century racialist thinkers, Roosevelt was enthralled with the idea of a superior Anglo-Saxon race. He believed not only that linguistic purity was essential to racial purity, but that it was also necessary to maintain the unity of a race. Racial mixing was objectionable in part because it would lead to the loss of a shared language and thus threaten racial unity. By 1905, even though he had discounted the existence of an Anglo-Saxon or Aryan race, Roosevelt's continued use of the concept of an "English-speaking race" became something of a stand-in for the Anglo-Saxon ideal. His evolving definition of race continued to allot a prominent place to linguistic unity that, together with a shared culture, constituted "the essence of racialness."[48] The use of the term *English-speaking race[s]* reflects an assumed link between language and race, however broadly and inconsistently Roosevelt and his contemporaries conceptualized race. Indeed, for Roosevelt as for other Americanizers, races could be made. The creation of an American race hinged on the English language that was, in Roosevelt's words, "the crucible [that] turns our people out as Americans."[49]

Roosevelt's belief in the transformative powers of English, which would become a defining feature of the Americanization movement, anticipated the widespread post–World War I adoption of the idea of a Nordic race that displaced any remaining vestiges of the superior nineteenth-century conception of the Anglo-Saxon. As the twentieth century progressed, race became increasingly correlated with color, but the ability to speak English remained a mark of Nordicism.[50] However, although Roosevelt and others believed that the English language could create Americans out of the new immigrants, it could not transform blacks, Asians, and Hispanics who were seen as unequivocally nonwhite.

The number of attempts to sever the connection between language and race is itself suggestive of how the two remained linked well into the twentieth century. As late as 1947, the social scientist and former president of the American Eugenics Society, Henry Pratt Fairchild, wrote *Race and Nationality* in response to the continued popular confusion regarding distinctions between race and culture. "Language," writes Fairchild, "was the most insidious pitfall."[51] In her 1940 publication *Race: Science and Politics*, the cultural anthropologist Ruth Benedict felt compelled to argue against the ready equation of language and race: "From earliest times . . . language and race have had different histories and different distributions; in the modern world they are shuffled like suits in a pack of cards."[52] Even Madison Grant's *The Passing of the Great Race*, the 1917 publication that became a manifesto in the 1920s for racialist fearmongers, argued against confusing language, nationality, and race. Although the first half of the book is devoted to disentangling the two, the book underscores the way that Americans continued to link language and race. Noting that "language is ever a measure of culture and the higher forms of civilization are greatly hampered by the limitations of speech imposed by the less highly evolved languages . . . which include nearly all the Non-Aryan languages of the world," he devotes the three concluding chapters to demonstrating that the Aryan languages originated with the Nordics rather than the Mediterraneans or Alpines that together formed the three great races of Europe.[53]

A pointed challenge to the prevailing wisdom on the relationship between language and immigrants can be found in the little-known early work of Margaret Mead on Italian immigrant children in the United States. For her 1924 master's thesis in psychology and later articles based on her early graduate studies, Mead, who later became a student of Franz Boas at Columbia University, questioned the results of intelligence tests that consistently found Italian children in the United States deficient. Mead noted the popularity intelligence tests were enjoying at the time and the degree to which they were used to reinforce contemporary notions of racial hierarchy. Italians held a decidedly low place in that hierarchy. She writes that intelligence testing had "allocate[d] to the Italian a place below the negro."[54] However, intelligence tests were not only used to justify racialist public policies such as Jim Crow and immigration laws. As Mead noted, average citizens drew upon them to justify popular notions of race. Mead's main concern, however, was with the practice of placing children in the public schools according to their performance on tests, which she believed put the children of immigrants at a disadvantage.[55]

Mead studied Italian children in the public schools of Hammonton, New Jersey, a farming community with a large Italian population where her mother, Emily Fogg Mead, had conducted her own fieldwork as a sociologist. She found that Italian children did indeed fare poorly on intelligence tests. Mead saw a correlation, however, between low scores and the use of Italian by the parents in the home. Conversely, the more English the Italian children heard spoken in the home, the greater the likelihood that they would perform better on the intelligence tests. The child's linguistic environment rather than his or her ethnic background was at the root of disparities in test scores. Mead also recognized the importance of comparing groups of equal social status as well as the possibility that other social factors helped account for differences in test scores between different national groups.[56]

Mead was not the only one to note a correlation between language environment and low scores on intelligence tests. Clifford Kirkpatrick, for example, recognized that language was a factor, but he along with others, minimized its influence. In his influential 1926 study, he determined that the lower scores on intelligence tests given to children of immigrant parents including Italians were indicative of inherent mental deficiencies: "the total evidence," he concluded, "with certain exceptions, is unfavorable to the 'New Immigration,' especially the Italians, so that the effect of immigration on American intelligence might be viewed with some concern."[57]

The most forceful challenge to the association between language and race came from Boas himself.[58] As a member of the 1911 Immigration (or Dillingham) Commission, Boas was one of the few voices of opposition to its restrictionist recommendations. While other linguists simply used modern European languages as a standard against which to measure all other languages, Boas recognized the importance of language to the study of culture and the need to study languages within their own cultural context. Indeed, his work foreshadowed the development of comparative linguistics as a discipline. He argued that it was a fallacy to single out certain languages—and peoples—as superior. He specifically challenged the connections made by racialist thinkers between "the blond type" or Aryan people and so-called "Aryan languages": they argued that just as the blond northern European or Aryan was superior to other races, so too were the Aryan languages. Boas went so far as to contest the belief in the need for linguistic unity to maintain a national community. A nation, he argued, was formed not through common language or heredity but through "the community of emotional life that rises from our every-day habits, from the forms of our thoughts, feelings, and actions."[59] Clearly, Boas had little impact on the commission and its influential forty-two volume report on the new immigration.

The confusion over the relationship between language and race that reflected the inconsistent understandings of how culture and biology operate is evident in the commission's *Dictionary of Races or Peoples*. Published in 1911, the *Dictionary* recognized five "great races"—Caucasian, Ethiopian, Mongolian, Malay, and American, also known as "the white, black, yellow, brown, and red races"—and drew distinctions within these categories "largely upon a linguistic basis." The rationale given for using this classificatory system was twofold: it reflected the thinking of anthropological and linguistic authorities of the day such as A. H. Keane and Daniel G. Brinton, and it was in keeping with the practices of immigration officials and census statisticians who used language to track different groups. The *Dictionary* acknowledged the uncertainty surrounding this system of classification (the title itself, which cannot settle on either "races" or "peoples," is an admission of the confusion surrounding the subject). He noted that "the sciences of anthropology and ethnology are not far enough advanced to be in agreement upon many questions that arise in such a study" and that, "finally, it may be that neither the ethnical nor the linguistic school has reached the ultimate word, but that a more natural and acceptable classification of peoples will be based in the future upon continuity of descent among the members of a race or of a stock, whether such genetic relationship be established by somatological, linguistic, sociological, or historical evidence, or by all combined."[60]

All European languages were considered to have been Aryan in derivation; so according to the *Dictionary* that was based on linguistic evidence, there was no question southern Italians were members of the European race, which was synonymous with the Caucasian race. However, as the *Dictionary* explains, the European and Caucasian races were most closely identified with the Nordic as opposed to the Alpine or the Mediterranean race to which southern Italians were thought to belong. (This followed William Z. Ripley's three-tiered division of the European races that was widely used at the time.) The *Dictionary* notes as well that Caucasians are "also called the 'Aryan' race by Lapouge, but includes little more than the Teutonic and Celtic divisions of the Aryans as defined in this dictionary."[61] That is, some believed that Teutonic peoples, including the Anglo-Saxons or Nordics, were most closely associated with the Aryan race and the English language. In the entry for English race, the *Dictionary* hints at the popular belief in the superiority of the English language and the prestige the language extended to its speakers.

The author of the definition of the English race, which includes a discussion of the origins of the English language, notes that "it is today the language . . . [of] two of the greatest nations of the world, the British Empire and the United States of America."[62]

The impact of the commission's report was far-reaching. A reading of the landmark *Thind* decision reveals that as late as 1923, the courts referred to the "scientific" understanding of language and race synthesized in the *Dictionary* to define whiteness. The Supreme Court accepted the more recent definition of Aryans put forth in the *Dictionary* that identified them as a purely linguistic group, yet it went against the definition of Caucasian by the very same authorities that relied only in part on linguistic evidence. The definition of Caucasian (which contains discussions of Caucasic, European, Eurafrican, and White race) includes "the dark Gallas of eastern Africa . . . partly on linguistic grounds, partly because they have the regular features of the Caucasian," and, of particular relevance for *Thind*, "the dark Hindus and other peoples of India still more emphatically because of their possessing an Aryan speech, relating them still more closely to the white race, as well as because of their physical type." Like the entries for other contested terms, the author of the *Dictionary* goes on to elaborate the various recent (and tortured) definitions of Caucasian and related terms. The most lucid portion of this entry reads: "Although the white race would be supposed to be the one best understood, it is really the one about which there is the most fundamental and sometimes violent discussion." Even though the Court rejected a linguistic premise for determining race in the *Thind* case, resorting instead to a popular understanding of whiteness based on color, that it entertained such a definition at all suggests that the tie between language and race had yet to be severed.

Literacy and Race

Just as language and race continued to be linked in the period of mass migration, so too were literacy and race. The Dillingham Commission deemed literacy in any language a racial trait. Although the commission's report discussed the effects of environment and class, the high rate of illiteracy among the new immigrants was ultimately attributed to "inherent racial tendencies."[63] This conclusion bolstered the case for a literacy test as a way to restrict the new immigration. The legislation was finally passed in 1917 over President Wilson's veto, following three previous attempts to override presidential vetoes in twenty years. Laws restricting Chinese immigration were already in effect, but the Literacy Test represented the first effort to limit immigration for a broader base of immigrants that was followed by the restrictive immigration legislation of the 1920s.[64] Formed in 1894, the Immigration Restriction League was instrumental to the implementation of the test and to fostering the belief in a racial basis for literacy. As Matthew Frye Jacobson notes, "race was central to the league's conceptions of literacy from the beginning, and it became more prominent over time in its rhetoric of Americanism and civic requirements."[65]

Literacy was the subject of some concern throughout the early decades of the century when a great number of the immigrants arriving in the United States were illiterate in their own languages. Indeed, the stereotype of the poorly educated, illiterate immigrant who was easily corrupted likely has its roots in this period.[66] In the early 1920s, voter literacy laws aimed at immigrants were enacted in northern states.[67] At the polls, suspected illiterates were required to read aloud an extract from the Constitution. Before they were allowed to vote, they had to write ten words of English chosen by the election inspector.[68] Some questioned the efficacy of a test of voters that relied solely on knowledge of English. In an editorial entitled "A Real 'Americanization' Law," John Finley, former commissioner of education in New York state and longtime editorialist for the *New York Times*, advocated that the test should be administered by teachers rather than election officials. The teachers' version of the test would include questions regarding U.S. history and government. Unlike the election officials' version, which would simply test the reading ability of the candidate, the teachers' test would "disclose the acquaintance of the candidate with his duties as a citizen."[69] Finley and his supporters won the day. In 1923, New York became the first state to authorize the schools to issue formerly illiterate voters "Certificates of Literacy" that defined voter literacy more broadly than English language ability.[70]

Both native- and foreign-born illiterates were targeted by a nationwide adult literacy campaign under government auspices in the 1920s, although in the context of these literacy campaigns, *illiterate* when applied to the foreign-born was generally used to mean non-English speaking.[71] As with newly arrived immigrants, native-born adult illiterates were identified—in this case via the census—and put in contact with the nearest adult education facility. The 1930 census was eagerly awaited by those active in the illiteracy movement in thirty-nine states because it would provide figures on illiteracy. The goal of the National Literacy Crusade, a private organization that counted Jane Addams and Ida Tarbell among its board members, was to wipe out illiteracy in the United States by 1930, a date the crusade later pushed back to 1940.[72]

Gendered notions of literacy are evident in discussions of the particular challenge that immigrant women were thought to pose in the effort to make all Americans and would-be Americans literate. Immigrant women were the largest group of illiterates and were considered more foreign in terms of language and culture than were immigrant men. As one member of the National Advisory Committee on Illiteracy wrote, "the tradition-bound women who belong to another century in their ideals of civic responsibility is numerically the largest in the entire nation and far more difficult [to work with than] the native-born illiterates who possess our language and our backgrounds."[73]

The importance attached to literacy in part reflected the sense that a literate citizenry was necessary to vote and to fulfill other civic duties required in a democratic society. Literacy in any language was also important, particularly in the years leading up to the passage of the Literacy Test, because literacy was linked with intelligence. As such, it provided some indication of the immigrant's ability to learn English. Indeed, the Literacy Test, which required that immigrants read and demonstrate comprehension of a selected piece of text translated into their own language or dialect in order to enter the country, was partially based on this logic. Restrictionists believed that the illiteracy of southern and eastern Europeans in their own languages was an indication that they were inherently less capable of learning English. Literacy was used to demonstrate the capacity to acquire English and the superior traits associated with the English-speaking races.

Many different and sometimes overlapping groups, including Progressives, Americanizers, nativists, organized labor, and eugenicists, were represented in the congressional hearings on the Literacy Test. These groups contributed to a discourse on literacy and immigrants that encompassed diverse and contradictory elements. A test of literacy may have suited the refined sensibilities of patrician politicians, and it may well have been considered the most effective way to exclude temporary migrants that included many southern Italians.[74] However, the particular means chosen to limit immigration reflected a belief in the racial basis of literacy that was formed in part in response to the new mass immigration. It stemmed from the conviction that literacy in any language was a sign of character and intelligence. Two years prior to the founding of the league, for example, Henry Cabot Lodge was already calling for the exclusion of "the illiterate foreigners" whom he distinguished from "intelligent and thrifty immigrants."[75]

Although no specific nationality was identified as the target of the Literacy Test legislation, the hearings and reports on the proposed legislation make frequent reference to southern Italians. Given that southern Italians constituted perhaps the largest group of temporary sojourners or "birds of passage" in America and had one of the highest illiteracy rates of all immigrant groups, they were consistently grouped among those that some congressional representatives referred to as "the illiterate races."[76] In testimony presented in the hearings, these Italians were also often accused of working for less money than native workers. Americans considered them particularly foreign in their resistance to shedding their native ways and especially in their refusal—some would say their inability—to learn English.

In congressional discussions of the Literacy Test in 1916, literacy, like other socioeconomic and cultural characteristics of different national groups, was conflated with race. Congressmen discussed the illiteracy of the new immigrants within the larger context of their ambiguous racial position. There are a number of allusions to the difficulty of assimilating southern Italians in particular and suggestions of ambiguous racial status. Comments by the chairman of the U.S. House Committee on Immigration, John Burnett of Alabama, illustrate the assumptions of congressmen who favored the literacy test as a means of racial exclusion. Burnett reported that the Italian minister of education explained to him that the reason that northern Italians had much higher rates of literacy than southern Italians was because "the north Italian is white; the south Italian is not white." In interpreting these remarks to a bewildered Italian community leader who testified before Burnett's committee against the imposition of the Literacy Test, Burnett stated, "I suppose the meaning of it is that the people in the south of Italy have mixed their blood with the people across the Mediterranean and they are not entirely white."[77] Burnett and like-minded legislators drew on the racialist thinking of northern Italians, who had long insisted on the racial inferiority of southerners, to justify their own racial impressions of immigrants in the U.S. context.

Even though Congress debated the racial positioning of southern and eastern Europeans, the undisputed "whiteness" of northern Europeans was plain. Similarly, the literacy of northern Europeans was also beyond question. In the same hearings, Senator Nelson of Minnesota rhapsodized over the northern European immigrant who, unlike his southern European counterpart, had no problem learning English and fitting easily into American society: "The literacy test . . . does not affect any of the immigrants from northern Europe. They can all read and write. . . . Many of them come from countries in which the principles of free government prevail to as great an extent as they do in this country. So it is no difficulty for them when they come here to assimilate themselves with our institutions. . . . I have noticed they readily acquired the language of this country; and under the operation of our naturalization law recently, which requires that they must be able to speak the English language before they can become naturalized, it is wonderful to see how readily they adapt themselves to that situation."[78] In keeping with contemporary notions of Nordic supremacy, the linguistic superiority of northern Europeans was an indication of their superior political evolution and their racial predominance. They were clearly among the literate races.

Although Americans and their legislators offered many reasons why the new immigration should be restricted, the means they chose to do so reflects the assumptions of the time regarding the relationship between language, literacy, and race. These assumptions underlying the legislation may help to explain why many congressmen advocated the Literacy Test as a means of restricting immigration when other options were available and when the test—as predicted by some at the time—proved ineffectual. The same 1917 bill that authorized the use of the Literacy Test also restricted the entry of specific groups by using geographical boundaries to demarcate areas from which no immigration would be allowed. This was a blatant attempt to restrict the immigration of Asian peoples who were perceived as unambiguously nonwhite. Only four years after the imposition of the Literacy Test, racial quotas discussed as numerical quotas that limited immigration to a percentage of a group's prior immigration were in effect imposed upon southern and eastern Europeans. The initial use of a test of literacy to restrict this immigration suggests both the special resonance that literacy and English held in this period as well as the uncertainty regarding the assimilation of the new immigrants.

Assimilation through Language

While some were struggling with the question of how to racially define the newcomers and on what basis, Americanizers were attempting to integrate them into American life. The call for foreigners to Americanize gained urgency with American entry into World War I and the related hysteria over national loyalties and carried into the early 1920s. In the words of one scholar, Americanization in these years "became an all-consuming passion."[79] Because these two efforts were occurring simultaneously—the attempt to racially define southern and eastern European immigrants along with an intensive Americanization campaign— nationality and race became intertwined. That is, for some immigrant groups, Americanization implied a change in the perception of their racial status as it was then understood, as much as it required a transfer of national allegiance. Americanizers viewed the English language as one, if not the primary, means of incorporating the new immigrants into American society. The nineteenth century's confused and often contradictory understanding of the relationship between language and race, including in particular the raced trait of intelligence, was more subtly reprised in the central role that English language instruction was allotted in the Americanization movement.[80] By learning the English language, "stupid foreigners" would be reborn as intelligent Americans.

The Bureau of Naturalization, the forerunner of the Immigration and Naturalization Service, along with the Office of Education, led the charge. The records of the Immigration and Naturalization Service reveal how widespread the connection between language and entry into American society was and the lengths to which numerous organizations went to make sure that as many immigrants as possible learned English. In May 1918, Congress passed broadly worded legislation authorizing the Bureau of Naturalization to "promote instruction and training by the public schools of foreigners who are candidates for naturalization."[81] In practice, the bureau interpreted this to include supplying the names of aliens applying for citizenship to local school boards who would in turn encourage the immigrants to enroll in evening English and civics classes. The public schools also received material support from the bureau to prepare aliens for naturalization.[82] The bureau was so involved in this effort that, in at least one instance when it was dissatisfied with the pace at which New York City public schools were being supplied the names of aliens applying for citizenship, the bureau threatened to relieve the district superintendent of these duties and replace him with its own staff member. The agency widely promoted the evening classes, sending out letters to local mayors, leaders of the Chamber of Commerce, labor leaders, immigrant organizations, and patriotic groups, informing each of the benefits to be gained by the education of aliens.[83]

The bureau promoted the evening citizenship courses in other ways. It encouraged and helped organize mass meetings on behalf of churches, schools, employers, and other organizations with the aim of spurring foreigners to enroll in evening classes and generally raising awareness regarding citizenship. These efforts were supported by the federal government, which proclaimed July 4, 1915, "Americanization Day." July 2, 1916, became "Good Citizenship Sunday," when churches around the nation devoted their sermons to the benefits of becoming American.[84]

What did it mean to become American? Learning the English language was a key component of the Americanization process; Americanization would naturally proceed from knowledge of the national language. As one author of a civics text wrote, "unity of speech will bring unity of thought, unity of feeling, unity of patriotism."[85] The centrality of English to Americanization efforts is evident in a 1918 speech submitted by the commissioner of naturalization to the famous Four Minute Men whose task was to rouse patriotic fervor during World War I through their brief street corner addresses. In this instance, their efforts were directed toward the Americanization of foreigners. The speech is pointed in its equation of English with entry into American society. After noting the vast numbers of immigrants who could neither speak, read, nor write English and who were ignorant of American government and institutions, the speech continued that in the evening classes for citizenship preparation, "the first thing they teach them is how to speak, read and write in our tongue. Every foreigner wants to learn to do that. He is ambitious to be told he *speaks United States like an American*" [italics added].[86] (It is telling that the notion that the English language was distinct from "American" gained currency in these years for the first time since the Revolutionary Era.) The Four Minute Men were not obliged to stick with the bureau's script, but they were advised to present the "advantages" of knowing the national language. These included, "the advantage to the community to flow from an all-American language and sentiment community; the advantage to the Nation in the prosecution of this war, that will flow from a united allegiance in comparison to the danger to the Nation from a divided language and allegiance."[87] The idea was simply captured in the slogan suggested by the bureau, "One language, one country, one flag."[88]

The same document suggests that one could only learn the true meaning of what it means to be an American from someone fluent in the English language: "Often the only source thru [sic] which they can gain impressions of our customs and habits and standards of living, is the self appointed member of their nationality or race, who has learned to speak some English, and induces them to believe that he is a competent instructor in Americanization. A high standard of true Americanism can be taught only by American people whose blood tingles with patriotism, loyalty, love and honor for America alone."[89] Apparently, a few words of English would not suffice; only someone who was fluent in English could make Americans out of foreigners. The image of blood here is suggestive as it hints at a racial basis for nationality along with the transformative power of English.

English was clearly associated with national unity and the essence of what it meant to be an American, but it was also linked with what some saw as the raced quality of intelligence that was also considered necessary to fully enter American life. Returning to the Four Minute speech, anyone unwilling to "become thoroughly American in thought and deed" by clinging to foreign customs, including language, threatens to "lower the standard of intelligence." Fortunately, "the public school [*sic*] have worked wonders in teaching English and Citizenship—in the making of intelligent and loyal Americans."[90] The bureau encouraged the evening adult education schools that were professionalized in this period to offer prizes to those who were most proficient in English, so that "their transformation from uninformed foreigners, not comprehending our language, customs or governmental institutions, to intelligent, loyal, and productive members of society" could be celebrated.[91]

The adult evening schools were not the only places where immigrants learned English. English courses were provided on the job; some employers even made night school compulsory for immigrant workers. Still others offered monetary incentives or compensatory time to learn English.[92] Settlement houses and other social work organizations also encouraged immigrants to learn English. English was even taught to some immigrants in their homes—by their own children. Public School 62 in New York City conducted an experiment in "'home teaching'" whereby second-generation children would teach their "foreign-language parents" how to speak, read, and write English for fifteen minutes each day. The foreign-language parents would benefit, but the secondary gain would be the increase in "the pride and patriotism of the pupil teacher, who feels that he is rendering some service to his city and its people and the American nation."[93] Young people were targeted by a 1918 New York state law that mandated all minors ages 16–21 who could not speak English to enroll in adult classes to complete at least the fifth grade. Penalties were set for the recalcitrant students as well as their employers, but the measure was never enforced.[94]

Women were as much targets of the Americanization program as men. Indeed, immigrant mothers were deemed of such importance to the Americanization of their families that they were considered barometers of assimilation.[95] Americanization efforts aimed at immigrant women placed strong emphasis on reinforcing American gender hierarchy and inculcating immigrant women with American standards of child rearing and home-making. However, mothers provided an American home not merely by adopting American household habits; Americanizers also emphasized English language instruction for women even though they could not become naturalized independently of their husbands.[96] The role of women in the home made it particularly important that they learn English and participate in the Americanization process: "The influence of things American which permeate so pronouncedly the American public school may be taken from the school into the home surroundings with even more potent results by the wife and mother."[97] One approach the bureau took to promoting its campaign was to suggest that if immigrant parents learned English, the real beneficiaries would be the immigrant sons who were then abroad fighting the war: "Every American soldier has the right to demand and be given the opportunity to come home to an American home with American speaking and thinking parents upon his return from the great adventure across the waters. He should not be compelled to return to an alien home when he is himself in all of his speech and nature American."[98] The degree to which some Americanizers equated speaking "American" with thinking "American" suggests the profound transformation that they sought to make in the immigrants through English language instruction.

The premium that the Americanization movement placed on the English language developed against the backdrop of world events and technological developments that contributed to a heightened awareness of language and English in particular. The Treaty of Versailles was negotiated largely in English, placing the English language, specifically its American variant, on the world stage. (Georges Clemenceau was reported to have spoken English with an American accent.)[99] There were even those who felt that English should become the official "language of diplomacy."[100] Indeed, a movement to make English the international language arose in the second decade of the century and received support from prominent Americans. American English was thought by some to be more uniform in pronunciation than British English and thereby more suitable as an international language. In a period that saw major advancements in communication, such as the telephone, telegraph, radio, and motion pictures, which brought the different nations and peoples of the world into closer proximity, the notion of establishing an international medium of expression had some currency.[101] The fact that Great Britain and the United States constituted the two greatest imperial powers of the time made the choice of English the obvious one for an international language. As late as 1936, in a revised version of his 1919 book, *The American Language*, H. L. Mencken predicted that "American English" would overtake standard English as America gained predominance worldwide. The fact that the field of linguistics began to establish a place for itself in U.S. academia in the 1920s further highlights the degree to which language was at the forefront of the national consciousness.[102]

Nevertheless, there was some opposition to the emphasis on the exclusive use of language to Americanize the immigrants. The critique of social scientists and others challenged the connections between language and race that continued to permeate popular thought and influence the Americanization movement. In his landmark study of immigration, *Old World Traits Transplanted*, published in 1921, the sociologist Robert E. Park emphasized the role of immigrant "heritages," composed of "values and attitudes," in explaining differences between the immigrants and native-born Americans. This cultural relativist approach that stressed environment over genetics undercut any notion of racially superior and inferior peoples. The book also deflated contemporary ideas about language. Language, according to Park, was important for the assimilation of immigrants, but no more so than a knowledge of the history of America so that immigrant and native could come to share "similar apperception masses," defined as "all the meanings of past experience retained in the memory of the individual."[103] Park criticized Americanizers who demanded of the immigrant the "quick and complete Americanization through the suppression and repudiation of all the signs that distinguish him from us," including language.[104] He also recognized the role that language played in his day as a signifier of difference: "Where color exists, it is the mark specially singled out by prejudice, but since our immigrants are mainly not colored, language becomes the most concrete sign of unlikeness and the foremost object of animosity."[105] Suppressing the immigrant language was not the answer and actually worked against assimilation. Park pointed out the absurdity of discarding one's own language before mastering another. The retention of the foreign language was necessary to gain information about American life through, for example, the foreign language press that the immigrants otherwise could not obtain. Park speculated that forcing immigrants to give up their languages could easily result in greater resistance to becoming Americanized.[106] Even though Park and other members of the Chicago school were critical of Americanizers who insisted on the immediate and complete assimilation of the immigrant, they were not cultural pluralists. Rather, they were so convinced of the ultimate ability of American society to absorb the immigrants that they saw the aggressive Americanization campaign as unnecessary and even counterproductive to assimilation.[107]

The cultural pluralism articulated by Horace Kallen in 1915 found its nearest approximation in the settlement house movement. The writings of Jane Addams reveal a more humane approach to Americanization that included a respect for immigrant languages even if the ultimate goal of even the most culturally sensitive settlement workers was the assimilation of the immigrant. Addams clearly felt that learning English was important, if not critical, to the Americanization of immigrant children and their families. In an essay on the role of the social settlement, she negatively contrasted Italian boys who happily reverted to speaking Italian at the end of the school day to those boys "who are teaching the entire family and forming a connection between them and the outside world, interpreting political speeches and newspapers and eagerly transforming Italian customs into American ones."[108] She saw English language acquisition as an important means of integrating immigrants into American society, yet she deplored the attitude that "all persons who do not speak English are ignorant." Rather than succumb to the implicit connection many Americanizers drew between English and intelligence, Addams believed that settlement workers themselves could benefit by learning the languages and customs of those immigrants who came to them to learn English.[109] Despite her sympathy for the plight of immigrants, Addams was a product of her time, which is evident in her easy characterizations of different "racial" groups. Thus, in her estimation, southern Italians, "more than any other immigrants represent the pathetic stupidity of agricultural people crowded into city tenements."[110]

Americanizers who hailed from academia also challenged the majority view on language and immigrants. They argued that the English language could not be imposed on the immigrant nor was the suppression of foreign languages appropriate. Each of these related approaches would serve only to further alienate the immigrant. Instead, immigrants had to be enticed to learn English based on the practical advantages that the language conferred on its speakers. For example, in *Essentials of Americanization*, Emory S. Bogardus, head of the Sociology Department at the University of Southern California and editor of the *Journal of Applied Sociology,* took a sympathetic approach toward immigrant languages that went against the grain of many involved in the Americanization movement: "When you strike at the language of a person you strike at his feelings, his mother tongue, his childhood memories." Similarly, Frank V. Thompson, assistant superintendent of schools in Boston who supervised immigrant education and was a nationally recognized specialist in vocational and immigrant education, criticized the reduction or outright elimination of foreign languages in elementary schools across the country in the wake of the First World War as being "un-American." Thompson also attacked the ready equation of English language acquisition with Americanization, insisting instead on the need to teach American civics as well as English.[111]

Although the adult division of the New York City public schools focused on teaching immigrants English and civics in preparation for naturalization, there were those in the educational system who provided options for immigrants that suggest a different understanding of the connection between language and Americanization. Henry Leipzig, himself an immigrant, was the architect of the popular free Public Lectures series that offered evening classes on a variety of subjects in addition to American civics and history. The real innovation of the series was that the lectures were given in the major immigrant languages—Yiddish, Italian, and German—rather than in English alone. Contrary to many American-born educators who conflated English speech with American thought, Leipzig emphasized the importance of content in education rather than linguistic form. Even though Leipzig agreed that immigrants needed to learn English, he felt it was more critical that they develop an appreciation for American ideals. According to Leipzig, this was best achieved by teaching them what America had to offer rather than by giving them English lessons exclusively. As he put it, "to give the masses a concept of the true democracy and what it means to each individual man who shares its privileges is the only way to raise the level of citizenship."[112]

The Public Lectures series was envisioned as a "People's University." This is reflected in the wide range of purely academic areas covered, including sociology, biology, and music. Lectures were given by notable speakers on subjects selected specifically to suit the needs and interests of the various immigrant groups. Italians could sign up for a lecture series on "Great American Inventors" that included a lecture on "Marconi and Wireless Telegraphy." Another offering was "How to Improve the Social Conditions of Italian Women." These were offered in addition to subjects such as "What Immigrants Must Do in Order to Adapt Themselves to the New Environment" and "Why Every Italian should Learn the English Language."[113] Although the lectures were well-attended beginning with their institution in 1889, and reached their peak in 1914 with an enrollment of 1,295,000,[114] the city cut funding for the lectures by 40 percent, even as spending on all other areas of public education increased. Predictably, attendance began to decline.[115] The Public Lectures series continued until 1928, but in 1918, the New York City Board of Education decreed that no lectures would be given in foreign languages from then on, possibly reflecting the nativist hysteria generated by World War I.[116]

Despite the existence of alternative views to the relationship between language and Americanization, many Americanizers continued to believe that their language, like their political institutions, was superior. They glorified English and attributed transformative powers to it that suggest the desire for a more profound change in the newcomers than merely learning another language. George Gordon, a proponent of Americanization through English, spoke of the role of learning English in the Americanization process in almost mystical terms: "Let no American citizen hug his foreign tongue . . . and shut out the light of the great English language which carries all our ideals as Americans! The very vessel of the Lord it is. . . . This tongue consecrates the immigrant who would be a citizen; he can never be a citizen of the United States without that, never."[117]

By the early 1920s, Americanizers had come to see their movement as a failed one. Although much of the bureau's promotional material insisted that immigrants were anxious to attend evening school, they also acknowledged that it was difficult to get immigrants to the first class and even harder to get them to return. According to one estimate, less than half of those who enrolled in citizenship classes completed them. In some communities, the attrition rate may have been as high as three-fourths of the estimated one million foreign-born who participated in Americanization classes nationwide.[118] The particularly low levels of enrollment in adult education classes by southern Italians no doubt contributed to the image of them as unintelligent and therefore incapable of learning English and assimilating.

Americanizers may have been frustrated, but at least some members of the Italian community felt that the emphasis on English language usage was so successful that it was taking a toll on Italian families. The editor of Chicago's *L'Italia* forwarded a report to immigration officials detailing his readers' responses to a 1924 editorial in the *Chicago Tribune*, "Keep the U.S. American." The report notes that although most Italian immigrants have "done their best to learn the language, acquire the customs of this country," it should come as no surprise that they harbor "some recollection of 'their mother land.'" However, what most astonished Italian immigrants, according to the report, was the suggestion that their children were somehow less American than native-born children. The *L'Italia* report goes on to note that the children of Italian immigrants "are so American that for the most part they forget the language of their parents and grandparents and use nothing but English even at home."[119] To the Italian immigrant parent, the English language had already succeeded in Americanizing the next generation and, in so doing, distancing children from their parents and grandparents.

Ironically, the Americanization era, a period of relative tolerance, only led to a more forceful resurgence of racialist thinking; the perceived failure of the movement seemed to confirm the inability of the newcomers to Americanize. English had not failed the Americanizers; the immigrants had. The possibilities for the immigrants to make the change from members of foreign-language speaking races to English-speaking and -thinking Americans had narrowed. A dramatic example of this backlash can be found in the person of Gino Speranza, an Italian American who was a major voice in the Americanization movement and a longtime advocate for Italian immigrants. Although he had originally championed the assimilation of Italian immigrants, by the 1920s he had come to view them as inherently incapable of becoming Americans.[120]

Linguistic and Racial Purity

As Americanizers sought to transform immigrants through instruction in the English language, educators attempted to defend the language from the pernicious influence of immigrants and their children. The emphasis on linguistic purity is illustrated by the pedagogical practices of the New York City public schools. Educators and school administrators harped on the need to teach immigrant children how to speak, read, and write English. Civics was subsumed under the study of English: "The time for this [civics] work should be included under English as a part of the child's necessary instruction for social membership."[121] Becoming American was inseparable from learning English for the children of immigrants as well as their parents. As one study of Jewish children in the early twentieth-century New York City public schools notes, "linguistic transformation was central to making Americans out of immigrants."[122]

Yet merely learning English was not enough. The language had to be learned correctly to avoid its debasement by foreign speakers. One 1921 guidebook for English instructors notes "the necessity for safeguarding the purity of English speech in our great port city, into which immigrants stream from every quarter of the globe."[123] Deviations in usage were not tolerated. Teachers with any trace of a foreign accent were not permitted to instruct courses in English. As late as 1931, educators still saw themselves combating "those tendencies which in a cosmopolitan city like New York tend to debase accepted usage and to inject into English speech foreignisms of pronunciation and intonation."[124] Nor was the interest in guarding the purity of the English language limited to the public schools. In 1928, the American Academy of Arts and Letters gave out awards for best diction to stage actors and radio announcers. In his acceptance speech, one of the winners of the medal referred to the "'demoralizing seepings from every part of the globe'" that were sullying the language.[125]

This emphasis on the proper use of English in the public schools ensured that those who failed to demonstrate mastery of the language would be stigmatized. As Paula Fass notes in her study of the public schools and second-generation children, "in the U.S., 'English' was a code word used to describe the urgency of schooling for those who were considered poor, and assumed to be less intelligent." In fact, the practice of placing second-generation or immigrant children in the so-called "steamer" classes for slow learners and keeping them back a grade was widespread. The children of immigrants often found themselves placed on a vocational track instead of being encouraged to pursue academic studies under the presumption that they were incapable of performing well academically. Their imperfect command of English was a mark of intellectual inferiority.[126]

Concern with proper usage extended beyond the practical benefits that immigrants might gain by learning English. Rather, the insistence on speaking unadulterated English was part of the process of transforming the racial perception of the immigrants that was a prerequisite for full entry into American society. At the same time, American fears regarding the defilement of the language reflected anxieties over the threat of racial mixing posed by the new immigrants. In explaining why the midwestern accent came to be accepted as the standard in American speech beginning in the 1920s, Thomas Paul Bonfiglio points to the country's fears of linguistic contamination by the mass immigration of southern and eastern Europeans who were concentrated in the eastern seaboard cities. This helps to account for the fact that, contrary to most other nations, it was not the speech pattern of the great industrial and cultural centers—New York or Boston—that became the models of standard American speech, but rather that of the heartland that was associated with a Nordic type. As Bonfiglio describes it, "Americans gravitated toward the pronunciation associated with a 'purer' region of the country, and they did so in a largely non-conscious manner."[127]

Though other immigrant groups were caricatured based on their poor command of the English language or their accents, these traits were especially prominent in the stereotype of the Italian immigrants who were also viewed as particularly difficult to assimilate into American society.[128] A 1922 cartoon recalls the stereotype of Italian immigrants at that time, rooted in poor command of the English language, but it also hints at the ways in which immigrants may have capitalized on that stereotype. In the cartoon, which appears under the heading "Another Day of Suspense," an exasperated woman chases after a workman who is ambling away from her at the end of the workday, shovel in hand. He is perhaps her gardener. She asks him when he will return, presumably to finish some work. Her manner and question suggest that she has little control over him. The workman responds without turning to face her, "I *no* speak-a-Da English."[129] The multiple meanings attached to English and the ways in which it was manipulated depended upon which side of the linguistic divide one was on.

• • •

In the early years of the twentieth century, language was one of the means used to help determine who would be fully incorporated into American society and who would be marginalized. The immigrant language was a signifier of racial difference, as it was then understood. The English language provided a means through which those immigrants considered capable of assimilating—or at least their children—could eventually gain complete entry into American society. Through language, the state, in the form of the Bureau of Naturalization, the Office of Education, and the public schools, actively initiated a process that in part helped to transform the racial perceptions of the new immigrants, though this transformation remained incomplete at the end of the Americanization campaigns. Although from a contemporary perspective they would have been considered unambiguously white, Americans at the time questioned the racial identity of southern Italians and other new immigrants even though the state granted them the legal privileges of whiteness. Popular as well as "scientific" perceptions of the racial identity of southern Italians were the outcome of lengthy and complex negotiations that ultimately drew clearer racial distinctions between European groups and African Americans along with other darker-skinned immigrants who were seeking legal and civic rights at the same time that the southern and eastern Europeans were entering the United States. Some prominent members of society opposed the equation of Americanization with English and offered different ways of thinking about immigrants, race, language, and supposedly linked raced traits such as intelligence. Nevertheless, language became an important component in the construction and reconstruction of the racial and later ethnic identities of the new immigrants and their children. This process took place within an America that was unwelcoming at best (save for the more sympathetic wing of the Americanizers) toward immigrant languages and their speakers, one that linked American nationality to the English language to a degree that had not been seen before. This context marked a sharp break from the relative linguistic tolerance that characterized America from its inception up until the late nineteenth century and made it unlikely that language would remain a significant component of ethnic identity for most European groups. It was against this backdrop that the linguistic experiences of Italians and other immigrants and ethnics were played out.

PART TWO

THREE

"He could not explain things the way I tell it": The Immigrant in Translation

> Until yesterday I was among folks who understood me. This morning
> I seemed to have awakened in a land where my language meant little
> more to the native (as far as meaning was concerned) than the pitiful
> noises of a dumb animal. Where was I to go? What was I to do? Here
> was the promised land. The elevated rattled by and did not answer. The
> automobiles and trolley sped by, heedless of me.
>
> —Bartolomeo Vanzetti

Sometime between 1907 and 1910, a teenaged girl from northern Italy who spoke an obscure dialect arrived at Ellis Island. According to one of the interpreters, the young Fiorello La Guardia, the girl hesitated in replying to the questions of the immigration inspectors. None of the interpreters spoke her dialect; most likely, she had some difficulty understanding her interlocutors. She was sent to the hospital where she was examined, probably at least partially disrobed, by an unattended male doctor. La Guardia described the effect of such examinations on the girl: "Imagine this girl who had always been protected, according to the custom of her province (medieval?) and who was perhaps never in the company of a man alone, suddenly to have a doctor rap at her knees . . . tickling her spine to ascertain normal reflexes. Of course this child rebelled and how! It was the most cruel case I have ever witnessed. In two weeks time this child was a raving maniac, although she had been perfectly sound and normal in her own standard when she arrived at Ellis Island."[1]

This example vividly illustrates the dissonance that can occur when two social worlds, constructed in two different languages, encounter each other. Translation is an attempt to smooth over that dissonance. Of necessity, many immigrants experience their new worlds in translation. Their experience is mediated through an interpreter who can take many forms: official interpreters, conationals, often their own children. An examination of the role of the interpreter in various contexts and the phenomenon of translation more broadly offers a window through which to view the immigrant perspective on living in translation. Ellis Island, the point for many immigrants of the initial encounter with translation, is the first site. The next is the courtroom, where language barriers could prove detrimental to an immigrant's case, but examples from the courts also suggest that immigrants could be adept at turning a seeming disadvantage to their own ends. Finally, first- and second-generation narratives allow for a consideration of a more expansive definition of translation. In addition to the literal sense of translating from one language to another, this includes the translation of the self through the encounter with another language, raising the question of the relationship between language and identity. Viewing the phenomenon of translation from the perspective of the immigrant complicates our understanding of assimilation as it is commonly thought to operate and find expression through language (i.e., English language acquisition as an indicator of assimilation). An analysis of these narratives suggests that becoming American did not always correspond with English language fluency nor did the inability to speak English necessarily preclude identification with mainstream America.

These sites provide access to the subjective experience of translation for the immigrant. Although disparate, each suggests the limitations of translation, not merely because of errors in translation, but because of the relationship between language and lived experience; a life shaped in one language cannot be fully transposed into another language. The immigrant in some sense then experiences his or her new environment at a remove, similar to the way the immigrant is experienced by members of the dominant society. Translation can also act as a kind of veil for the immigrant that, depending on the situation, can be lifted to reveal or lowered in an effort to conceal. The immigrant, somewhat incongruously, is sometimes able to exercise power through the translation event just as it is exercised over him or her.

Translation upon Arrival

The first major translation event for the Italian immigrant occurred upon arrival. At Ellis Island, legions of interpreters were on hand to translate the numerous languages and dialects represented by the immigrant newcomers. LaGuardia spent three years as a translator on the island. His writings on his years there touch on the effect of translation on the immigrants, revealing the truly dire consequences inadequate translation could have for the immigrant. He makes this clear in his recollections of his experiences translating "mental cases" such as that of the northern Italian girl. Immigrants found to be mentally ill were deported as a matter of course at Ellis Island. According to La Guardia's estimates, over half of the deportations for mental illness were the result of the inability of the attending physician "to understand the norm or the standard of the particular immigrant."[2] This inability to appreciate the immigrant's perspective had its basis in poor translation, not merely in the literal sense of understanding the exact words used, but in the larger sense of being able to translate one's mental and emotional frame of reference.

La Guardia was not alone at the time in suspecting that problems of translation were behind the tendency to label some southern and eastern European immigrants mentally deficient or, in the parlance of the day, "feebleminded." Advocates for immigrants, such as the Italian St. Raphael Society, and prominent Italian Americans, such as Dr. Antonio Stella, took issue with Ellis Island physicians whom they accused of mistaking problems of language and culture for mental deficiency.[3] The implications of such mistaken judgments were significant not just on an individual basis, but for the whole question of immigration and American racial identity. A major argument of immigration restrictionists at the time of mass immigration was that by allowing the free flow of immigrants into the United States, the entire gene pool was put at risk because of the perceived mental inferiority of the recent arrivals. Nor were fears regarding the mental inferiority of immigrants and their potential to debase the gene pool limited to restrictionists. In its *Manual of the Mental Examination of Aliens*, published in 1918, the Public Health Service (PHS) stated the dire importance attached to its work of weeding out those immigrants who were considered mentally impaired: "Each mental defective may become the progenitor of a line of paupers, vagrants, criminals, or insane persons which will terminate only with the extinction of the race. Were the expense to be purely financial it would be deplorable enough, but to the cost in dollars and cents must be added the ever-present moral degeneracy and its pernicious influence upon society."[4]

Based on the procedures the authorities at Ellis Island claimed to follow, they would have argued that they were well aware of cultural—or, in their words, racial—differences and took them into account in assessing the mental status of immigrants. Yet, as the following excerpt suggests, the difference in "races" recognized by officials on the island was based on stereotypical impressions of immigrants, couched in the Progressive Era's scientific approach: "Experience enables the inspecting officer to tell at a glance the race of an alien. There are, however, exceptions to this rule. It occasionally happens that the inspecting officer thinking that an approaching alien is of a certain race brings him to a standstill and questions him. The alien's facial expression and manner are peculiar and just as the officer is about to decide that this alien is mentally unbalanced, he finds out that the alien in question belongs to an entirely different race. The peculiar attitude of the alien in question is no longer peculiar; it is readily accounted for by racial considerations."[5] The philosophy of the immigration officials is readily captured in a 1917 quote from E. H. Mullan, a surgeon for the PHS: "If the Italian responded to questions as the Russian Finn responds, the former would in all probability be suffering with a depressive psychosis."[6]

A wide range of unremarkable speech patterns and mannerisms were used as criteria to determine mental illness in the immigrant. For example, "an active or maniacal psychosis" manifested itself through such traits as "talkativeness, witticism, facetiousness . . . impatience in word or manner . . . smiling, facial expression of mirth, laughing . . . boisterous conduct, meddling with the affairs of others." Conversely, "psychoses of a depressive nature" were suggested by "slow speech, low voice, trembling articulation, sad facies [sic], tearful eyes, perplexity . . . delayed responses."[7] The display of these behaviors by immigrants not known for them was enough to have an immigrant sent to the "mental room" for a more detailed examination by the PHS.[8] Confirmation of mental illness by the PHS in turn was grounds for deportation.

Immigrants also risked deportation due to inaccurate translations of conversations or of necessary certificates. Besides the very real possibility of deportation, which could result from problems of translation, La Guardia also noted the humiliations that immigrants suffered as a result of their inability to speak English. As part of his job, La Guardia sometimes accompanied couples to City Hall in New York so they could be married and secure the entry into the country of a spouse. He described a typical scene at these marriage ceremonies: "The alderman was drunk. He would insert what he considered funny or sometimes lewd language in reading the ceremony, much to the amusement of other redfaced . . . politicians who hung around."[9]

The PHS recognized both the necessity and the limitations of employing interpreters in determining the mental health status of immigrants. The PHS

Manual for the Mental Examination of Aliens indicates a preference for nonverbal "performance tests" usually involving puzzles that eliminated the need for an intermediary although even these were not without a language bias; significant differences existed between illiterates and literates who took the tests. The limited applicability of these tests necessitated verbal examinations that required the use of interpreters even though the examiners were strongly encouraged to learn at least a few stock phrases in other languages for use in the interview. The manual notes some of the issues that could arise with the use of interpreters based on the experience of the examiners. The difficulty of obtaining exact translations is an obvious example but one with multiple causes. It could be the result of the interpreter's imperfect knowledge of a given dialect. The tendency of some interpreters to filter out information based on their own sense of what was relevant was also problematic. As the manual notes, "time is wasted . . . when the interpreter engages the subject in several minutes' conversation and then instead of stating what was actually said gives his analysis of the alien's remarks by informing the examiner that the alien says 'yes' or 'no' or does not think he is being persecuted. Such an interpreter has made up his mind that the subject is normal and his services, so far as the case in question is concerned, may as well be dispensed with."[10]

Yet, even in the case of highly qualified and conscientious interpreters, the PHS recognized that translations resulted in the loss of important subtleties that could mean the difference between a diagnosis of mental illness or a clean bill of mental health: "Even with a careful, well-trained interpreter much is lost in any examination of an insane person. Certain significant expressions and tones of voice can not be translated, and many things which would be of great significance to a psychiatrist mean nothing to an interpreter, and therefore remain untranslated."[11]

The manual highlights the issue of dialects, lending credence to the observations of LaGuardia and others regarding the mishaps that occurred during the mental examination due to faulty translations. Interpreters were loath to admit that they did not understand a given dialect even when it became obvious to the examiner that there was a communication problem. The manual notes, "this confusion often occurs and seems to be in a measure unavoidable" leading to situations where mental illness might be overlooked as well as cases where "a bright, intelligent alien may, because of faulty interpretation, appear stupid or demented."[12] These substantive issues surrounding the interpretation of immigrant responses call into question the validity of the entire mental examination process.

The problem of correctly evaluating responses was further complicated by the illiteracy or semiliteracy of many immigrants. Degree of literacy had a direct bearing on test performance. For example, as a way to test reasoning, immigrants were questioned regarding hypothetical situations. In one bizarre example given by the manual, subjects were told that the body of a woman was found cut up into eighteen pieces. They were then asked if, as the police indicated, she was a suicide. In assessing the responses generated by such questions designed to test abstract reasoning, the manual again points to the problem of faulty translations, but it also notes that immigrants often missed the point of these hypothetical questions. In the case of the slain woman, "it is not unusual to get such answers such as 'Indeed. I was not there.' 'It was a great sin for her to kill herself.'" The manual explains that such responses were common among illiterates and suggests that they did not indicate mental deficiency so much as a lack of schooling and thereby an inability to think abstractly. The discrepancy between the situations posed by the examiners and the responses of the immigrants also suggest profound cultural differences. Tests that relied on numbers were also biased in favor of literate immigrants. Testing of "superficial memory and attention" by asking immigrants to repeat digits was considered "one of the best tests and should be given to every alien who comes to secondary examination." Even so, the PHS recognized that literates and illiterates would perform differently on the test, with illiterates able to repeat fewer digits than could literates. Distinctions were also drawn on the basis of race so that Anglo-Saxons along with all adults from English-speaking countries could be expected to perform as well as adult, educated Americans. Illiterate adults from southern Europe, on the other hand, could be expected to perform poorly, repeating on average four digits as compared with more than seven by their English-speaking counterparts, indicating below normal intelligence although not necessarily a mental defect.[13] These differences with regard to expected test performance suggest the degree to which language and race continued to be conflated.

In addition to the mental examination, translation and misinterpretation were at the center of a fabled aspect of the immigrant experience of Ellis Island: name changing. Although stories of family names being changed at Ellis Island are a staple of the nation's immigrant lore, it appears unlikely that name changes actually occurred in this way.[14] Immigrants arrived with written documentation that would have precluded the possibility of name change due to a clerk's inability to spell a foreign name or to understand the way a name was pronounced by an arriving immigrant. In any case, the army of translators employed at Ellis Island—even if problematic as far as conducting mental examinations—made it unlikely that names could become so mangled. The inspectors themselves spoke at least one foreign language they could use in their work with arriving immigrants and many of the inspectors were second-generation Americans with native fluency in an immigrant language. There are a number of more likely explanations of how and why immigrant names were altered. If names were changed at any point in the emigration process, it was likely at embarkation because Ellis Island officials depended on the passenger lists drawn up on board the ships for their information. Given that these lists were usually created in the home countries of departing emigrants, misspellings of names were probably fairly rare. Changing ships in the course of the journey did increase the odds of misspellings of names because a new ship manifest had to be completed for each voyage. Many immigrants may not, in any case, even have had consistent spellings of their names because they had been living in largely illiterate or semiliterate communities. Name changes were more likely the result of contacts with English-speaking representatives within American society—teachers and employers, for example—whose misspellings over the course of time led to permanent name changes. Nor were these changes necessarily unwelcome. Some immigrants undoubtedly favored anything that might facilitate their entry into the United States and ease the process of assimilation, which accounts for name changes initiated by immigrants themselves.[15]

Italians rarely changed their surnames of their own accord; however, it was not uncommon to translate Italian first names into their English equivalents in an American context. In cases where surnames were changed, their anglicization took several characteristic forms: the abandonment of final vowels or the conversion of pronounced vowels into silent ones (the use of the final *e* in Menine rather than an *i*), the use of an Anglo counterpart (Chester for Cestaro), the inclusion of prepositions or articles into the name proper (Deluca instead of de Luca), the clipping of names (Trenta for Trentadue), or phonetic respellings of the original (Cherry for Cerri).[16]

More to the point is not whether name changes actually took place on Ellis Island, but that the process of immigration, symbolized by the famed immigration inspection station, became identified in the popular imagination with translation. The widespread acceptance of this myth suggests an understanding of immigration as a translation event; the immigrant must be translated from one world and its language to another. Language in the form of the translated name has come to represent immigration in this period and the incorporation of those immigrants into the host society. That the name changing myth involves an element of coercion—central to the myth is that immigrants were involuntarily given new names by representatives of the dominant society—can be read as an allusion to the violence of the translation process and the transformation in identity that it represented.

Translation and the Law

The nature of litigation, which is based on carefully recorded exchanges between different parties, makes the courts a logical site for examining the experience of translation. Unquestionably, the most famous court case involving Italian immigrants was the six-week trial in 1921 of Nicola Sacco and Bartolomeo Vanzetti, Italian immigrant anarchists who were convicted and executed for their alleged participation in an armed robbery and murder in South Braintree, Massachusetts (Vanzetti was tried for a separate robbery in Bridgewater as well). The case, which occurred during the height of the Red Scare and anti-immigration sentiment, became a cause célèbre of the Left, a kind of political litmus test that drew international attention to an immigrant shoemaker and a fish peddler. It was widely believed that Sacco and Vanzetti were prosecuted, convicted, and executed not for the crimes of which they were accused, but for their political beliefs and their immigrant status.

Much has been written on the injustice of the proceedings even though a few researchers question whether Sacco at least may have been guilty.[17] Given that the defendants as well as many of the witnesses were immigrants with a poor command of the English language, little attention has been paid to how issues of language and interpretation may have affected the outcome of the proceedings.[18] An examination of the transcripts of the case reveals that poor translations due in part to the variety of dialects spoken by witnesses and the defendants as well as to conscious manipulation by a pro-prosecution interpreter contributed to the swift guilty verdict handed down by the jury. The proceedings also suggest the difficulty immigrants could face in presenting themselves in translation via a "proxy." In this case, in addition to the defendants' loss of control over meaning throughout the proceedings, their very lives were at stake.[19]

Problems regarding translation were recognized and taken up during the trial. The defense questioned the translations of the court interpreter on numerous occasions and even went so far as to secure its own interpreter to monitor the accuracy of the translations. At the center of this dispute was the colorful figure of court interpreter Giuseppe Rossi or, as he translated himself to the courts, Joseph Ross. The defense had reason to be suspicious of Ross.

A former radical who later moved sharply to the right, Ross was personally connected both to Judge Webster Thayer, who presided over the Sacco and Vanzetti case as well as the burglary case against Vanzetti in Bridgewater, and to the district attorney, Frederick Katzmann. Ross named his son after Thayer, and Katzmann served as godfather to the child. The degree of his connection to the prosecution and the judge may not have been fully appreciated at the time, but it was common knowledge that Ross drove Thayer to the courthouse every day of the trial. In later years, the basis of Ross's friendship and generosity was revealed. Apparently, Ross would make stops at private homes while the judge was riding with him under the pretext of some errand or other. The individuals he visited turned out to be Italian immigrants awaiting trial or sentencing. Ross used the presence of Thayer in his car to demonstrate his influence with the judge, thus securing bribes in exchange for putting in a good word for the defendant. Some time after the trial, Ross was convicted of extortion on the testimony of an Italian immigrant who felt he had not received his money's worth when given a stiff sentence from Thayer. Although Ross's activities may have been unknown to the American participants in the trial, they were no secret to the Italian community.[20]

Examples of faulty translation by Ross and other interpreters abound within the transcripts of the trial. Although some instances may seem relatively minor, a poor translation of even one word could significantly alter the meaning of a question or a response. In the context of a legal proceeding, such a misunderstanding could have serious consequences, especially in this case which was as much, if not more, concerned with the character of the defendants than their actual guilt or innocence. Indeed, in the absence of substantial physical evidence, the two were convicted largely according to the legal precept of "consciousness of guilt." That is, because they behaved at the time of their arrest as if they were guilty, then they must have committed the crimes. That they behaved strangely is not surprising given that they were radicals who had reason to fear persecution for their political beliefs in an era of heightened repression. Moreover, the two were never told why they were under arrest and no interpreter was made available to translate their initial interrogation.[21] Hesitating or vacillating on the stand could easily be interpreted in this context as further evidence of "consciousness of guilt" rather than language difficulties.

The degree to which the two men were conversant in English at the time of their trial is a crucial question that is difficult to ascertain. Secondary sources make note of the fragility of their English, yet both men insisted on being examined directly on the stand and only called on the interpreter when absolutely necessary.[22] Whether this decision was based on their distrust of Ross, the desire to represent themselves, an unrealistic appraisal of their language skills, or a combination of the three is not known. When asked directly by the district attorney if he wanted an interpreter because he did not seem to understand the line of questioning, Vanzetti answered resolutely, "I should speak as long as I can understand you and I can answer to you."[23] An exchange between Sacco and the judge suggests that he was dissatisfied with the way his testimony was being translated. In explaining to the judge why he continued to resist employing the interpreter, Sacco insisted, "the interpreter, could not explain things the way I tell him." When told by the judge that the interpreter had worked in the court for the past twenty-five years, Sacco responded, "I don't care if the interpreter was in this court for forty years, if he could not explain things the way I tell it."[24] It bears mentioning that Sacco and Vanzetti each spoke in their respective regional dialects.[25] Besides the likelihood that Ross favored the prosecution, he may not have been conversant enough with Vanzetti's northern and Sacco's southern dialects to interpret them accurately.

Although the transcripts reveal a number of instances where Sacco or Vanzetti struggled to understand the questions and to express themselves, overall they give the impression of being fairly articulate for two immigrant laborers. This sense may be heightened by the way the court stenographer transcribed their speech patterns. The distinct rhythm of their speech and unique grammatical structure is preserved in the transcript, but we cannot know if their pronunciation and word choice were left intact. Although hundreds of pages of the transcript record their participation in the trial, the true "voices" of Sacco and Vanzetti are lost to us. Ironically, their imperfect knowledge of English should have worked in their favor; a major witness at the trial claimed that at least one of the two defendants spoke "clear and unmistakable English."[26]

The prosecution effectively took advantage of the defendants' imperfect knowledge of English to discredit them before the jury. Sacco, whose English was more limited than Vanzetti's, was particularly damaged by the district attorney on the stand. In testimony explaining how he ended up coming to the United States with his brother, Sacco said, "I was crazy to come to this country, because I was liked a free country, call a free country. I desire to come with him."[27] Katzman, the district attorney, refashioned Sacco's phrase "like a free country" to mean that Sacco claimed to love the United States. This change in meaning easily allowed him to make Sacco out to be a liar and a hypocrite. He successfully contrasted Sacco's "love for the U.S." with seemingly contradictory behavior such as avoiding the U.S. draft, actions that would not necessarily have carried a negative connotation had Sacco's original meaning—that he came to the United States because he had heard that it was a land of freedom—not been twisted. His lack of ease with English made it easy for the district attorney to impugn his testimony.[28]

Vanzetti's greater facility with English is evident, for example, in his close monitoring of the interpreter whenever Sacco took the stand. In one instance, Vanzetti called out, "no," when he felt the interpreter had mistranslated Sacco's meaning.[29] He also questioned translations of his own words on several occasions. When presented with a translation of a political speech he had given in Bridgewater, he noted, "maybe the man who translated thought it was very nice in the intention, but he did not catch my thought."[30] Nor was he blind to the ways in which the prosecution tried to take advantage of his imperfect knowledge of English. When the district attorney attempted to catch him in an inconsistency, Vanzetti replied, "If I said that, it is because I don't speak good English enough to explain myself or am mistaken in explaining myself because the fact is I don't know."[31] Yet he, like Sacco, was occasionally forced to rely on the interpreter.[32]

Other Italian immigrants who testified through the interpreter were subject to questionable translations that appear to have gone unnoticed or unchallenged by either the court or the defense. During the cross-examination of a witness who claimed that neither Sacco nor Vanzetti committed the murder he witnessed, the prosecutor aggressively questioned the witness on the type of cap the murderer was wearing. At one point, the prosecutor asked if the cap was "checked" (had a checkered pattern) to which the witness at first responded that it was and then seemed to deny that, giving the appearance of an unreliable witness. However, a reading of the transcript suggests that the witness either did not understand the initial question put to him by the interpreter regarding whether or not the cap was checked or the interpreter had misled the witness:

Q. How is your memory?
A. My memory is good to-day.
Q. Good is it? Now, did you say within five minutes that the cap was checkered?
A. Probably I did not understand you well—
The Interpreter: Meaning that to me. . . .
Q. Did the interpreter use the word "checked" to you? Did this gentleman say "checked" to you, asking you if the cap was checked?
The Interpreter: He says he don't know, he don't remember, he did not understand the question.
Q. And your memory is good this morning. . .[33]

Contrary to the popular notion of a neutral interpreter who attempts to approximate the meanings of the two parties as closely as possible, court interpreters sometimes actively intervened in the proceedings. Ross intervened to such an extent that even the prosecution, which most often benefitted from Ross, was compelled to take him to task. For example, while questioning an eyewitness to the shooting, the district attorney entered into a confrontation with the interpreter who questioned the witness's reading of a map of the area where the shooting occurred.

> Mr. Katzman: One moment. That is for the jury. The Interpreter says he thinks he got the wrong one. I say that is for the jury, not for the Interpreter.
> The Court: Yes.
> The Interpreter: Pardon me. I says he got it wrong on the map.

Even after the interpreter was warned to "simply interpret what he says and nothing else," and the questioning resumed, the interpreter was heard to make a remark that was inaudible to the stenographer, but called forth an objection from the defense.[34]

Even though it is reasonable to suspect Ross of purposely giving inaccurate translations, problems also arose with other interpreters. In Vanzetti's earlier trial for the holdup in Bridgewater, the interpreter, a Neapolitan named Menine, was not always able to understand the Italian witnesses who came from different regions of Italy. William Bernagozzi, who was brought in by Vanzetti's defense lawyer, John P. Vahey, to monitor Menine's translations, testified during the 1927 Governor's Advisory Committee hearings that "it was impossible for the witness to understand the interpreter and it was impossible for the interpreter to understand the witness because it was in entirely different dialects."[35] Bernagozzi also testified to the poor impression these witnesses made on the jury as a result of their struggling to understand and make themselves understood by the interpreter.

The issue here, however, is not simply whether or not Ross intentionally mistranslated or whether Menine did not understand the dialects well enough to interpret for the immigrant witnesses. As translation studies scholars note, there is no such thing as a simple one-to-one correspondence in translating from one language to another; subtleties of meaning are inevitably lost or transformed. Lawrence Venuti writes of the "ethnocentric violence of translation," suggesting the contingency of meaning and the impossibility (indeed, the undesirability) of aiming for transparency in translation that masks rather than reveals difference and suggests a false compatibility. These insights can be applied to the spoken as well as the written word. To some extent, then, whether speaking for him- or herself or through an interpreter, the immigrant cannot be fully present in the American courtroom due to the nature of translation itself.[36] Sacco and Vanzetti would have been convicted even if they did not have to rely on translators to interpret their testimony in the courtroom. The translations did, however, provide the prosecution with another tool with which to chip away at the testimony of non-English-speaking immigrant witnesses, including the defendants. Moreover, this courtroom drama provides an opportunity to explore both the experience and the consequences of living in translation.

An examination of commonplace encounters with the legal system reveals that other Italian defendants faced similar issues. The records of the Municipal Court of New York City in the early decades of the century reflect the ways in which language could, not surprisingly, be used against the immigrant, much as it was in the Sacco and Vanzetti case. At the height of the Italian immigrant presence in the early decades of the twentieth century, contemporary commentators took note of the plight of the largely non-English-speaking Italian immigrants in the courts. Italian-born attorney and advocate for immigrants, Gino Speranza, clearly understood the problematic relationship between the court translator and the immigrant defendant. In an article entitled "The Interpreter Service in our Courts," in which he discussed the situation in the New York City court system, Speranza cites a number of issues. To begin with, few translators could be expected to be familiar with the many and disparate dialects of Italy and yet this assumption was often made, creating situations where an interpreter was present although incapable of rendering accurate translations. More subtle issues of translation plagued the immigrant in the courtroom as well. Court interpreters often lacked sufficient facility to translate idiomatic expressions, for example, relying on barely literal translations that failed to convey the full meaning of a phrase. Additionally, the complete court proceedings were not translated to Italian defendants so that their right to know the evidence against them and to check translations was regularly violated. Interpreters in municipal courts were chosen by individual judges and permanently assigned to a specific court. This meant that even when the local immigrant population changed, no new interpreter familiar with these languages could be brought in. Examinations for interpreters in the magistrate courts were not designed to ensure that well-trained people entered the profession. Generally poor salaries did not help the situation. Interpreters for magistrate courts spent much of their time as assistant clerks, limiting their already inadequate time to interpret in the courtroom. So few interpreters were available that none were on hand for the arraignments of non-English speakers. The lack of resources to hire qualified interpreters led to such practices as having police officers or lawyers who were prosecuting the immigrants serve as unofficial interpreters in cases. Speranza notes instances where bootblacks and other poorly educated workers were literally pulled off the street to serve as impromptu interpreters. He also hints at the fact that many interpreters seemed to be unscrupulous, due in part to the low pay and minimal qualifications required for the job. The ability of defendants to enlist interpreters to help mislead judges and so win their cases supports this contention.[37]

Speranza, like other Americanizers, saw the courts as one of the best-placed institutions to Americanize the foreigner. Immigrants who experienced firsthand the American rule of law and the blind dispensation of justice in the courts would perhaps be inspired to become citizens out of an appreciation of this most American of institutions. Speranza's plea for fairness for immigrants in the legal system was made within the larger context of Americanization efforts of his time. The inequities Italian and other immigrants faced as a result of being denied adequate translators threatened not only their legal rights but their view of America itself.[38]

Problems of translation worked against defendants in numerous ways. Court records reveal exasperating exchanges between attorneys and witnesses through court interpreters over the precise translation of words that could dramatically alter a witness's testimony. If an impasse was reached, the judge might make the final call. In the 1902 *DeMasso* murder trial, for example, the ambiguous testimony of a young boy who witnessed the murder of a patron of a clam bar by its owner was decided by the judge. The dispute centered on whether the boy had heard a group of other youths threaten to kill or only to beat the defendant, Dominick DeMasso:

> The Interpreter: To kill and to beat is the same word in Italian.
> The Court: It is 'killing'; that is what it is.
> The Interpreter: I can't tell if he means to say killing or beating.
> The Court: Translate it according to the dictionary translation, and that
> is, 'to kill.'[39]

When the witness tried to clarify his testimony by using different language suggesting that the youths only wanted to "punch" the defendant, the judge ruled on the interpretation of the boy's testimony:

> The Court: Strike that all out. I am not going to allow a boy testify [sic]
> what they wanted to do.[40]

The *DeMasso* case also exemplifies the way attorneys attempted to discredit immigrant witnesses based on their lack of knowledge of the English language. An attorney could call into question the entire testimony of a witness if he could show that the witness was lying about his or her capacity to understand English. It is not surprising that immigrant witnesses sometimes claimed to be able to understand or speak a few words of English, but were not fluent in the language. Yet attorneys harped on this apparent discrepancy to their advantage. The following excerpt of the questioning of a witness in the *DeMasso* case through an interpreter exemplifies this practice:

Q. Do you understand this 'That is the man'?
A. I don't understand you.
Q. I want you to answer me in English: Do you understand this: 'That is the man'?
A. Don't understand.
Q. That question you don't understand?
A. No, I don't understand.
Q. You can understand a little English, can you not; a little?
A. No, sir.
Q. Can't you speak English at all?
A. (In English) No.
Q. Now, answer my question. I asked you if you could not speak English at all, and you answered me in English and said 'No.' Answer that question.
A. (In English) Don't understand.[41]

Of course, not infrequently, language difficulties played a direct role in landing a non-English-speaking immigrant in jail. When Michalagio Russo found himself accused of exposing himself to a young girl and attempting to lift her skirt, he was unable to respond to the charge made by the attending police officer. Instead, according to the officer, "he pleaded he did not understand English."[42] Ultimately, his obvious inability to speak English considerably weakened the case against Russo because the girl in question testified that her assailant spoke to her in English and the defendant was clearly unable to testify without an interpreter. Indeed, as with the *DeMasso* case, some effort was expended by the prosecution in trying to get Russo to admit that he must have known some English, particularly because he worked as a barber in a shop that catered largely to Irish Americans. Russo explained that even though the other barbers in the shop spoke English with the customers, he was teased by them for his inability to speak beyond a few words: "A. I would go as far as this in English, I would say 'shampoo', 'hair cut,' 'massage,' and no further than that."[43] According to Russo, he was himself the victim of a crime that night. He testified that while urinating on the street due to a kidney condition that rendered him unable to contain himself for any length of time, two men attempted to steal his watch. It was at this point that a police officer accosted him. Once on the stand, Russo testified through an interpreter: "I find myself here at this present time because I am ignorant of the language, and had I been able to tell the police in English at that time, I would have told him to place those two men under arrest."[44]

Problems of communication and translation that could result in legal proceedings extended beyond the spoken word to include hand gestures. In a case in North Carolina, which attracted the attention of Speranza and other advocates for Italian immigrants, eight Italian immigrant workers were accused of threatening to kill their superintendent and blow up the work camp because they had not been paid. At the center of the charges was a questionable hand gesture that one or more of the defendants made toward the superintendent. The defense claimed that the gesture was meant to indicate that the workers would starve if they were not paid, but the prosecution contended that it was a death threat.[45] Hand gestures are a common feature of southern Italian communication and are used to convey a wide range of meanings. As one early scholar of Italian immigrants has noted, "south Italian culture differs from American culture, therefore, not only in assigning to gestures a more important role in communication, but also in the specific form of whatever gestures are used."[46] It is perhaps not surprising that Americans would assign physical gestures of communication the most exaggerated meanings because the use of such gestures is comparatively rare by American standards and thus something likely to be associated with extremes of emotion. The translation of Italian immigrants then—and the possibility for miscommunication—extended beyond spoken or written language to nonverbal communications that were outside of the normal range of communicative behaviors of Americans.

More surprising than the frequency with which miscommunications could prove disastrous for Italian immigrants are the examples of Italian immigrants who successfully used the confusion over language to their advantage. Immigrant defendants used a variety of strategies to confound prosecutors' efforts to impugn their testimony. Take the 1906 murder trial of Biaggio Calandra. Calandra was accused of shooting his wife's brother, with whom he worked. The shooting took place in Calandra's apartment, apparently in the presence of Mrs. Calandra. Excerpts from Mrs. Calandra's testimony on the witness stand suggest that she feigned ignorance of English to shield her husband from prosecution. The district attorney contended that Mrs. Calandra unmistakably pointed to her husband when asked by the police officer at the scene of the crime to identify her brother's assailant. By playing on the question of the degree to which she understood English, Mrs. Calandra—through an interpreter—did her best to subvert this damning evidence against her husband:

> Q. Now, did he ask you who did the shooting? Yes or no, please?
> A. He didn't say anything to me, because I wasn't talking English; I didn't know how to talk English.
> Q. Now, please, didn't this officer ask you who did the shooting?
> A. Well, but if I don't understand English, how can I know whether he asked me or not?
> Q. Well, you understand English somewhat, do you not?
> A. I don't understand anything at all.
> Q. Why, you have answered some questions here in English, to-day [*sic*].
> A. Well, what answer did I give in English? Do you call it to talk in English, when a person says, yes?[47]

Even when presented with, according to the attending police officer, the words she spoke in broken English to him, Mrs. Calandra stood by her claim of not knowing English and never having implicated her husband at the murder scene:

> Q. Now, did you say, in the presence of the officer, as you were walking up and down the room, 'What for you kill my brother? What for you shoot my brother?' in broken English?
> A. No.
> Q. Did you use those words in any language at all?
> A. No.[48]

Unfortunately, the record does not indicate whether Mrs. Calandra's ruse was successful.

A 1928 story in the *New York Times* suggests a perhaps more common scenario of how immigrants sought to protect themselves from the law by feigning ignorance of the language. A young Italian immigrant, an iceman, was accused by his customers of cheating them. When hauled before the judge, the youth adamantly protested his innocence by claiming that he did not know enough English to cheat anyone, though others contradicted his story. Although it is difficult to pass judgment based solely on a newspaper account of this case, it is not difficult to imagine an immigrant taking recourse in such a defense. That the image of the foreigner who claims not to know English in order to evade the law is a well-worn stereotype suggests that there is a at least a kernel of truth in it.[49]

Clearly, immigrants played with the question of English fluency when faced with criminal prosecution. They also actively pursued legal action when necessary; they did not allow their lack of familiarity with English to keep them from claiming their rights to property or money in the civil courts. Instead, immigrants sought out Italian-speaking lawyers such as Speranza or enlisted the help of English-speaking relatives and friends to translate and press their claims in court. Just as they were subject to the vagaries and inconsistencies of court-appointed translators when facing prosecution, immigrants sought to use translators and translation to their own advantage when initiating proceedings. Although the weight of evidence suggests that immigrants suffered from the language disadvantage they faced in the courts, it is also doubtless that some managed successfully to exploit linguistic ambiguities on the witness stand.

Translation in First- and Second-Generation Narratives

Immigrant and second-generation narratives often raise the issue of translation, either directly or indirectly. An examination of these narratives allows for an exploration of translation itself as well as the larger issues involved in translating the self into another language. Even though there are a number of continuities between the authors in terms of their experience of language, their stories also reveal significant differences.

Language holds a prominent place in Jerre Mangione's *Mount Allegro*, an autobiographical narrative of Italian immigrant life in the early decades of the twentieth century. In a chapter devoted to "Talking American," Mangione looks at language from the perspective of the second generation. He reveals the way language delineated his life into two separate worlds and his experience of himself as a translator between them. Of all the differences between the Italian world of the home and the American world outside, Mangione notes, "the difference that pained me most was that of language, probably because I was aware of it most often."[50] Mangione's mother insisted that her children only address her in Italian although she took pride in their ability to speak English. Conflict, along with intense embarrassment, arose for

Mangione only when his two linguistic worlds collided, such as when his mother called to him in Italian while he was playing on the street where his non-Italian friends could hear. This separation between the private and the public was formalized through naming: Mangione was Jerre to his friends, but Gerlando at home.

Yet even within his own home, Mangione experienced a split with regard to language for he realized early on that "the language we called Italian and spoke at home was not Italian. It was a Sicilian dialect which only Sicilians could understand." As a second-generation child, Mangione manifested an acute sensitivity to the regional differences of Italian and the implications of their use. The differences between the Sicilian of his home and standard Italian were not lost on the young Mangione: "Proper Italian sounded like the melody of church bells and it was fresh and delicate compared to the earthy sounds of the dialect we spoke." Not only did the two languages sound different, they carried very different connotations. He agreed with an observation made by his uncle who claimed that "the only reason Sicilians ever addressed each other in proper Italian was to show off their schooling and prove to each other that they were not peasants." Mangione himself observed that most Sicilians would stop speaking standard Italian once they had spent any time together or if they had any interest in becoming friends. Anyone who insisted on continuing in standard Italian "was considered a prig or, at least, a socialist."[51] The observations of Mangione and his relatives suggest the special sensitivities that Italians brought with them to America regarding the significance of language and the many clues to identity imbedded in language usage.

Mangione's relatives could not speak standard Italian, and they could not even claim to speak a pure Sicilian dialect. Like many Italian immigrants, they spoke a mixture that included English, other Italian dialects, and Italianized—or Sicilianized—words, including some words from other languages they encountered in the United States. As a child, Mangione had no way of knowing this. His knowledge of Sicilian dialect was shaken when as an adult visitor in Sicily he asked to use the *baccauso*. Through the uncomprehending looks of his hosts, he realized that this word that he had been using his entire life was not a Sicilian word at all. Rather, it was an Italianization of the phrase "back house," synonymous in the minds of his immigrant relatives with outhouse and later the toilet.[52]

Mangione's book also captures his parents' experience with English. As in many immigrant families, Mangione's father had a greater facility with English than did his mother, mainly because he worked with non-Italians.

Nevertheless, Mangione's father made only a minimal effort to learn English, in his case just enough to tell off his Irish boss. Once he had accomplished this goal, he remained contented to speak his unique brand of English. According to Mangione, his father "developed a system of speaking English which defied all philological laws but could be understood by most Americans after about five minutes of orientation. Probably the most astonishing aspect of his system was that he used only one pronoun—'she'—and only one tense—the present."[53] Despite its inaccuracies, Mangione claimed that his father's English was more easily understood than that spoken by most of his other relatives, including his mother. Unlike his father, his mother "spoke the language without any system, groping for nearly all the words she used, without any of my father's wonderful sureness."[54] Like his father, Mangione's mother apparently felt little need to learn English. Most of the stores she frequented were run by Italians, and the Jewish and Polish immigrants who made up a sizable part of their town also kept to their native languages. Not only was it unnecessary to know English to get by, but an inability to speak the language could actually be expedient. Mangione's mother, who seems to have had little interest in attending weekly mass, used her lack of familiarity with English to ease her conscience: "'Who in the world has time to learn enough American to understand what they say in those sermons?'"[55]

Mangione's Uncle Nino provides another example of how the Italian immigrant experienced life in translation. Mangione surmised that Nino never learned English because he resented being cajoled into emigrating by his wife and behaved as if any day he might return to Sicily. However, Nino himself is quoted as saying, "'Why should I try to master a language as difficult as English? By the time I learned to speak it properly, it would be time for me to die. If your demands are as simple as mine, it is not hard to get whatever you want without knowing the language.'" He then went on to recount a story that reads like a fable of how the Italians came to establish themselves in the fictional Mount Allegro, a stand-in for Mangione's native Rochester, New York. Nino explained that the first Italians were poorly received; storekeepers refused to sell their wares to them and landlords would not rent to them. Initially, the Italians prayed to God for help, but when that failed, they marched en masse to the largest grocery store, brandishing pickaxes. The leader of the group, not knowing any English, pantomimed their needs for food and shelter, which were conveyed to the town authorities. In short order, these basic needs were satisfied. Nino concluded the story by saying, "'There's no doubt about it: you have to ask for whatever you want in this world, and prayer isn't always the way to ask.'"[56] Nor apparently was language necessary. Mangione's and Nino's explanations, however, fail to adequately account for the resistance of Nino and his fellow immigrants to learning the language of their adopted home. As we have seen, Italian immigrants brought with them a complex linguistic history that was more likely to impede rather than facilitate the acquisition of a new language.

Not all Italian immigrants eschewed English. Perhaps the most literary and moving autobiography of Italian immigration is Pascal (originally Pasquale) D'Angelo's *Son of Italy*.[57] How D'Angelo came to master the English language figures largely into his story. D'Angelo begins with a description of his childhood in a small pastoral village in the Abruzzi region of Italy, but the bulk of the story takes place in the New World where he performed arduous manual labor as a "pick and shovel man" throughout the northeast. In his free time, D'Angelo managed to teach himself English (in addition to standard Italian and French) and became a recognized poet in the English language. He was well on his way to a career in letters when his promise was cut short by his untimely death at the age of thirty-eight while undergoing a routine appendectomy.[58] His is the story of an uneducated laborer's literary and spiritual awakening. In a sense, language is the story here because English becomes for D'Angelo the catalyst for this dual awakening. The importance he attaches to learning English is captured in his reference to his "struggle to acquire a new language and a new world."[59] Even though D'Angelo's acquisition of the English language and his development as a writer are central to his story, he does not equate his linguistic conversion to English with becoming American. English was not so much a vehicle for entering American society as it was a means of transcending the worker's life. The essential transformation wrought through language was not D'Angelo's movement from Italian to American but from workingman to worker-poet, for he never gave up his identification with his fellow Italian laborers. As William Boelhower notes in his study of Italian immigrant autobiography, D'Angelo plans to "safeguard the ethnic space of his subaltern culture."[60] In D'Angelo's own words, written in a letter to the editor of *The Nation*, "I am not deserting the legions of toil to refuge myself in the literary world. No! No! I only want to express the wrath of their mistreatment. No! I seek no refuge! I am a worker, a pick and shovel man—what I want is an outlet to express what I can say besides work."[61] Perhaps this attitude helps to explain why he seemed not to experience any tension between his English-speaking world (limited mostly to his written work) and the largely Italian world of his fellow workers. For example, the translation of D'Angelo's name by the

Americans he comes into contact with elicits little comment: "He greeted me, 'Hello, Pat!' Everybody called me Pat."[62] For D'Angelo, "Pat" was merely a moniker that he donned (or was given) in the English-speaking world, one which he could easily shed at the end of the working day. In D'Angelo then, we have a very different interpretation of the effects of language change. He represents another type of identity change besides the traditional understanding of English language acquisition as an index of assimilation.

D'Angelo expresses the cultural dissonance that the immigrant experiences as a linguistic confrontation between Italian and English. D'Angelo arrived in America utterly ignorant of the English language. As the following suggests, from practically his first moment in America, the problems—in this instance, comical—posed by language and translation for the immigrant form a significant theme in his narrative: "And now, just before we reached the station, I began to notice that there were signs at the corners of the streets with 'Ave.! Ave.! Ave.!' How religious a place this must be that expresses its devotion at every crossing, I mused. Still, they did not put the 'Ave.' before the holy word, as, in 'Ave Maria,' but rather after. How topsy-turvy!"[63] This example illustrates how translation for the immigrant is not simply a matter of literal understanding but of comprehension in the largest sense. Here, D'Angelo's misinterpretation of the meaning of *Ave.* leads him to draw an inaccurate conclusion about the nature of American society. In another humorous account of translation gone awry, D'Angelo tells the story of how he tried to buy eggs in a store. He enters the store intending to ask for "aches," just as his compatriots had instructed him, but the word comes out as "axe." After acting out a chicken laying eggs and making an egg shape with his fingers, the proprietors finally came to understand his request. He concludes, "I went home in triumph."[64] Other mishaps with translation, however, are remembered by D'Angelo as moments of great humiliation and shame. He recounts an incident when he asked his Italian foreman to help him come up with a suitable explanation for a black eye that D'Angelo had received in a fight. The foreman instructed him to explain to anyone who asked that he had fallen down, which D'Angelo heard as "faw don." By the time he had an opportunity to give his explanation, "faw don" had become "you damn." He continued to proffer this explanation until someone took pity on him and explained to him what he was actually saying: "When finally one man made me understand what I had been saying, I was so ashamed that I hurried straight home. And on the way I met Filippo, also angry, and we had another fight."[65]

This story and the one preceding it are also notable for revealing the means by which Italian immigrants learned the scanty English that they knew: through others with a similarly limited ability to speak English. Not only did immigrants in this way often learn the words incorrectly, but this was also compounded by a tendency for the words to become transformed between the time of learning them and the occasion to speak them, resulting in the confusion illustrated above. The immigrant's seeming unwillingness to learn more than rudimentary English words and phrases needed for ordinary life resulted in a peculiar isolation, one that was tinged with defiance. As D'Angelo explains, "none of us, including myself, ever thought of a movement to broaden our knowledge of the English language. We soon learned a few words about the job, that was the preliminary creed; then came 'bread,' 'shirt,' 'gloves' (not kid gloves), 'milk.' And that is all. We formed our own little world—one of many in this country. And the other people around us who spoke in strange languages might have been phantoms for all the influence that they had upon us or for all we cared about them."[66] In the last two lines of this passage, D'Angelo specifically equates the self-imposed isolation of the immigrants with their disinterest in learning English. D'Angelo's self-contained "little world" held no place for English, nor did the larger English-speaking world hold any fascination for the immigrants. However, the hesitancy to make greater efforts to learn the language seems to be based, at least in part, on the sense that English is very difficult to learn. Upon tasting a new fruit for the first time, what stands out for D'Angelo and his compatriots is the ease with which they could pronounce the word: "He told us that they were called bananas. The name was easy to pronounce."[67]

D'Angelo's narrative confirms Italian sensibilities regarding language. In keeping with the traditional Italian appreciation of verbal display, D'Angelo makes a point of commenting on the verbal dexterity of a fellow Italian worker. D'Angelo describes Giorgio Vanno, an otherwise undistinguished character in the narrative, as "the champion talker of the gang. Sometimes the rest of us would launch a verbal attack upon him, and he all alone, would defend himself and probably defeat the whole crowd of us with his clever repartee."[68] Vanno's eloquence may have been especially noteworthy for the contrast it formed with the halting, imperfect English of most of D'Angelo's fellow Italian immigrants. D'Angelo as well as Mangione evinces a sensitivity to regional differences in language. For example, D'Angelo remarked on someone who spoke "a weird Calabrese," a "loud-mouthed, but good-natured Neapolitan" and a speaker of a "soft Abruzzese dialect that is so much like ours of the uplands." A special reverence was reserved for anyone who could speak standard Italian: "He was an intelligent man and spoke in excellent Italian. . . . But now, old, the foreman took him on more in pity than anything and because he could talk so nicely to them."[69]

D'Angelo poignantly captures the experience of incomprehension that plagues the immigrant who cannot understand the host language and instead must rely on other cues to interpret a given situation. In the following description, D'Angelo gives the impression of watching a pantomime: "A group of men came past shouting in a strange language. That was probably the American language, which I had heard on my arrival in New York. A fight started up. Two men were pummeling each other. There were shouts, and their foreman rushed toward them white-faced with anger."[70] He also illustrates how communication on a nonverbal level can be confusing for the immigrant. On first seeing crowds on a Manhattan street, he says "Where did they all come from? And why their silence? Who had cast the spell over them all? . . . Nobody nodded good evening to me or to my companions."[71] In each instance, the silence in the face of a strange language and a strange land is pronounced. D'Angelo eventually escapes the silence that envelopes many of his conationals by finding an English language voice.

Even though D'Angelo never explicitly explains why he determined to take up the study of English, it is clear that the language offered the possibility of expression that would give his life meaning beyond the daily drudgery of his work. Shortly before he decided to learn English, he found himself wondering about his situation: "Why, I am nothing more than a dog. A dog. But a dog is silent and slinks away when whipped, while I am filled with the urge to cry out, to cry out disconnected words, expressions of pain— anything—to cry out!"[72] Despite his obvious longing for self-expression and the ability to transcend his laborer's existence, D'Angelo described his turn toward English as a fortuitous accident rather than as a conscious strategy to gain access to English-speaking America. Through his encounters with some Mexican laborers, his interest in language was piqued, first by listening to them speak, and then by reading their Spanish language newspapers in an effort to identify words that resembled Italian. "Somehow," he writes, "I found English more to my liking than Spanish" and so he began to teach himself English by reading newspapers.[73] Before long, he became a curiosity in the rail yards, where he lived in a boxcar and worked clearing wrecks from the tracks, for his ability to write and tell jokes in English. The American brakemen and conductors referred to him as "that queer Italian laborer." These Americans took to testing him by finding obscure English words for him to define. The reactions of his fellow immigrants to his new familiarity with

English are telling. His coworkers argued among themselves as to whether knowing English was an advantage for D'Angelo. Some claimed that it would help him get ahead, but others insisted that laborers like themselves could never hope to advance under any circumstances. This latter position was articulated in Italian by Felice, an old man who was physically misshapen by years of hard labor: "And you, who they say can write English—what good does it do you to know the language of America while working here? You are not getting a cent more than a parrot like me who goes wherever they take him. You live in the same box car. You eat the same food. And if you stay here long enough you will become the same as I."[74] Felice's advice to D'Angelo is to try to get an office job; only the possibility of betterment of one's living conditions justified learning English for these immigrant laborers. Again, one is struck by the utter indifference to learning English as a way to enter American society.

D'Angelo's story concludes with his winning a writing contest that marks his literary coming of age. More than the accolades of American reviewers, what most impressed him was the praise of his fellow workers "who recognized that at last one of them had risen from the ditches and quicksands of toil to speak his heart to the upper world."[75] His linguistic triumph had an entirely different meaning for his working-class compatriots than it would have had for native-born Americans who would only have seen in D'Angelo a successfully Americanized immigrant.

Language is also a theme in Constantine Panunzio's 1928 autobiography, *The Soul of an Immigrant.*[76] Panunzio, who was born in 1884 in the south of Italy, came from an upper-middle-class family. Although he could probably have enjoyed a comfortable existence in his hometown, he decided to emigrate to the United States against his family's wishes.[77] Language figured largely in Panunzio's earliest notions of America, or rather in his reconstruction of them. The first impression of America that he notes was of a local man who had returned to their town after living in America for some years. Yet the language that Panunzio first associates with America is not English: "I remember him as clearly as if it were to-day. He could not speak our dialect any more. What little of the language he spoke was the pure Italian, which he had learned in America."[78] America had transformed a local villager not into an American through English, but into a proper Italian, signified by the use of standard Italian.

Unlike D'Angelo, Panunzio developed a desire to learn English before he even decided to immigrate to America. His first acquaintance with English was through drunken American sailors who visited his port town of Molfetta and whose speech sounded like "funny jabbering." He was particularly impressed by a local man who, although blind, stood out in Panunzio's mind because of his singular ability to speak English: "To me the most striking thing about this man was that he was the only person in Molfetta who could speak English, and he always acted as interpreter when English or American vessels chanced to come to the city. It was this man who first awakened in me a desire to learn the English language. I used to think that if I could learn English and become an 'interrupter' [sic] myself, I would be in the height of my glory."[79] The idea of learning enough English so that he could return to Molfetta as an interpreter motivated Panunzio's early and very difficult years in America, though he had little leisure for study upon arrival. The desire to become an interpreter is perhaps a reflection of the liminal position Panunzio came to occupy and the wish to integrate the two worlds of which he was a part. Indeed, he would go on to become an interpreter of sorts between the immigrants and the larger American world in his work as a Methodist minister.

As the first English words he learned in America, "pick and shovel . . . possessed great charm . . . I practised [sic] for a day or two until I could say 'peek' and 'shuvle' to perfection."[80] Panunzio's account of his experience with language in the New World shares other similarities with D'Angelo's. He too, learns "English" from conationals with whom he works. He paraphrases one *padrone* who explained a job to him in a mixture of Sicilian and "English": "The company has a 'shantee' in which you can sleep, and a 'storo' where you can buy your 'grosserie' all very cheap. 'Buona paga' [good pay] . . . and you only have to pay me fifty cents a week for having gotten you this 'gooda jobba.'"[81] As with D'Angelo, Panunzio's employer gave him an American name, but the meanings they each attached to their new names differed, perhaps because of the different circumstances under which they worked. D'Angelo always worked with a crew of other Italian immigrants, but Panunzio labored as a hired farm hand in rural New England communities where he was usually the only Italian. At one point, he went three years without hearing or speaking Italian. Thus, when he was given the arbitrary name of "Frank Nardi" by an employer in Maine, it represented a completely new identity for him rather than something that could be left behind at the end of the work day. (At least it was an improvement over "Mr. Beefsteak," which his employer called him for three months until Panunzio figured out what it meant and demanded a new name.)[82]

To a much greater extent than D'Angelo, Panunzio entered the American mainstream, first through school, then through the army, and later through his conversion to Methodism. He maintained a remarkable optimism about America, its language, and its people, despite the gross injustices he suffered at the hands of his American employers. English came to represent for Panunzio full entry into American life, something that he clearly prized for himself and for others. If only Italian immigrants would immerse themselves in English, claims Panunzio, they would "come to understand the advantages of mingling with American people and to develop a wholesome attitude toward America and all things American."[83] Panunzio's infatuation with America in the face of his exploitation by Americans suggests an element of identifying with the oppressor. For all of Panunzio's protestations to the contrary, his early life in America is one of almost unrelenting suffering and humiliation. These accounts dominate the first half of the book, but by the second half, when Panunzio has learned English and obtained a formal education, his story becomes a mere collection of commentaries and reflections. Boelhower suggests that Panunzio's price for becoming American is the loss of his physical self.[84] He is given to abstraction, suggesting perhaps a certain distance from his new, English-speaking self. This emotional distancing within the speaker of two or more languages reflects the propensity for splitting among polylinguals, a central theme in the writings of those psychoanalysts who have dealt with issues arising from the abandonment of the mother tongue. Knowledge of a second language can result in a defensive splitting off of emotions and situations experienced in the mother tongue or their complete repression.[85]

D'Angelo and Panunzio tell the story of the immigrant's first encounter with the ways of the New World from a male perspective. Not surprisingly, it is far more difficult to find narratives by Italian American women in this period given their higher rates of illiteracy and lack of English language fluency relative to their male counterparts. Traditional gender roles made it even more difficult for women than men to pursue educational or literary pursuits. The lack of literacy among southern Italian immigrants overall is born out by the strong oral tradition that the immigrants brought with them to the New World.[86] Thus, the available narratives by women are largely transcriptions—and translations, to varying degrees—of oral accounts.

Rosa, the Life of an Italian Immigrant is the first-person account of Rosa Cassetari, an immigrant woman from the northern Italian province of Lombardy who arrived in the United States in 1884.[87] Rosa Cavalleri, as she is called in the book, came to the attention of Marie Hall Ets, a social worker at a small settlement house in Chicago, toward the end of World War I. Rosa was the cleaning woman at the settlement house, and according to

Ets, the two were "staunch friends" who saw each other daily for thirteen years and then visited with each other after Ets left the settlement house until Rosa's death in 1943.[88] Impressed with Rosa's skills as a storyteller, which were widely recognized within Chicago's social work circles, women's clubs, and even some local universities that offered storytelling classes, and perhaps with some prodding from Rosa herself,[89] Ets decided to take down her stories.

Although written in the first person, Rosa, the person and the book, is heavily mediated by Ets both in terms of the material offered and its delivery. Ets notes in her introduction that most of Rosa's stories were traditional ones, often funny and irreverent, that Rosa learned from male storytellers she heard as a child in her hometown of Bugiarno, where they entertained villagers gathered in barns with their animals for warmth during cold winter nights. However, these stories held little interest for Ets, who appreciated Rosa's embellishments and acting out of the stories but felt that "when written down these stories held little that would interest moderns." What interested Ets and other "moderns" was the story of Rosa's life and "the fears and superstitions and beliefs of the people of her village. . . . These did seem worth taking down and passing on." She quickly adds "and Rosa was anxious to have me do so,"[90] though one wonders if Rosa would have preferred to tell the traditional tales that had been passed on for generations rather than indulge the moderns' fascination with what they considered the primitive lives of Rosa and her *paesani.*

Just as the content of Rosa's stories was controlled by Ets, so too were her actual words. Because Rosa could neither read nor write English and had very little formal knowledge of Italian, Ets had to rely completely on her own note taking during Rosa's storytelling sessions. As she explains, "she just had to tell me things as she remembered them, *and let me put them in order*" [italics added]. For an earlier version of the book, Ets claims to have taken down Rosa's words "in heavy dialect, as she spoke them," by which I assume she means a heavy Italian American dialect as the text is in English, albeit imperfect. However, for this later version, Ets decided that a literal transcription of Rosa's stories was too difficult for the reader so she "corrected and simplified the text, trying at the same time not to lose the character and style of her spoken words."[91] Ets attempts to convey the "character and style" of Rosa's speech by, for example, using the present tense as often as possible, but it is clear that Rosa's style of speaking has been heavily sanitized. The following sentence is only one example of an unlikely construction: "Maddened by their disapproving silence Santino stalked across the room, snatched his hat from the nail, and went out."[92] Thus Rosa comes to the reader filtered and censored through Ets.[93] It is impossible to know how much of Rosa is lost in translation.

In her mediated state, Rosa has little to say specifically about language. It is only at the end of her tale that traces her childhood beginnings in a Milanese orphanage through her travails in America as an immigrant mother, wife, and worker that Rosa comments at length on the meaning of the English language to her: "Only one wish more I have: I'd love to go in Italia again before I die. Now I speak English good like an American I could go anywhere—where millionaires go and high people. . . . I wouldn't be afraid now—not of anybody. I'd be proud I come from America and speak English. . . . That's what I learned in America: not to be afraid."[94]

Fred Gardaphé has noted that the oral tradition from which Rosa and other Italian immigrants arose left little room for expression of the individual self. This is partly the result of the noted tendency of Italians, particularly in the South, to guard personal secrets and partly because storytelling served specific purposes such as educating the young in the traditions of the group as well as providing entertainment, goals that were not well-served by personal stories. A hallmark of Italian American autobiographical writing is the development of an identity as an individual that is linked to greater facility with the English language. According to Gardaphé, "control of the American language—something immigrants of the oral tradition did not have—means greater control of the self as American." With this greater ability to control the language comes the possibility of forging and articulating an Italian American as opposed to an Italian identity.[95] Rosa's concluding words seem to suggest the beginning of such a transformation for herself, a transformation closely linked with knowledge of the English language, which more than anything else signifies for Rosa her newfound identity as an American. By the end of her narrative, Rosa is no longer one of the millions of Italian immigrants who came to America with their rigid notions of class hierarchy and deference expressed through their local dialects; she has become an individual American armed with a language that makes her second to none.

In her article on autobiographies by Italian women, Maria Parrino offers the possibility of a different interpretation. In keeping with other scholars of women's autobiographies, Parrino draws a distinction between the autobiographies of men and women. She claims that the autobiographies of Italian men are more prone to stress identity conflicts and discontinuities between pre-and postmigration lives. For immigrant women, life was defined much more by gender than by immigration. Life in Italy, as in the United States, centered on household chores and the care of men and children. Although some Italian women such as Rosa did work outside the home, their lives were organized around the private space of the family to a larger degree than men's lives. Parrino concludes that Rosa's ability to assert herself in America is less a function of the transformations wrought by immigration than a question of finding a space that allowed her to express her existing personality. Although she makes no mention of language, Parrino's conclusions suggest that although English, and through it Americanization, may not have been responsible for the development of Rosa's identity, her newfound language made it easier for her to assert her forceful personality. The identity issues implied in the adoption of a new language and culture are perhaps less central to Rosa's life and the lives of other Italian American women.[96]

Rosa's account does provide some indirect clues as to the meanings she and other Italians attributed to language. As a natural storyteller, it is not surprising that Rosa displays an early fascination with language. When she was only four years old, she took delight in learning prayers in Latin from her adopted mother and drew praise for her agility with the language of her religion: "I just loved the sound of those Latin prayers. The words were like music. . . . Pretty soon I was saying them with Mamma Lena. When she heard how good I said them she helped me—she taught me all the words and what the words meant too. The old women were so surprised. They thought I was wonderful. They couldn't say the prayers themselves; they could only say the responses."[97] That Rosa earned so much praise for her facility with Latin prayers suggests the degree to which her *paesani* respected such linguistic fluency. Regarding the storytellers Rosa heard as a child, she notes, "those poor men had never been to school to learn to read and write but they were smart the way they told the stories. They made everyone bust out laughing."[98] Yet it is clear that even though storytelling gave the men a certain amount of status, actual knowledge of how to read and write was what distinguished a person. So Rosa notes that her father knew how to count and read somewhat because he had worked on an American ship "so he was not so stupid."[99] Rosa equates the fear of the villagers for their superiors with ignorance. Intelligence, which came with the formal knowledge of language, made people fearless. Still, Rosa notes that Mama Lena, although she could read, was still fearful, unlike her adopted father whose scant bit of knowledge endowed him with the courage to question "the high people." Indeed, the theme of language—whether standard Italian in her childhood or English in her American incarnation—as the great social leveler appears at several points in Rosa's narrative. Knowledge of standard

Italian provided the means to erase distinctions between "the high people" and Rosa's peasant community in Italy, and English offered the possibility for social elevation not only in the United States, but in Italy as well. On a return trip to Italy, Rosa puts on airs at the local bank by speaking English phrases to an uncomprehending bank officer. As she explains, "that Italian [bank] officer wouldn't know that the words didn't fit and I wanted to show him that I was learning to speak English."[100]

Italian Immigrants wrote autobiographies in Italian as well as in English.[101] Two such examples are Carmine Biagio Iannace's *La scoperta dell'America* (The Discovery of America) and Antonio Margariti's *America! America!* Although translation is not an explicit theme as the authors write and largely live in their original languages, each of these works provides insight into language and its relationship to ethnic identity in the lives of the first-generation arrivals. The stories they tell and the language they use to tell them suggest an uncomplicated relationship to language. Nor does either of these narratives follow the trajectory of the typical immigrant autobiography in which the narrator undergoes a transformation from immigrant to American ethnic marked in part by learning English.

Iannace immigrated to the United States in 1906 while still in his teens from the southern village of San Leucio del Sannio in the region of Campagnia. He passed through Ellis Island and went to Pennsylvania where he joined some fellow *paesani* to work in the rail yards of Meadville. The somewhat disjointed narrative largely consists of scenes of village life from Iannace's youth in Italy either related directly by the author or as recalled in the many stories told by the *paesani* when gathered around the table at the boardinghouse. The scenes of his life in America most often revolve around work with his coethnics, leaving the reader with little sense of the wider world outside of the immigrant community.

This ethnic insularity is reflected in the language of the book. Iannace's autobiography, like Margariti's, is written in a combination of dialect and what the literary critic and the book's translator William Boelhower describes as a "lively but often rudimental" version of Italian notable for its "essentially oral and highly idiomatic style," interspersed with mixed Italian and English words and phrases. Along with his own dialect, Iannace also recreates the speech of fellow Italian workers speaking different dialects such as Sicilian and Neapolitan. Iannace's use of language suggests not just the various linguistic influences on the immigrant's life and their limited education, but also the "double value" of the immigrant's life. As Iannace observes, "it was like living a double life. Not two different or contrasting lives, but one having a double value."[102] As Boelhower notes in an afterword to the book, Iannace's sense of entitlement to write his autobiography in his version of Italian underscores his appreciation for and recognition of the duality of his life, a life lived in his Italian village as well as in the rail yards of Meadville, Pennsylvania, where in any case he was continually surrounded by fellow *paesani*. Unlike the authors previously discussed who wrote in English, Iannace's work was not directed to a broad American audience. Iannace himself, who was in his seventies when he wrote the book in the latter part of the 1960s, suggests that he did so for his grown children and his grandchildren.

There are moments in the narrative when language surfaces as an explicit issue. The inability of the immigrants to speak English is the butt of several comic stories, as is often the case in immigrant narratives. However, language—English, used interchangeably with "American"—is also used in several places to symbolic ends. On the very first page, for example, Iannace relates a story about the all-purpose English word rendered here as "Atzawright": "When my brother Gioacchino arrived at Willas, Pennsylvania, Michelangelo [Iannace's cousin] was already a veteran American and knew how to say 'Atz-awright.' This was an American word that meant many different things. It meant: yes, that's all right, good, very good, not bad, you did a good job, did we do all right? And it had a hundred other nuances that depended on the way it was spoken. He knew only that word, but it was enough. You only had to reply 'Atzawright' and everything was fine."[103] His brother's status as an American is symbolized here by his mastery of this versatile "American" word. This story also suggests the disinterest in English demonstrated by some of D'Angelo's coworkers. As long as he was able to function in American society, Iannace's brother and other immigrant workers were satisfied with their limited knowledge of the de facto national language. At a later point in his narrative, Iannace relates a story that highlights his first words in English. While working in the rail yards, at not more than seventeen years of age, Biagio (the young Iannace) is approached by a revered non-Italian boss who the Italians had nicknamed "Tatone"—"grandfather" in some southern Italian dialects—because of his asthma and chronic cough, although this is an honorific as well. When Tatone tries to encourage Biagio in his arduous and sometimes dangerous work by raising his fist in a gesture meant to spur him on, he says, believing that Biagio has misinterpreted him, "don't be afraid," to which Biagio quickly retorts in English, "I am not afraid. I knew you were joking." Iannace goes on to write, referring to his bewildered Italian coworkers who were awed by his audacity in talking back to Tatone, "to tell the truth, I knew less English than they did, namely, not a single word, but when I heard something, I was often able to remember the way it sounded."[104] Biagio's pluck is symbolized by his willingness to exploit what little knowledge he has of the language of his new home, a language that enhances his status among his own people.

Antonio Margariti was born in Ferruzzano in Calabria, but he spent most of his long life in Philadelphia and later in nearby Willow Grove where he died in 1981 at the age of ninety. He was twenty-two years old when he arrived in the United States in 1914. Margariti, who became an ardent socialist and years later an anarchist sympathizer, largely through his own experiences as a laborer and soldier both in Italy and in America, was an autodidact who taught himself to write after his own fashion. He tells his story through a combination of the Calabrese dialect interspersed with Italian, English, and mixed words. To give some sense of the idiosyncratic nature of his use of language, the book, published in Italy, provides an Italian language translation of Margariti's narrative followed by a replica of his typewritten text. Like Iannace, Margariti tries to capture the dialects of his conationals as well. Unlike Iannace, however, Margariti does not reflect on his life first in Italy and then in America in terms of the doubling that Boelhower saw refracted in Iannace's choice of language. Rather, his story reads like one seamless tale of hardship and exploitation regardless of geographical location. There is little reflection on language or living in translation. He uses Italo-American dialect unselfconsciously and without comment, using, for example, *machina* to refer to a machine (the Italian word is *macchina*) and "una box di candy."[105] The English language receives little mention, appearing either when he is describing American phenomena ("state road," "the Victor Talking machene [sic]") or when spoken by the occasional non-Italian figure in his story ("what she said you know").[106] Indeed, his indifference to the language of his new home is symbolized by the first words of English that he learned on the boat over: "'you speak italiano?'"[107]

One of the few stories dealing with language involves an incident in France when he was a U.S. soldier. He narrates proudly how he was able to fool the other soldiers into thinking that he knew French. However, as he writes in his own idiosyncratic version of Italian, "*laverita era che io non parlavo, ne il Francese e ben poco L'Inglese ma comprendeva il Francese molto meglio degli americani perche' era vecine all Italiano*" ("the truth was that I didn't speak French and very little English but I understood French much better than the Americans because it was close to Italian").[108] He appears to take pride in being able to understand when the Americans do not, an apparent inversion of his usual situation in America.

Neither Iannace's nor Margariti's narrative delves deeply into questions of identity. In an uncharacteristically self-conscious passage, Iannace salutes the American ideal of work, a testament, according to Boelhower, to his

Americanization or, at a minimum, a way to "claim his rights as citizen."[109] It reads, however, more like an afterthought, an attempt to justify the struggles and deprivations he and his compatriots silently endured. This impression of Iannace as having a limited identification with America is bolstered by the structure of the narrative that begins with a scene from Iannace's life in his small southern Italian village and concludes when he is about to leave Italy again for the second of many trips to America. His choice of (primarily) an Italian dialect and the limited audience he chooses to address further supports an identification with, if not Italy and Italians, then with the well-defined circle of family and *paesani* that inhabit the narrative from beginning to end, whether in Italy or in America. This is not to say that Iannace does not appreciate the benefits of America, which he defines exclusively in material terms, but his narrative does not suggest a profound transformation in ethnic identification. Iannace's double lives appear to have remained largely separate, save for some linguistic overlap.

Margariti's lack of attention to language is indicative of his disinterest in the whole question of ethnic identity. It is a nonissue to him best illustrated by his response to the village priest of his hometown who asks him, upon a return visit to see his mother, if he is an American: "*Io? Sono nato in questo paese. In America mi chiamano italiano, qui in Italia mi chiamano americano.*" ("Me? I was born in this country. In America they call me Italian, here in Italy they call me American.")[110] Unlike Iannace, he takes a more critical view of his conationals, at several points leveling a harsh critique of Italians and southerners in particular, although he is careful to lay the blame for their shortcomings on "the system." Margariti's depiction of southern Italians as a violent people who took advantage of each other was likely colored by his occasional run-ins with the Philadelphia *mafiosi* who bombed his brother's bar not once, but twice. America for Margariti is at once the center of the capitalist system he despises as well as the source of opportunities—education, housing, steady pay—that were unimaginable in Italy. Yet the impression his book leaves is that he enjoyed those benefits from the margins of American life, separated as he was not only by language, but also by political ideology and culture, a separation that he does not once bemoan.

That language receives such short shrift in both of these accounts can most simply be accounted for by the striking lack of contact that the Italians have with English-speaking Americans. The worlds that Iannace and Margariti inhabit are largely peopled by relatives and *paesani* and secondarily with Italians from other parts of Italy. When non-Italians do make an appearance in these narratives, they are often members of other recognizable immigrant/ethnic groups. Margariti, for example, tells the story of getting into a fight with one of his German coworkers in a Philadelphia bakery because the Germans *"ci parlavano con tono arrogante"* ("they spoke to us in arrogant tones").[111] One wonders whether the Germans spoke to the Italians in English or whether Margariti and others could detect the derision the Germans had for them even when speaking their own (German) language. However, Margariti is silent on this point.[112] The most likely place that Italians encountered the English language was on the job, as Iannace does in the rail yards and Margariti does whether working in the bakery or as part of a road construction gang. English in these contexts is almost entirely utilitarian.

• • •

The three sites of examination reveal the mixed outcomes possible for the immigrant in translation. As the examples of Ellis Island and the courtroom suggest, relying on translators involved a loss of control over self-representation that could have serious consequences including deportation or incarceration. However, translation could also lead to opportunities for gain. Immigrants used the ambiguity of their linguistic situation to their advantage just as it was used against them. The writings of first- and second-generation Italian Americans reveal that the translation of the self into the American context was not a simple matter of linguistic adaptation. The easy equation of learning English with becoming American is inadequate to account for the variety of linguistic experiences depicted here, as exemplified by Rosa's use of English in Italy to enhance her social status as an Italian. Nor did speaking Italian imply an uncomplicated identification with Italy, as Margariti's text illustrates. Moreover, the construction of a new ethnic identity took place within the context of a variety of language encounters, not simply those between Italian immigrant and native English speakers. Speakers of various Italian dialects and members of other immigrant groups were also an important part of the linguistic landscape that informed the construction of Italian American linguistic and ethnic identity. The use of the Italian immigrant idiom suggests even more permutations of the language/identity equation.

FOUR

The World Turned Upside Down in Farfariello's Theater of Language

The Inglish [*sic*] is the Italian language up side down.
—"Italian Language" by Eduardo Migliaccio

Italians, like other immigrant groups in the early decades of the twentieth century, had their own theater that ranged from Italian language productions of Shakespearean dramas to Sicilian puppet shows.[1] Comic theater, however, was the most popular Italian form. The undisputed leading performer of the Italian American comic stage was Eduardo Migliaccio, also known as Farfariello (literally, "Little Butterfly," but with the added connotation of a little devil, i.e., a womanizer). Farfariello mined the immigrant encounter with the American way of life for his comic character sketches known as *macchiette coloniale*. He played the Bowery theaters of the Lower East Side, although his fame extended from the east coast to the west coast and even to Italy, which he toured at least once.[2]

Farfariello's comic skits and songs, many of them written in the Italian immigrant idiom, often relied on confusions of language for their punch. His work constitutes an especially rich source for examining issues of language for Italian immigrants from the perspective of the immigrants. His papers, consisting largely of the material used in his acts, may well be the only significant body of writing in the Italian American vernacular. Indeed, it is clear from the multiple revisions that Farfariello made to his sketches and song lyrics that it required some thought on his part to determine how best to transcribe the sound of a language that previously did not exist in written form. The rarity of this source coupled with Farfariello's popularity among working-class Italian immigrants who left few written records makes his work an invaluable site for the examination of immigrant subjectivity and the relationship between immigrant identity and language in particular. An analysis of these pieces reveals both the centrality and the complexity of language in the immigrant imagination as well as in daily life. Major aspects of immigrant life were expressed as problems of language that echoed the issues faced by his immigrant audience. These included social tensions of gender and class within the immigrant community itself, tensions that had their basis in the Old World, but that were uniquely a part of the changing social relations in the New World. Farfariello's characters use language to assert themselves within the immigrant community often in novel ways— women over men, lower class over upper class. His intricate use of language illustrates aspects of linguistic power that would have been familiar to the immigrants, but that were given a new twist in America. Farfariello's language humor also poked fun at immigrant ways of speaking. Coming from a sympathetic insider, this humor offered the audience a way to transcend the hardships of immigration represented by the inability to speak either standard Italian or English. His work vividly illustrates the transformations of identity the immigrants underwent that are reflected in the Italian American vernacular. These identity changes wrought by and reflected in language were not necessarily unidirectional, from dialect to English, or from Italian to Italian American, but were considerably more complicated.

Il Re dei Macchiettisti

Migliaccio, who was born into a well-to-do family, grew up in Cava dei Tirreni near Naples. He studied design and sculpture in Italy and immigrated to the United States sometime in 1897 or 1898. By the early 1900s, he had become the king of the Italian immigrant theater, a position he would maintain through the 1930s, although he continued to perform to live and radio audiences until his death in 1946.[3] His *macchiette* owed much to the modern Neapolitan variety theater that also relied on this form.[4] A contemporary of Farfariello's described this art form in an article for *The American Mercury*: "The *macchietta* is a character sketch. If well done, the character with all its peculiarities is recognized as soon as the comedian appears on the stage. It can be satirical, ironic, tragicomic, or sentimentally ridiculous. As it is done by the majority of the *macchiettisti* it has usually a double sense, relying upon the spectator to catch a hidden pornographic meaning. The *machietta* is mostly written in verse, with spoken passages of prose. The verses are put to music."[5]

Farfariello portrayed a variety of characters, male and female, from the lowly immigrant *cafone* to the great Caruso (a friend of his) with an artistry that drew the attention of uptown patrons of the arts as well as Italian immigrant laborers. There is some indication that he was also known to the larger American society; he was referred to by some as the Italian Harry Lauder, a well-known Scottish vaudeville performer of the era.[6] Italian language humor did not originate with Farfariello. Italy has a long tradition of theatrical comedy that relied on plays on language. The contrast between the various Italian dialects and in particular the high-low juxtaposition of Florentine with what were considered lesser dialects was standard fare in Italian theater, including the *commedia dell'arte*, at least as far back as the 1600s. Language humor has also characterized Italian American comedy throughout the twentieth century, from Farfariello to the contemporary comic, Floyd Vivino.[7]

However, Migliaccio's singular contribution to the Italian American theater was his use of the Italian immigrant idiom. He, along with others whose songs he performed, wrote in this idiom. The interweaving of standard Italian, Italian dialects, English, and Italianized English reflected the actual speech styles of his audience rather than mere caricatures.[8]

Migliaccio's initial experience with Italian immigrants in the United States is worth noting in considering how he came to develop his distinctive art form. He came to the United States to work with his father in a bank in Hazleton, Pennsylvania. His job was to write letters for the largely illiterate Italian clients of the bank to their relatives overseas. He naturally wrote the letters in standard Italian, as any educated Italian would, but this prompted at least one bewildered immigrant to demand of Migliaccio's father, "*Ma questo figliolo in che lingua scrive?*" ("In what language does this boy write?").[9]

Migliaccio later moved to New York City where, following a series of jobs as a manual laborer, he secured another position with a bank located on Mulberry Street. Once in Little Italy, he began frequenting a local cafe that featured live entertainment. His career began when he spontaneously started entertaining the cafe's patrons with a comic sketch and song involving the character Farfariello. This character was based on the idea of a buffoonish peasant attempting to become Americanized: "He [Farfariello] was a familiar character, typical of the *cafone*, who adopted American clothes, aped American manners and even took over a few American colloquialisms, but who was still Italian to the core."[10] The sobriquet stuck because it was the refrain of the song for which he received many encores. Though he occasionally toured, most of his performances took place in the theaters of the Lower East Side such as the Fugazy on Houston Street or the People's Theater in the Bowery.[11]

Unlike some other groups, notably Jewish immigrants, Italians in New York City were more likely to attend their own theater rather than mainstream vaudeville shows.[12] Italian theaters presented some dramas and melodramas written by Italian playwrights. At least one contemporary of Farfariello argued that the highest form of artistic expression in the Italian American theater was reached by some of the marionette theaters.[13] However, there was little in the way of new works of any genre that drew specifically on Italian American life. Comedy emerged as one, if not the favored, form of entertainment. The mainly comic nature of the Italian American stage did not lend itself to the use of theater as a self-conscious vehicle of ethnic pride. Unlike the Yiddish theater that made language a central subject in dramas to encourage its preservation, language in the Italian comic theater was more often than not the butt of the joke. Critic Giuseppe Cautela, writing in the *American Mercury* in 1927, explained the difference between the two ethnic theaters: "The Jews, it seems, keep up the living tradition of their tongue by sheer force of intellect, whereas the Italians seem bent upon forgetting whatever culture they bring along." Even though Cautela attributes the difference to "the tremendous struggle for existence" that left Italian immigrants with little time or interest in cultural enrichment, the greater disparity between Jewish and Italian immigrant culture is in the cohesive function that Yiddish traditionally served for Jews that contrasts sharply with the linguistic diversity and rivalry of the dialects of Italy.[14]

Initially, Migliaccio's material was derived from Neapolitan sketches that poked fun at the poor grammar of the lead characters. This type of humor was rooted in the North-South tensions in Italy that included a derisive view of southern dialects. Migliaccio had been an avid theatergoer in Naples, attending numerous performances of the famed Neapolitan *machiettista* Maldacea. These early forays into the art of the *macchiette* were probably based on Maldacea's work. However, Migliaccio quickly realized that the jokes fell flat on his poorly educated, working-class immigrant audiences who could not always make subtle distinctions between good and poor Italian grammar. Nor could they understand the references to contemporary Italian politics and culture.[15] These experiences ultimately contributed to Migliaccio's development of a uniquely Italian American theater that not only incorporated the language of the immigrants, but also the events of their daily lives. Indeed, the interrelatedness of the two—language and lived existence—required that he use both.

It was Farfariello's development of the *macchiette coloniale* that led to the birth of Italian variety theater in New York, a form that has been compared to American vaudeville by at least one Italian American critic of the time. We know something of the scene in the Italian American variety theaters in which Farfariello performed, although there are some discrepancies in the accounts. One observer in 1926 noted, "the real performance in an Italian theater, especially the *varietà*, is given by the audience. It runs the house. From the pit to the gallery the battle of approval and disapproval rages." He describes the audience as mainly laborers with their families, including women and children. In addition to the women and children who formed a significant portion of the audience, author Carl Van Vechten noted the presence of different classes at a performance he attended in 1919.[16] Although his work appealed to various segments of the Italian immigrant community, it is not surprising that the lower class constituted the bulk of his audience given the preponderance of uneducated laborers who formed the core of the community and the variety theatergoing public. Audiences responded forcefully one way or another to Farfariello's performances. It was not unusual for members of the audience to interact with the performers on stage by talking or hissing.[17] Yet a reviewer for the *Christian Science Monitor*, also writing in 1919, commented on the way the audience became silent when Farfariello came on stage and remained so even between costume changes, which suggested a certain popular reverence for the performer.[18] Whether silent or animated, it seems that Farfariello's audiences paid close attention to his performances.

The performances consisted of an opening song, then a monologue followed by another verse of the opening song. Unlike other vaudeville and variety performers, Farfariello's character sketches were not just crude caricatures. One observer also objected to the term impersonation, saying: "The word impersonation is used advisedly, for Farfariello's character studies were, in each of these four phases, examples of a thorough blending of the player's individuality with that of the personage represented. With each change of character, there was a change in the style of speaking, a subtle but effective change in the matter of slide, pause and attack which represented the instinctive response of his voice to the mentality of the individual being impersonated. Farfariello's gestures are varied in the same way."[19]

In addition to his skill as a lyricist and performer, Migliaccio had a talent for making masks and wigs that helped him create a panoply of diverse but equally believable characters including both sexes (he was well-known for performing in drag) and different nationalities. He even developed a means of fitting all of the pieces of one costume together to facilitate the many costume changes—as many as six in one-half hour—he had to undergo in the course of a single performance.[20] His characterizations of everyday types from New York's Little Italy seem to have been most popular with his audience, much more so than characters taken from Italy itself. As another contemporary noted, "for in Farfariello his audiences find a congenial expression of themselves." This ability to recognize themselves in Farfariello's art seems to have been a central component of the appeal for his immigrant audience. The character of the ice man—a New World figure who sings old Neapolitan songs—was his most popular impersonation, encapsulating as it did immigrant life that was characterized by both novelty and nostalgia.[21]

Farfariello's ability to capture these immigrant characters was the result of careful study, much of which took place at the Caffe Ronca near his home where he would begin each day with his morning coffee: "Unobtrusively sitting at a corner table, he would sip his black coffee with anisette. Taciturn and never smiling, he would listen patiently to any one of his admirers who approached and spoke to him. Thus he studied the types and characters that some days later had new life on the stage."[22] So effective were his character studies that at least one contemporary reviewer has remarked on the power that Migliaccio exerted on the immigrant community through his art. His satiric impersonation of the Italian immigrant patriot who was given to parading through the streets of New York in ill-fitting Italian army uniforms apparently brought this practice to an end.[23]

The attention he devoted to his craft was rewarded; his popularity among Italian immigrants is unquestionable. In 1919, while performing at the New Palace, the Italian theater in Boston, he presented four performances each day for over two weeks. A contemporary newspaper critic noted that when he attended, the seats were filled with over fifty additional people standing. Carl van Vechten captured Farfariello's stature within New York's Italian immigrant community: "I doubt . . . if there is a single Italian in New York—and are there not more Italians here than in Rome?—who would not genuflect before the name, [Farfariello] the name behind which Edoardo [*sic*] Migliaccio has become *il re dei macchiettisti*."[24]

The Problem of Language

Migliaccio's careful study of his compatriots gave him a feel for the lives of average Italians in the United States that is clearly reflected in the songs and skits that explicitly address the problems the immigrants had with language.

Some songs suggest a sense of chaos through language best expressed in the image of New York (and America more generally) as a tower of Babel where it is impossible to comprehend anything and it is easy to misunderstand or be misunderstood. In "Che suonno" (What a Dream), the narrator describes a dream in which he ascends to heaven but at one point finds himself in *"un nuovo mondo"* (a new world, the implication being *the* New World) *"non era piu' il paradiso, era la torre di Babele, na specie Nuova Yorca, parlavano tutte le lingue... io no ho capito niente"* ("it wasn't heaven anymore, it was the Tower of Babel, a type of New York, they spoke all languages . . . I didn't understand anything").[25] In "Chrley" [*sic*] (Charley) a young Italian dandy asserts, *"intanto siccome l'America e' la torre di Babele sono stato costretto a imparare tutte le lingue"* ("because America is the tower of Babel I have been forced to learn all of the languages").[26] This sense of the difficulty of communicating is one that is depicted as a problem internal to the Italian community as well as in relations with non-Italians. "'O Cucchiere Napulitano," about a dolt who fancies himself a lady's man, opens with the narrator's dubious assertion in Neapolitan dialect that he can speak Italian, French, English, *and* "American." When he addresses a man in French, the response he receives is *"Io so' cchiu' napulitano 'e te . . . E allora, vatte'."* ("I'm more Neapolitan than you. . . . So get lost").[27] In the New World that Migliaccio depicted on stage, one never knew what language to use and this could create comic, but ultimately disturbing possibilities.

This theme of miscommunication was not unique to Migliaccio. In a play found among his papers entitled *Sabato Santo*, Vincenzo and Nannina, an older Neapolitan couple living in the United States, await the arrival of their newly widowed son and his daughter who have been living in northern Italy for years. Vincenzo explains that his son has forgotten how to speak Neapolitan and his granddaughter never learned it so it is up to him and his wife to speak standard Italian. Although Vincenzo makes an effort and goes so far as to claim *"Il Napoletano e un dialetto volgare,"* his wife refuses to even try and is delighted to find that her son does speak some Neapolitan in spite of himself. The running "joke" is in the fear that members of the same family will not be able to understand each other.[28]

The confusion generated by English words that have entirely different meanings in Italian is another element in Migliaccio's humor that again speaks to the disorientating experience of living in America for the immigrant and that provides an opportunity to skewer American values. In *Il Calandriello* (The Greenhorn), Migliaccio writes in dialect: "The language then, it is like Italian! . . .The 'piani' then, are called floors [play on *fuori* in

Italian meaning, 'outside'] because when your friends come and visit you they are usually kicked out. . . . The bed ['letto'] is called *bed* because in the American language bed means bad, and the bed is no good, it makes you an animal! . . . The chair [*cera* pronounced 'chair-a'; Italian for 'wax'] because people wax it so that you don't sit on it, because, if you ever sit down in this country, you don't eat."[29] While Farfariello's material reflects the difficulties brought about by the use of multiple languages in America, including different versions of Italian and the slippage between English and Italian, the Italian language in some form is held up as the superior one, reflecting a common sensibility among the immigrants. The contrast between English as a crooked (*storto*) language vs. Italian as smooth (*liscia*) appears in several songs and suggests the ease of expression possible in Italian and particularly in the Neapolitan dialect as opposed to English, which the immigrant experiences as awkward and halting. In "'a Lengua 'Taliana" (The Italian Language), the narrator speaks to the difference in sound between the two, with Italian cast as the more pleasing alternative: "*Pane significa pane nun gia' ca come l'inglese me lo chiamate prete*" ("Bread means bread not like in English where they call it *bread*," a pun on the Italian word *prete*, which means "priest"). It is clear that the Italian word *pane* (pronounced pa-ney) is more pleasing to the ear than *bread* (which is pronounced as an Italian trying to speak English might say it—pret) because of the awkward sound as well as the reference to priests.[30] In an English version of this piece, the narrator uses the example of his name—Pasquale (Pas-kwal-eh) in Italian as opposed to Patsy in English—to demonstrate that Italian is more *liscia*. Similarly, he objects to the English word *beans* ("Like something that escpolodes" [*sic*]): "See how *liscia* is in italian. *Pasta e fasule*. See that's *liscia!*" Of course, these are comic pieces and Farfariello is poking fun at this immigrant attitude at the same time that he is representing it. This same piece, for example, ends with the narrator's wife swearing at him in Italian to which he responds, "see *come e liscia!*" ("See how smooth it is!") Another version of this song has the narrator claim that it is not that English is an ugly language (though it is "crooked"); the problem is that it is just not Italian. That the word *storto* also means "wrong" certainly adds to the comic affect while also revealing something of the immigrant sensibility regarding the English language. [31]

Just as Italian is preferable to English, so are other dialects even though they can be notoriously difficult to understand for an outsider. In one song, the narrator claims he would even take Calabrese (which other Italians sometimes equate in difficulty with Chinese) over English. The idea of English as a difficult language seems to parallel the idea that America is a difficult place in which to live when one considers all of the images of the New World presented in these songs: as a place of confusion, excessively hard work, and so on. The advantage of any Italian language over English is clear—"*Qualunque dialetto che parla il taliano / Si tu non 'o capisce, se fa capi' cu 'e mmane*" ("Whatever dialect the Italian speaks / If you don't understand, he can make you understand with the hands").[32] The Italian—and particularly Neapolitan—use of hand gestures as an eloquent means of communication is good for many laughs in these pieces even as it provides a commentary on the southern Italian sensibility vis-à-vis communication.[33] In psychoanalytic terms, giving up any version of Italian for English is equivalent to a kind of linguistic dismemberment: one has to symbolically lose one's hands and the greater possibilities for communication that they allow.

The use of hand gestures forms a part of a larger southern Italian sensibility regarding self-expression that includes an appreciation for variety. Not only does Italian offer an additional repertoire for communication in the form of hand gestures, but the Neapolitan dialect in particular also contains rich possibilities for expression, especially when it comes to stronger emotions such as love and anger. The narrator of "'a Lengua 'Taliana" comments on the greater number of swear words in Italian (and especially Neapolitan) than in English: "*nu migliaro . . . senza contare quelle ca sape muglierema*" ("about a thousand . . . not counting those that my wife knows"). However, as in most of Farfariello's pieces, there is much playfulness and good-spirited self-mockery here regarding immigrant attitudes toward language. The stock Italian characters Colombine and Pulcinella give some sense of this in a song named after them:

Col.	*Si' venuto a stu paese,*	You came to this country
	Senza manco parla' inglese?	Without even knowing English?
Pul.	*Pe gira' 'o munno sano,*	To travel the world safely
	He 'a sape' 'o napulitano.	You must know Neapolitan.
	E si tu nun me capisce,	And if you don't understand me,
	Io te parlo pure inglisce	I'll even speak to you in English.
	Parlo 'alengua 'e stu paese,	I speak the language of the land,
	'o turesco e 'o francese.	whether Turkish or French.[34]

The absurdity of the idea that Neapolitan is the only language one need know to travel the world pokes fun at immigrant provincialism expressed as language pride.

The content of this material suggests that the problem of language for Italian immigrants was not limited to the difficulty of learning English, as might be expected, but encompassed a broad range of linguistic issues including the meanings attached to various languages, both pre- and postmigration, and the greater opportunities for communication offered by the use of Italian hand gestures. Figuratively, Farfariello employed the theme of the linguistic confusion encountered in the New World to signify the disorder of immigrant life. The use of language as a comic theme represents the difficulties associated with immigration, but it also suggests a kind of continuity from Old World to New, not only in terms of the history of the Italian stage with its use of dialect humor, but in addressing the familiar issue of language itself for southern Italians. Linguistic subordination was a staple of life for the dialect-speaking southern Italians, whether in Italy or in America.

Gender Trouble

The theme of misunderstanding and miscommunication due to differences in language evident in Farfariello's *macchiette* was common in ethnic theater.[35] A number of Farfariello's skits and songs involving women and relations between the sexes make use of the same premise of miscommunication, but they also reveal additional themes. Three specific themes include: (1) the way in which communication problems men had with women—both Italian and American—reflect the language problems immigrants faced in everyday life and the profound dislocation they experienced between their lives in southern Italy and their new lives in the United States; (2) how conflicts regarding issues of language for the immigrants such as the use of dialect versus standard Italian, or Italian versus English usage, were projected onto women and treated again as problems between the sexes; and, (3) the use of the comparative freedom to court women in the United States to represent the differences between southern Italian and American life illustrated through language usage. The male anxieties regarding gender relations in the New World expressed in these works suggest more generalized male immigrant fears regarding the experience of immigration.

A bit from the piece entitled "Italian Language" illustrates the degree to which women, language, and the experience of immigration were bound up in much of Farfariello's work. The male Italian immigrant narrator, making a pun on the similarity between the English word women and the Italian word for men (*uomini*), notes (in English), "The Inglish [*sic*] is the Italian language up side down. For instance in English woman means woman in Italian *women [uomini] means men* . . . see . . . up side down."[36] Punning, a recurring device in Farfariello's language humor, and other attempts to subvert language have been discussed in terms of "a refusal to submit to linguistic discipline, a momentary tactic by which the linguistic system is raided and used 'trickily,' disrespectfully."[37] The "interlinguistic play" that characterizes Farfariello's work is an example of what Michael Fisher calls "inter-referencing." This refers to the use of the language (or in the Italian case, "languages") that the immigrants brought with them as well as the language of the host country in the same speech event, also known as code-switching, along with references from the two cultures to form a unique communication fully accessible only to insiders who have direct experience of living between two cultures.[38] However, this upside down world that Farfariello invoked was not only a function of words, but also of the very different social and economic circumstances that enabled Italian immigrant women and especially their daughters to assume new, nontraditional roles in America—as wage workers, consumers, and participants in American popular culture.[39] Immigration presented Italian men with a host of challenges, not the least of which was the perceived threat to traditional notions of masculinity presented by this new reality, no laughing matter for a people who historically had lived and, in some cases, died by the codes of honor and shame.

Farfariello's language humor expertly captured these gender tensions. A common scenario involves the idea of a male narrator being taken advantage of, usually in terms of money, by a woman capitalizing on the confusion over language. "Come Darling" tells the story of an Italian with upper class pretensions who courts a woman in Naples whom he mistakenly thinks is English, but who turns out to be an Italian born in the United States.[40] He wonders how he will court her "*Con dieci parole che so'?*" ("With the ten words I know [of English]?") In the refrain, he croons "Come darling I love you, y [*sic*] love you . . . give me a kiss, j [*sic*] love you." He takes her out to dinner and she racks up a bill while ignoring his amorous overtures. At one point she turns her back to him and he is filled with murderous rage, wishing to "*strangolarla come un tacchino insolente*" ("strangle her like an insolent turkey"). He tries to touch her and she gives him "*un formidabile schiaffo*" ("a formidable slap") at which point "*la bellissima inglese cosi si esprimeva nella sua lingua nativa* ("the English beauty expressed herself like this in her native language"). Using very rough-sounding dialect, she answers: "*Ueh e chi t' 'o ffa fa? Tu 'a ggente pe chi ll' he pigliate? . . . e si cu quatte cienteseme ca 'e spiso, te vulive suzzulia' 'sta pullanchella . . . So' 'taliana ma so' nato America.*" ("Eh, who made you do it? Who do you take people for? and if with those four cents that you spent you wanted to nibble this girl . . . I'm Italian but born in America [i.e., she understands English]"). There is some ambiguity about the question of who the audience is meant to sympathize with, the rebuffed gentleman or the common woman who puts the womanizing dandy in his place using the language of the street. However, the conclusion reasserts the supremacy of gender over class solidarity. The Neapolitan offers this advice for others *"quando vi capitera' una avventura simile, cercate d'essere sicuri se e' inglese o americana, o se e' americana figlia d'italiani, o se proprio e' una di quell figlie di"* ("when a similar event occurs to you, try to be sure if she is English or American, or if she is an American daughter of Italians, or if she's really one of those daughters of a [whore]"). Even though in this case the action is transposed to Italy and complicated with overtones of class antagonism, the theme that predominates is that of being defrauded by a woman through language—a literal and symbolic male immigrant fear reflecting the sense of powerlessness in the New World where confusion, signified by women, reigned.

Men could sometimes also benefit from this linguistic confusion, though ultimately women seem to be more adept at using the ambiguities of language and nationality to their advantage. In "Mi no spicco guddo inglisce" ("Me no speak good English"), a womanizing immigrant narrator explains how he is popular with presumably American women but avoids any requests for money by saying:

Mi no spicco guddo inglisce	Me no speak good English.
So taliano e no capisce	I'm Italian and don't understand
no spik evri bari	don't speak everybody
Mi no long in dis contri	Me no long in this country
Mi no gare tu mocce moni	Me no got too much money

However, the tables are turned on him when he courts a girl who seems American with her bobbed blond hair and make up, but who turns out to be Italian. She demands marriage or else *"Te taglio 'a capa iu capisce?"* ("I'll cut your head off you understand?") *"Uariu min . . . mi parlo poco poco taliano mi no stend."* ("What do you mean . . . me speak little little Italian me no understand"). He elaborates in the concluding rhyme:

"Mi no spicco guddo 'taliano	Me no speak good Italian
mi parlo little bit	me speak little bit
mi tok sulo 'mericano	me talk just American
no tok Mulberi' strit	no talk Mulberry Street
Mi so nato a stu contri'	Me born in this country
Scuse scuse mai dir Meri'	Excuse excuse my dear Mary[41]

While he tries to pull off a version of his usual routine with the Italian woman, one gets the feeling that he will not have too much luck with it this time. This piece is also indicative of how Italian women who speak in their dialects are portrayed by Farfariello: as sharp-witted and somewhat menacing to men; they are a force to be reckoned with that cannot easily be dismissed. This view stands in stark contrast to the stereotype of Italian immigrant women as passive and subordinate to men.[42] This example functions, as do others, as a kind of warning to the male immigrant to resist the temptations of the New World represented by American women. Despite her threats, the revelation that the seductress is in actuality Italian, and a southern Italian at that, may have been a source of reassurance, an indication that the immigrant had not strayed as far from the motherland—and the mother tongue—as he might have feared.[43]

Women are presented in these skits as alternatively more likely to speak either English or standard Italian or as traditionalists who resist speaking anything but their dialect. The ambivalence of the immigrants over the necessity of learning English and their loyalty to their traditional languages—and what each of these positions implies for identity—is projected onto women. The inability to speak standard Italian as opposed to dialect, an Old World issue for these immigrants, is also reflected in the dual role given women in these pieces. The next two songs exemplify this last point.

In the song "Mary," the narrator says he loves Mary, but complains of her insistence that he stop speaking Italian and speak English instead:

Conosco a na guagliona,	I know a girl
c' overamente e' bbona,	who's really good
ma nun me vo' senti'	but she doesn't want to hear me
Le parlo italiano,	I speak Italian to her
Risponno americano	She answers in American

So the narrator attempts to accommodate her with:

"Mary . . . Mary . . .
With the red, with the green jellow cloths
J [*sic*] bought a wedding ring
To put on your fing
J'm [*sic*] waiting now to hear
Thos [*sic*] wedding bells ring.[44]

The narrator is clearly self-conscious about his English, which explains in part his reluctance to speak it, but there is also a sense of impending loss at the thought of having to give up his language (dialect) to have his bride. In this case, the woman is the Americanizer and the man her reluctant follower.

A parallel process occurs in "A Lengua d' 'a Dummeneca" (Sunday's Language), which features a Neapolitan dialect-speaking paramour.[45] He asks his Tuscan lover, who prefers standard Italian, to allow him to declare his love in Neapolitan. As in "Mary," Farfariello has the narrator move between two languages, in this case, standard Italian and Neapolitan. Using standard Italian for the first two lines, the narrator states:*"Vi parlero di rose di verbene / e cerchero il piu puro italiano"* ("I will speak to you of rose and verbena / and seek the most pure Italian"). However, he concludes in Neapolitan: *"ma quanno v' aggia di': ve voglio bene, / faciteme parla' napulitano"* ("but when I have to tell you: I love you / let me speak neapolitan"). The narrator's desire to express his love in his native dialect suggests an emotional anchoring to the language of origin (in this case, as for most immigrants, the dialect) and suggests the potential depth of the conflicts that are involved in adopting a new language. Again, as in "Mary," this struggle over language is presented as a dissonance between the sexes.

As in other pieces that pit the dialect against standard Italian, there is a tone of mockery directed toward the language purists. Using a reference to Manzoni's *I promessi sposi* that he wrote in then contemporary Florentine Italian in order to promote its adoption as the national language, the narrator of "A Lengua d' 'a Dummeneca" claims (again, mixing dialect and standard Italian): *"Ho risciacquato in Arno 'a lengua mia / pecche' ve voglio tantu tanto bene"* ("I've rinsed my tongue in the Arno [river] / because I love you so so much").[46] The closing lines of the song reassert the supremacy of the dialect while again poking fun at the affectations of his mistress. Speaking one line in standard Italian and the last in Neapolitan, he says: *"Ed accettate un mio consiglio sano / mparateve a parla' napulitano"* ("And accept my sound advice / learn how to speak Neapolitan").

The woman as language traditionalist appears in "Pasquale Catena," a sentimental spoof of a hypernationalist, a common type presented by Farfariello.[47] He brags that everyone in his house knows Italian as well as English, his wife being the only exception: *"Sultanto la mia signora tiene un lengua, ma quella abbasta per cento"* ("Only my wife has one language but that is worth a hundred"). That language is clearly a dialect of Italian. Again, the dialect-speaking woman is presented as sharp-tongued and even abusive.[48] Women, in short, act as boundary figures in these pieces, either maintaining traditional linguistic and cultural limits or extending them.

The differences in courtship practices between southern Italy and America is another subject in Farfariello's work that reveals the interrelatedness of gender and language. These differences are signified by the use of English or the Italian immigrant idiom. In "'O Cafone c' 'a Sciammeri a," the immigrant narrator starts out by saying he loves America *"perche' qua siamo tutte quante eguale"* ("because here we're all equal") but, as it turns out, the ease of courting women is the best part of being in America.[49] In Italy, one has to be on the look out for fathers and brothers protecting the honor of their women, but suitors have a much easier time of it in America:

Ma qua ll'ammore e' olrraite,	But here lovemaking is alright,
Overamente e' bello,	Actually it's beautiful,
Il padre penza e' dollare,	The father thinks of dollars,
Il frate penza e' ghelle	The brother thinks of girls
Percio la strada e' libera,	That's why the road is clear,
Aperta so' li porte.	The doors are open.
La chiamme: Come daune.	You call her: Come down.
T' a pigli e te la puorte.	You get her and you take her away.
Dezze bicose Franci',	That's because Frankie,
Mi laiche dis contri'.	Me like this country.

Similarly, once married in America, it is not as difficult to get out of a marriage as it is in Italy.

Ma qua dentro all' America,	But here in America,
Si nun te pare bbona,	If she doesn't seem good to you,
Scasse lu matremmonio	Break the marriage
E te la vai a cagna'	And go exchange her
Dice: misto no laiche.	Say: Mister, no like.

In these pieces, English, or some variant of it, is equated with greater social freedoms even as these more lax American conventions are mocked. American-style courtship practices are portrayed as being based on consumerism symbolized by the need for gift giving by the much put-upon suitor. In "Ammore All'americana," the male narrator laments the loss of his girlfriend due to her incessant demands for money and gifts.[50] The two are both Italians, but he accuses her (in dialect) of thinking just like some American girls:

ca vanno mazzecanno miez' 'a via,	who go chewing [gum] in the middle of the street,
Se mangnano 'o saciccio mmiez 'o ppane,	they eat sausage inside bread [hot dogs],
Vulive accatta' sempe . . embe' Lili' e ppezze 'a dint' 'a sacca 'e cacciavo i'!	you wanted to buy always . . . so Lili with dollars in [your] pocket I took out [paid]!

When he first asks her if she loves him (*"Ju' love mi?"*) she responds *"Sciu' Gare mony'?"* ("Sure, got money?") His musings on what happened and his descriptions are in dialect (even a hot dog is described using dialect), but he and his girlfriend speak in the Italo-American dialect, suggesting the Americanness of their romance—*"Iu' bai mi pere sciuse?"* ("You buy me a pair of shoes?") *"Ai laiche silche dresse"* ("I like a silk dress"). As further proof of the difference between a traditional Italian courtship and this love affair, he accuses his girlfriend of:

n'ausanza tutt' americana:	an American habit:
doppo ca m'he, spurpato buono buono	after you have used me
me lasse; embe', strignimmece	you leave me; so, squeeze
'sta mana!	this hand!
Te voglio si e' accussi' cerca' perduono?!	I want you so and this is how
	you ask forgiveness?!
Io, a penzo a' taliana bella mia;	Me, I think Italian style, my
	pretty;
tu, a pienze comme a certe americane . . .	you think like some Americans.

The final proof of her transformation into an American-style girlfriend is her promiscuity, which is revealed at the end of the song.

In "Picchetto d'Amore," the perceived absurdities of courting American style are spoofed by comparing courtship practices with union rules, both of which were foreign to these previously largely agricultural workers. At one point, the male narrator is told by a delegate of the union that he was denied a kiss by his girlfriend because it was 2:00 A.M.: *"Avete torto, troppo tarde dezz overtaime"* ("You're wrong, too late, that's overtime").[51] The strangeness of these customs to the immigrant is signified by the use of new English words (translated into the immigrant idiom) and equated with the novel concept of a union, which most southern Italians first encountered in the United States.

Although the male protagonist often suffers at the hands of a woman in these song lyrics, it is the Americanized woman and the newfangled gender relations that the immigrants encountered in America that Farfariello, and through him his audience, ultimately mocked. In this sense, Farfariello's language humor at the expense of women allowed for a reassertion of traditional notions of masculinity and male control by placing the linguistic and identity confusions they faced within the context of gender relations, a place where immigrant men continued to believe that they could, or at least should, prevail.

A Question of Class

In addition to gender, which figures prominently in a number of these pieces, class also surfaces as an issue. Differences in class are presented to the audience as a matter of language spoken. This is true in the Italian songs as well as those written in the immigrant idiom. This use of language to suggest class differences reflects a sensitivity about the relationship between social status and language as well as North-South tensions that southern Italian immigrants brought with them from the Old World. In "Pasquale Catena," the working class narrator takes offense at an Italian "*professore's*" remarks against the Italian people at a social club. The dialect-speaking narrator tries to address the professor in Italian, but cannot sustain it. As part of his defense of Italy and all things Italian, the narrator recounts how he told his fellow club members that he had all of his children learn Italian; he is greeted with shouts of "*E tu quanno t' 'o mpare?*" ("And you when will you learn it?"). The skit works on several levels. On the one hand, there is sympathy for the chauvinistic laborer. At the same time, many of the jokes are at his expense as they are with similar characters in Farfariello's repertoire.[52]

In this last piece, the class distinctions expressed through language are classic and familiar—the unschooled laborer confronting the professor. Other pieces depict the ways in which the immigrants try to use language to create a different kind of aristocracy in the New World. "Mastantonio" tells the story of a hapless immigrant who keeps missing his *accianza* (chance) in America. This does not stop him from bragging to his relatives of his riches to the point that he has to fend off their constant requests for money by writing to them that it is "*tutto stocco alla marchetta di Wollo stritto*" ("all stuck in the Wall Street market"). In a letter to his son he writes, "*plise no spicche abaut moni*" ("please don't speak about money"), knowing full well that his son does not understand "English." Like his fabled wealth, the ability to pretend that he has mastery over the English language is a way for the narrator to assert a higher status. Just in case his son might not understand him, the piece concludes: "*E fatti spiega' pure che significa Iu mecche mi sicche*" ("And have explained to you as well the meaning of *you make me sick*"). This example highlights the multiple uses and meanings of language for the immigrant beyond assimilation; the attempt to speak English here is less a matter of assimilating to the dominant culture than it is of asserting power over others within the immigrant community.[53]

"O Sunatore 'e Flauto" also features an immigrant narrator—in this case a flute player—who attempts to assert what he perceives to be his superior status through language.[54] In addressing his working-class immigrant audience, he attempts to use standard Italian instead of dialect though he quickly lapses into the latter. His type is skewered by Farfariello, who has him make a fool of himself even as he tries to show his superiority by speaking English:

Mentre li mericane,	Instead the Americans,
qualunque nota io caccio	whatever note I let out
mi sbatteno li mmane,	they clap their hands for me,
mi diceno accussi:	they tell me like this:
Iu' pplei veri naies	You play very nice
. . .	. . .
na vorda sola, un loffaro	only one time, a bum
dicette: iu mecco mi secco!	said: you make me sick!

The immigrant who tries to project the image of an upper class pedigree by using standard Italian instead of dialect is a popular subject for caricature. "Il Discorso Del Presidente Cornacchia alla Seduta Della Societa" has the president of a mutual aid society giving a speech in what he thinks is very refined and eloquent Italian, when in fact his Italian is laced with Italianized words and full of hyperbolic bombast.[55] At one point, he begs his audience to excuse him for not speaking to them in a more sophisticated way, *"perche mi trovo in mezzo a voi e mi piace parlare franco, cosi mi capite meglio, in qualche altra circostanza, vi parlero' con un altra lingua e usero' frazioni piu drammatiche"* ("because I am among you and I like to speak frankly, so that you will better understand me, in another situation, I will speak with another language and use more dramatic fractions" [he means to say phrases]). Whether through Italian or English, Migliaccio demonstrates sensitivity to the ways in which language can be used to dominate others, in this case both within the Italian community and between different groups, a sensitivity deeply ingrained in a people who historically spoke stigmatized dialects in their own country and found a comparable situation in their adopted one.

The Meanings and Functions of Language Humor in Ethnic Theater

Beyond the use of language humor to express social tensions within the community and anxieties about modern American life, an analysis of Farfariello's material requires a consideration of the meanings and functions of language humor along with the role of popular cultural forms such as the variety theater in the construction of ethnic identity. In keeping with

Frederik Barth's emphasis on boundaries in the formation of ethnic groups, scholars across disciplines have viewed humor as a way of delineating the line between "us" and "them." At the same time, humor reinforces the cohesion and exclusivity of the group, even if the content of the humor carries self-deprecating overtones. Freud has noted both the aggressive and liberating elements of humor that are also particularly relevant for the study of ethnic humor. While inducing a feeling of solidarity with those who are "in" on the joke, humor can express aggression toward outsiders. The liberating aspect of humor is in its ability to subvert pain and suffering, to transform it into a source of pleasure through laughter. As with dreams, jokes also reveal the Freudian processes of displacement and condensation at work.[56]

Farfariello's comic character sketches appear to serve all of these functions: the delineation and solidification of boundaries between his audience and the larger society, the expression of aggression toward that larger society, and the transformation of the disappointments of the immigration experience through humor into a source of pleasure. The last point seems particularly apt in considering Farfariello's use of language. Through language play, he transformed perhaps the greatest source of humiliation for his immigrant audience given the Old World antecedents of language conflicts for southern Italians, into comedy, subverting that humiliation in the process. As John Lowe notes on dialect usage in immigrant theater, "pride in dialect constitutes inversion, transforming an oppressive signifier of otherness into a pride-inspiring prism, one which may be used for the critical inspection of 'the other.'"[57] The inscrutability of the dialect by outsiders affords a measure of protection for the insider critic. In this view, the mere usage of the dialect, which in the larger society represents a clear marker of difference, is an act of unqualified assertion that holds the potential for retaliation. However, the deep ambivalence toward both southern Italian dialects and the Italian immigrant idiom suggests that Farfariello's dialect usage did not reflect pride so much as linguistic reality. One should not overlook the simple desire to hear one's original language spoken in a public forum.

It is worth following Farfariello's career as it moved from the stage to the airwaves to see how his use of language humor took on very different meanings and functions within and outside of the Italian immigrant community. This was the result not just of a change in the medium of performance, but changes in audience and time period. By the late 1930s and into the 1940s when Farfariello was performing on radio, the pressure on Italians to sever ties with their homeland and Americanize had reached new heights, particularly once Italy entered the war on the side of the Axis powers. The anti-immigration legislation of the 1920s had virtually stopped immigration from Italy, effectively cutting off the Italian community in the United States from the continual replenishment by newcomers it had seen in prior years. The first generation was aging in and gradually becoming eclipsed by the more obviously Americanized second generation.

Migliaccio's radio performances had a different flavor than his earlier stage shows. Farfariello's Italian and dialect stage pieces were performed primarily in front of an audience of "insiders," but the radio shows for which Migliaccio developed other characters had a broader audience that included non-Italian speakers as well. It is instructive to examine how his language humor took on different meanings when presented almost entirely in English for a mixed audience. This was reflected in the "hidden transcripts" embedded within the dialogue. For example, in the "Tony & Mr. O'Brien" skits performed by Migliaccio as part of the *P & R Variety Show*, the jokes come across as more self-deprecating and insulting than in Farfariello's dialect-"Italglish" stage pieces.[58] The former are sparer, both in the characterizations of Tony and Mr. O'Brien as well as in the dialogue. The shows' sponsors, Porcino and Rossi, "makers of true Italian-type macaroni products," suggest a largely Italian American though not necessarily Italian-speaking audience. The program is entirely in English except for an occasional outburst by Farfariello, who makes appearances here as "himself," and an occasional Italian language song or commercial. In one script, Tony the barber, played by Migliaccio, and his customer, Mr. O'Brien, get into an argument when, in discussing Tony's floors, Tony fails to distinguish between the words *knot* and *not*:

> Tony: (getting mad) They are *holes*, Mister O'Brien.
> O'Brien: (excited) Of course they are, but they're *knot* holes.
> Tony: (very angry) Mister O'Brien, maybe I can't speak very good English—but there's nothing wrong with my *eyes*—I can see! There are *holes*—holes all over this floor!
> O'Brien: (yells) I don't know why I waste time trying to teach a dummy like you anything! *Knot* holes.[59]

In this context, the confusion over language generates a humor of an entirely different tone than that of Migliaccio's stage performances. There is no sense here of a collective "us" versus the great tower of Babel outside of the theater. The fact that the piece is in English and that the dialogue involves a non-Italian lends it more of an oppressive air. A similar note of condescension is evident in the use of Italianized speech by non-Italians in some English songs about Italians that make fun of immigrant speech: the title "Pastafazoola" says it all.[60] (That the skit was not written by Farfariello or his collaborators helps explain this, but that he did not write it also says something about the place of an Italian-speaking performer in this newer medium and time).[61]

The fact that the audience for these radio shows was probably largely Italian American suggests the degree to which the community had internalized its devaluation by the larger American society. At the same time, the use of dialect in some of these performances can be seen as a sign, however feeble, of ethnic assertion. The notion of a hidden transcript helps explain why something that can be offensive if imposed on the immigrant group by the larger society can be the source not only of hilarity, but also of in-group solidarity and resistance when generated from the inside. Migliaccio offers a hint of this in a 1940 "Tony & Mr. O'Brien" skit that contains his handwritten notes over the typescript. He inserted some dialect phrases that are more or less innocuous—one character asks Tony, "Who are you," to which Migliaccio proposes to answer in dialect *"Chi song i?"* ("Who am I?") before identifying himself as Tony Fasuelo according to the script—and seem to add nothing to the script in terms of propelling the action. Yet it is easy to imagine the pleasure to be taken both in hearing the immigrant language spoken and especially to a non-Italian speaking character who offers no sign of understanding. It is a powerful means of achieving a fleeting sense of power over the host society as well as signaling inclusion within the ethnic subgroup.

However, as the content of the songs Migliaccio performed makes clear, Italians were not a monolithic or unconflicted group. The use of language in Farfariello's songs suggests the possibilities for upending the established order of the Old World. In America, to paraphrase Farfariello, up was down and down was up. Women could dominate men, and the lowliest *cafone* could make good. Because of the disorder they represented, women and immigrant types who transgressed traditional boundaries—often signaled by their attempted use of English or standard Italian—were most likely to be skewered. According to some scholars of ethnic theater and popular culture more broadly, Farfariello's theater of language can be read as a reflection of the transition his Italian audience was in the process of making from immigrant to American ethnic even as it facilitated that transformation.[62] However, the identity transformations that Italian immigrants went through were considerably more complicated. As Giorgio Bertellini's study of southern Italians' experience of popular culture in America and moviegoing in particular argues, the "southernist" character of Farfariello's theater reflected the immigrants' positioning between the Italian nation and the degraded Italian South, between Italian high culture and the diverse vernacular cultures of the South that included the use of dialects historically judged inferior to standard, Tuscan Italian. Immigrant encounters with popular cultural forms in America (as in Italy) in the early twentieth century, including Farfariello's theater, did not promote assimilation by contributing to the development of a national consciousness, but rather "implied a participatory performance of exilic identity."[63] The way Farfariello used language reflects the "double consciousness" that southern Italians brought with them from Italy and that only became more complicated through their exposure to modern American life, including the English language. The immigrants' use of language that Farfariello replicated for his audience signified the status of the migrant as both "an unassimilated stranger in America and an uneducated Southerner in Italy."[64] The construction of identity in America then entailed a dynamic process of engagement with both southernist discourses from Italy and American nativism that involved both appropriation and subversion rather than a linear progression from immigrant to ethnic American.[65]

For all of the ways in which Farfariello's theater may have inadvertently facilitated the assimilation of Italian immigrants by helping to create a specifically (southern) Italian American cultural form and bridging the gap between Old World languages and English, it served a larger and more critical function from the perspective of the immigrants. His theater provided a positive space for difference. It was a vehicle for expressing, through language play, the collective sense of bewilderment and the immigrants' distaste for American ways. Far from idealizing the New World, many of Farfariello's immigrant characters delivered a blistering critique of the materialism and perceived immorality of early twentieth-century capitalist America, a critique that was no less damning for being delivered in the "broken" language of the immigrants themselves.

FIVE

The Identity Politics of Language: Italian Language Maintenance in New York City, 1920–40

Chi sa due lingue, ha due anime.
(Whoever knows two languages has two souls.)

In the 1920s, at the height of the Americanization movement that placed a premium on the proper and exclusive use of English by immigrants and their children, two concurrent efforts to encourage New York City's Italian American students to learn Italian were underway. Some of the city's leading Italian Americans were advocating for the inclusion of Italian as a modern language option in all junior highs and high schools. They also sought to increase the enrollment of Italian American students in Italian language courses. At the center of this language-maintenance drive was the well-known Italian American educator, Leonard Covello. At the same time, Italy's Fascist government, through its Ministry of Foreign Affairs, was actively promoting Italian language instruction in the Italian "colonies" in America, particularly through the parochial primary schools.

As the founder and head of DeWitt Clinton High's Italian program, the first such program in any city high school, and later as principal of Benjamin Franklin High School with its community-centered approach to education, Covello was ideally situated to lead the drive to include Italian language classes at the junior highs and high schools. Covello was also a key member of a number of organizations that shared these goals, including the Organization of the Sons of Italy (OSIA) where he was a member of the education committee, and the Educational Bureau of Columbia University's Casa Italiana, which he led. Covello was driven by his belief that the public school offered the best hope for the Americanization of both the second-generation ethnics who attended them and their immigrant parents. By learning Italian in school, Covello believed that Italian American students would gain a greater appreciation of their heritage and enjoy better communication with their parents. Through language maintenance, children could introduce American ways to their parents as well as move more easily between the Old World of their parents and their New World home. His brand of Americanization was closer to the cultural pluralism first articulated by Horace Kallen in 1924 than to the complete cultural—including linguistic—assimilation of ethnic groups advocated by many Americanizers. Nevertheless, his ultimate goal was to fashion a new American through a blending of the different ethnic groups.[1]

Covello's views on what constituted an American were quite different from those of mainstream Americanizers. They also reflected a particular interpretation of what it meant to be Italian American. The drive to promote Italian language instruction within the Italian American community was an attempt to refashion the identity of Italian immigrants and their children. Although they claimed to want to preserve their community's Italian identity, Covello and other Italian American elites attempted to use language to create a new identity—an imagined, unified, pan–Italian-American community—out of disparate, local, linguistic, and cultural groups. As Covello himself readily admitted, standard Italian was not the language of most immigrant Italians who spoke distinct and sometimes mutually unintelligible dialects both in Italy and later in the United States where whole neighborhoods, even individual streets, were organized by linguistic and related regional differences.[2] The promotion of the Italian language was as much about creating a unified community of Italians as it was about weaving them into the fabric of American life.

Language was also critical to the Italian government's understanding of what constituted an Italian American. The efforts of Covello and others to promote the study of Italian among New York City's second-generation Italian Americans coincided and sometimes overlapped with those of Italy's Fascist government, which actively promoted Italian language instruction in the Italian communities abroad. The two differed in that the Italian government's main interest was in ensuring that the second generation become "'spiritually' tied to their ancestral country and fascism by linguistic bonds" in the hope that this allegiance could be put in service of Italy.[3]

Italian government officials felt that their best hope of heightening national consciousness was through the promotion of Italian culture and the Italian language in particular.

An examination of these two efforts to promote language maintenance among New York City's second-generation Italians Americans reveals the competing notions of identity that were circulating within the community at a critical moment in the creation of Italian Americans. In each case, language was at the core of identity. In addition to understanding how Fascist officials and Italian American leaders conceived of Italian American identity, the response of Italian immigrants and their children to these two language-maintenance efforts tells us something about *their* understanding of what it meant to be Italian and/or Italian American. Italians were not unique in attempting to forge a collective ethnic identity in America through language maintenance,[4] but I am using the prism of language maintenance to view the meanings attached to language by different segments of the same immigrant/ethnic community. The story of these two interrelated drives to teach Italian to second-generation youth reveals the assumptions and valuations regarding diverse languages within the same community—standard Italian, the dialects, and the Italian American idiom, along with the speakers of those languages—that permeated the Italian American community. The Italian language-maintenance efforts of Covello and other leading Italian American figures also suggest an alternative view of Americanization. Non-English-speaking immigrant and ethnic groups can have their own understanding of the role of language in American life that diverges from Americanizers of old and their descendants, the English-only propagators who continue to resurface. Covello and his cohort attempted to turn the Americanization movement on its head by insisting that Italian, not English, was the language that would make Americans out of Italians.

Uplift through Language

Until 1922, the New York City public schools offered French, German, and Spanish as modern foreign languages. In 1922, the Italian language achieved parity with these languages in New York City high schools. That is, Italian had to be offered in any school that had sixty or more students who wanted to study it. This change in public school policy was largely achieved through the efforts of the Italian Teachers Association under the leadership of Mario Cosenza and Leonard Covello. Although the Italian Teachers Association had begun a drive to initiate Italian at the public school level as early as 1912, the effort did not pick up momentum until after World War I. Prior to 1922, Italian, if it was offered at all, could only be chosen as a second language. It took two additional years to persuade colleges to accept Italian in fulfillment of language requirements. Even so, many refused to accept credits in Italian. Instruction in Italian at the junior high level lagged behind the high schools.[5] Still, more and more schools began offering Italian, and enrollment in Italian classes climbed from between five hundred and a thousand students in 1922 to its high point of over sixteen thousand students in about fifty schools in 1938. Many if not most of the students were of Italian origin.[6] However, this figure pales before the enrollment of New York City students taking French—a language without an immigrant base to support it—that hovered between seventy thousand and one hundred thousand in the 1930s.[7] The relatively low enrollments in Italian are especially noteworthy considering the size of the Italian population of New York City in the 1920s and 1930s. By one estimate, in 1939, there were three hundred thousand children of Italian origin in New York City's thirty-eight Italian American communities.[8] Indeed, Italian American advocates of teaching Italian in the public schools were baffled by this inconsistency. Moreover, because Italian classes could only be offered at the request of parents, community leaders were continually frustrated by the community's apparent apathy.

Even though the public school was the main forum for Italian language instruction, local community groups also sponsored their own Italian classes. Organizations formed for this purpose included the *Patronato Scolastico* and the *Scuola Gratuita di Lingua Italiana*. The *Patronato Scolastico* conducted language classes for Italian American children after school hours, and adults were offered the classes through the *Scuola Gratuita*. Smaller more localized groups were also part of the language-maintenance effort such as the Italo-American Educational Society, which offered free Italian classes in the Bronx. There was a great deal of cross-fertilization between the public school and private efforts to teach Italian.[9]

The timing of the drive to encourage Italian American children to enroll in Italian language instruction in New York City's public schools is related to a combination of developments on the domestic and international fronts. Anti-immigrant sentiment in the United States, much of it aimed at the large and visible urban Italian immigrant populations, undoubtedly contributed to a sense among Italian American elites that something needed to be done to counteract the negative stereotyping and animosity. The closing of the gates to new immigration through the restrictive immigration acts of the

1920s meant that Italians in the United States could no longer count on their language being maintained by a constant supply of new arrivals. This fact, combined with the coming of age of the second generation, further contributed to a belief in the need to foster ethnic pride through the preservation of the linguistic and cultural heritage of Italy.[10]

Central to the timing of Italian language-maintenance efforts in the United States was Mussolini's rise to power and the fervent nationalism that went hand in hand with Italian Fascism. Community leaders involved in the promotion of Italian language maintenance were not necessarily Fascist sympathizers, and indeed, some, including Covello, were opposed to Mussolini from the beginning. Nevertheless, Fascism laid the groundwork for the promotion of language maintenance by heightening Italian nationalist sentiment among immigrants and by bolstering institutional support for the movement.

Scholars have argued since, and it was recognized by many at the time, that popular Italian American support of Fascism was as much if not more an expression of ethnic pride as one of true political conviction. Italian Americans' attraction to Fascism developed in large part as a response to the powerful anti-immigrant sentiment of the 1920s within the context of widespread American fascination with the charismatic Mussolini that did not fade until his imperialistic ambitions surfaced in the 1930s.[11] Although a number of the *prominenti* had true Fascist leanings, most sought to enhance their own status by association with Italy's growing stature. The larger community was drawn to the national pride that Mussolini brought to Italian Americans prior to the war. As one Fascist supporter put it, Italians should appreciate Mussolini for "having raised Italians from despised 'barbers or fruit vendors' to 'a people respected all over the world.'"[12] Italian American attachment to Fascism may have had even less to do with politics than that statement implies. Stanislao Pugliese describes Italian American Fascist support as part of a "culture of nostalgia" that had more to do with local identities and loyalties than nationalism per se.[13] The comments of an Italian American fisherman from Monterey, California, convey the general and largely apolitical opinion that many Italian Americans held of Mussolini prior to the war: "Most people thought he was a pretty good guy."[14] Nor did Italian Americans support Mussolini during the war years to nearly the same extent that they had earlier. Once American sentiment turned against Mussolini after the invasion of Ethiopia in 1935 and particularly with the United States' entry into the war, Italian Americans, for the most part, abandoned at least any outward show of support for the Italian regime.

However, the Italian Fascist government provided more than the appropriate context for a revival of the Italian language in the United States. By the end of the 1920s, when the U.S. branch of the Italian National Fascist Party was threatening to turn American popular and government opinion against Italy with its increasingly violent tactics, Mussolini disbanded the American *fasci* and instead adopted a course of "cultural diplomacy" that relied on promoting the Italian language and culture among the second generation.[15] The Italian government came to focus their efforts on the parochial schools of parishes led by Italian priests, but they also supported language maintenance within the public schools. Organizations, such as OSIA and Columbia's Casa Italiana, that were active in promoting Italian language instruction within the public schools were under Fascist domination for a time.[16] OSIA, the prominent national Italian American organization, contributed resources toward promoting language instruction and lobbied the New York City School Board to introduce the classes.[17] Casa Italiana's involvement in language-maintenance promotion within the public schools peaked in 1933 with an intensive campaign that included a daily appeal to the parents of Italian American children in the local Italian language press. Printed along with the appeals was a coupon that parents were asked to return to Casa Italiana, which would in turn request that Italian be introduced in a particular school as soon as the necessary number of coupons had been received. Casa Italiana also sent speakers to Italian American societies throughout the greater New York area, gave various Italian entertainment programs in high schools, churches, and community houses, visited Italian families in their homes, established local committees, made radio announcements and programs, and produced posters, all in an effort to enroll Italian American children in Italian language classes.[18] Although not a Fascist sympathizer, Covello was involved in these organizations and used them to promote his own agenda with regard to language maintenance. Indeed, as Gaetano Salvemini's exhaustive documentation of Fascist activities in the United States reveals, it was difficult if not impossible during the interwar years to be active within the Italian American community without crossing paths with Fascist sympathizers.[19]

Covello's interest in Italian language maintenance was born of his own personal experience as someone who immigrated with his family when he was still a child and had his own hardships with learning English and adjusting to American life. Covello was born in the southern Italian mountain town of Avigliano to struggling parents. His father, after failed attempts working as a shoemaker and later as an upholsterer, immigrated to New York City in the latter years of the nineteenth century. Covello joined him in 1896 at the age of nine along with his mother and two younger siblings.[20]

Covello's autobiography, *The Heart Is the Teacher*, provides examples of his experiences with language, both English and Italian, while in Italy and later in the United States. His personal history clearly fueled his choice of career (he began as a high school instructor of Spanish and French) and the views he developed regarding education, particularly as they related to Italian Americans.

Even before arriving in America, Covello had an inkling of the transformative potential of language. He recalled the occasions when returning immigrants would try to impress their fellow villagers with their scant knowledge of English to enhance their own standing: "He spoke slowly and deliberately, as though his native Aviglianese dialect were an effort for him, and his conversation was spiced with such phrases as *Nuova Yorka! La jobba! Lu bosso! Alo—gooda-by.* And we hung on his words."[21]

Upon arrival at Ellis Island, Covello describes in vivid detail how his mother's inability to understand what was happening around her, including the separation from her sons when they underwent a physical examination, traumatized her. Covello's first encounter with a nonfamily member in the New World also centered on language. His father arrived to meet him and his family at Ellis Island with a young girl who had also come to America from Avigliano. What impressed Covello about her was the fact that "she could switch from our Italian dialect to English as she chose." It was she who gave him his first English lesson, insisting that he say "yes" when asked if he wanted a piece of candy rather than "*si.*" "'Good! Bravo!' the girl laughed. 'It is your first word in English and you will never forget it.'"[22] He would eventually marry her, the first person to initiate him into this new language and the new life it represented. She was the literal embodiment of his desire to achieve a mastery of English—and America—without sacrificing his Italian past, a personal goal that would animate his work within the Italian American community.

Covello's experiences as a student exemplify attitudes toward non-English speakers and Americanization in the early years of the century that he would later challenge. In grade school, his first teacher hit him on the head as he was pronouncing words written on the blackboard, "words which had absolutely no meaning to me. It seldom seemed to occur to our teachers that explanations were necessary. 'B-U-T-T-E-R—butter—butter,' I sing-songed with the rest of the class." The teacher later apologized to him, but never explained the source of her annoyance. More tellingly, Covello recalls being forced to sing a patriotic song, again without understanding its meaning; "I didn't know what the words meant but I sang it loudly with all the rest, in my own way, 'Tree Cheers for de Red Whatzam Blu!'"[23] Covello, like others in those years, was taught English as if the words in and of themselves, independent of any meaning, would be enough to make an American of him.

His most positive educational experience as a child came through a Protestant missionary who impressed Covello because she learned Italian before embarking on her work among the immigrants. This, apparently, was a first for Covello. The memory that she was well-respected and admired by his father's circle of friends also stayed with him. Miss Ruddy's willingness to speak Italian stood in marked contrast to the public schools where neither Italy nor anything Italian (except for Columbus) was ever mentioned, resulting in a sense of inferiority among the children and problems between the generations. "This," wrote Covello, "was the accepted process of Americanization. We were becoming Americans by learning how to be ashamed of our parents."[24]

Covello compensated for his sense of inferiority by striving to master the English language. In high school, he joined the literary club, the debating society, and the school newspaper in an apparent attempt to overcome the difficulty of being a nonnative speaker of the dominant language in a period of anti-immigrant sentiment. His initial acceptance of the era's zeitgeist is further suggested by his course of studies at Columbia University. Although he was drawn to languages, he chose to study French. As he explains, "it was fashionable to forget Italian."[25] While at Columbia, however, he fell in with a small group of Italian Americans who decided to reclaim their Italian heritage. Some reverted to their original Italian names although Covello did not opt to reclaim "Coviello," a name he gave up when a teacher gave him a version that was slightly easier for Americans to pronounce phonetically. Oddly enough, he explains the choice not to assume his original name by claiming "names have strength and a character of their own and are not played with easily." Even with the dropping of the *i*, "covello" retained its Italian sound, so he saw no reason to reprise his old name.[26]

While still in college, Covello joined the Young Men's Christian Association's Americanization program that emphasized teaching English to immigrants, but he quickly became frustrated by the standard methodology that prohibited the use of the immigrant language and insisted on English in the classroom at all times. His immigrant students were shy and unresponsive. "Finally," he writes, "I became impatient and let out a tirade of Italian.

'What is the matter with all of you? Did you come here to learn English or to sit like a bunch of cabbage heads? *Questa e una tavola*. This is a table! This is a table!'"[27]

Through these adult immigrant students, Covello became more aware of the language issues facing the different generations of Italian Americans. His students became much more comfortable in class once Covello revealed his knowledge of Italian, but they remained reluctant to bring their aging parents to classes. As they explained to Covello (in Italian), "They are old. They have known only the little village. It would be embarrassing. They do not even speak the same Italian as you."[28] Although younger, they may just as well have been speaking about themselves. Covello responded that he would then be glad to go to their homes and speak to them in dialect. He also commented on the fact that no matter how much at ease his students seemed to be, they always insisted on calling him "Mista Professore." These two points—the use of dialect in most immigrant families and the reverence accorded to educated people who were assumed to speak standard Italian—are critical to understanding the immigrant response to language-maintenance efforts.

Covello also realized the barriers his students faced when dealing with any issues concerning their children's education. Not knowing enough English, they were reluctant to come into contact with school officials. Covello summed up his experience teaching English at the "Y" this way: "I came to the conclusion that while it was important to teach English to immigrant people, it was equally important for me to find out about the problems they were unable to solve in becoming adjusted to a new way of life in a new country. And I could only do this through the use of their native language."[29]

It was the Italian American students at DeWitt Clinton High, Covello's first teaching job, who provided the final push to institute Italian language classes, at least in Covello's later recounting of his life. He began at DeWitt Clinton as an instructor in French and Spanish, languages that were much in demand following World War I. As the enrollment of Italian American students in the high school grew, they questioned the point of learning French or Spanish when they could not even speak their language of origin. In a rare direct reference to his own psychological turmoil around the issue of language, Covello writes, "Still I had no answer for them. How could I answer when I could not even understand the pattern of my own behavior as a teacher of languages?"[30] Following a stint in the army during the war as an interpreter of Spanish and French along with a brief interval working as an advertising executive, Covello returned to DeWitt Clinton in 1920 and started what was probably the only class in Italian in any American public high school. So began his long career as a promoter of the Italian language and an advocate of a central role for the public school in the life of the immigrant family.[31]

Covello's personal and early professional experiences developed into a fully articulated philosophy of education and Americanization that stressed the importance of immigrant languages. Much of Covello's thinking on language and Italian immigrants is laid out in a two-part article published in *Atlantica Magazine* in 1934. Based on a study of 593 Italian American boys at DeWitt Clinton and issued by Casa Italiana's Educational Bureau, of which he was then executive director, the article outlines Covello's views on the role of language in the life of the immigrant. Part II reviews the findings of a survey of language usage among the students interviewed, the most significant of which is that Italian or a dialect of Italian was the primary language in the homes of almost all of the boys. Actually, although Covello interprets the data this way, a breakdown of the questionnaire responses reveals that only 12 percent of the students responded that their parents spoke to each other exclusively in dialect. The majority cited a combination of languages including Italian and dialect; English and Italian; English and dialect; and English, Italian, and dialect. The latter combination was spoken by 19 percent of the parents, the highest percentage of any other "language." In any case, the point remains that English alone was the parental language in only 9 percent of the homes, thus justifying Covello's concern.[32]

Part I examines in detail the meaning of language for the Italian immigrant and the psychological strain the immigrant faced in trying to convey him- or herself in a new and imperfectly known medium. Difficulties with an unknown language are, according to Covello, "the most baffling and embarrassing that foreigners have to endure." Language—typically the dialect the immigrant brought over from his or her region of Italy or a variation of it—not only determined concrete matters such as settlement patterns, but was also at the heart of the immigrant's emotional and social adjustment.[33] Indeed, Covello discusses the linguistic experience of the Italian immigrant in dramatic terms. In leaving the familiar and comforting neighborhood peopled by his *paesani* to go to work in the multilingual, but primarily English-speaking world, the immigrant had to daily face "a confusing, perplexing sort of world in which the most unaccountable and incomprehensible things took place. The mellowness of life seems to have disappeared. Everything appeared hard, mechanical, tense, harsh. . . . And ever present was the boss who spoke an unknown language—a language in which human feeling seemed to be entirely absent."[34]

Covello argued against early Americanization efforts that centered on learning and speaking English exclusively. He noted the near impossibility of these often illiterate or semiliterate immigrants becoming fluent enough in a second language to express themselves fully, as well as the inhumanity of insisting that the immigrant stop speaking his native language altogether. Making the immigrant more fluent in his or her own language would have been more productive, according to Covello, especially if coupled with teaching the native language to the second generation. If parent and child could better communicate, even in a language other than English, Americanization could take hold more firmly in each. American ideas and traditions could penetrate into the immigrant home through the child. "In this way," argued Covello, "the school and the teacher could have reached through the child, into the very heart of the family group."[35]

Just as the adult immigrant faced a set of linguistic issues, so too did the immigrant's children. The pervasive hostility toward immigrant languages invariably filtered down to the child, who developed a sense of inferiority that was compounded by the low status that Italians themselves attributed to dialects, the form of language commonly used in immigrant homes. The school contributed to the linguistic burden of the second generation by its indifference or outright antagonism toward immigrant languages. Schools and teachers thus became "a disruptive force" in the immigrant family, separating parents from children who had internalized the anti-immigrant sentiment and turned against their heritage. However, in the same way that the schools had wreaked havoc on the immigrant family, Covello argued that they had the power to mend the rift both within families and between Italian Americans and the wider society. Indeed, Covello saw the resolution of such conflicts as "the major educational effort for the school in an immigrant community." This was the idea behind the community-centered school. One—if not the—critical way of aiding the two generations in their adjustment to American life was through language. His position is encapsulated in the following summation: "In denying the child the language of his parents; in showing, whether openly or covertly, hostility to the learning of the language, we have missed the wonderful educational opportunity of fostering Americanization on a positive, wholesome and unifying basis."[36]

Although many of his points may seem commonsensical to today's reader steeped in a discourse of respect for cultural diversity and sensitivity to the needs and concerns of immigrants, Covello was going against a formidable tide. In a sense, his was one of the earliest voices of multiculturalism in an era characterized by national chauvinism and intolerance for nonnatives. Although other American-born educators had begun adopting an intercultural approach to education as early as 1924, as one scholar notes, a more accurate description would have been "tolerance as a form of intolerance." That is, leading professional and governmental advocates of intercultural education were not so much interested in fostering any form of cultural pluralism as they were in inoculating against it; by introducing a small dose of pluralism into the schools, the society would develop immunity to the larger disease of true cultural pluralism.[37] Although more humane than the coercive Americanization foisted upon children, intercultural education did not represent as decisive a break with that tradition as did Covello's version.[38]

Covello's vision of intercultural education was given near-complete expression with his founding of the Benjamin Franklin High School in East Harlem in 1934. There, as principal of this ethnically diverse high school dominated first by Italian Americans and later by Puerto Ricans, Covello instituted his community-based model of public schooling. A multilingual approach to communication with the area's immigrant populations was central to bridging the gap between immigrant families and their children's school. Community bulletins that discussed local news were printed in several languages. All school presentations and materials were offered in the immigrant languages, predominantly Italian and Spanish. Such an approach was intended not only to facilitate communication, but also to affirm the immigrant cultures. Coupled with this sensitivity to fostering linguistic and cultural pride was a strong emphasis on the Americanization of the immigrant generation through their children. Benjamin Franklin High regularly sponsored naturalization drives and offered adult English and citizenship classes. Students even gave presentations to adults on the advantages of citizenship and assisted parents with the naturalization process. Covello was undoubtedly an Americanizer, albeit a culturally sensitive one who believed in the possibility of becoming an American while still retaining one's heritage.[39]

Although Covello was central to the drive to enroll Italian American students in Italian classes, the effort also involved other prominent Italian Americans. Alberto Bonaschi, a member of the New York City Board of Education in the 1930s who was active in the Italian Teachers Association, agreed with Covello that the main goal of language instruction was to facilitate the social adjustment of both immigrants and their children to

American life. As Bonaschi put it, "Italian is of inestimable value in civic and Americanization work, for the first approach to the Americanization of the millions of Italians in the United States must be through their own native tongue."[40] By learning Italian, children would not only regain the respect for their parents that is lost due to the child's sense of superiority in having the ability to speak English, but the child could "relay to the perplexed parents . . . all that the school and general social tact teach the youngster of American mores."[41] Educators such as Covello and Bonaschi stressed the value of language maintenance to a healthy Americanization process, one that would allow both parent and child to continue to identify with their Italian heritage. Others, likely under the sway of the fervent nationalism espoused by Italian Fascists, stressed the importance of language for maintaining a sense of *italianità* that would enhance the prestige of Italians in the United States by linking the immigrants to Italy's literary and scientific legacy.

"Perche non dobbiamo essere tutti italiani non solo di nome ma di fatto?" ("Why shouldn't we all be Italian not just in name but in fact?") Tomasso Russo asked this question in one of a series of 1932 articles in the New York Italian daily *Bolletina della Sera* on the teaching of Italian in the New York City public schools.[42] Russo was just one of a number of New York Italian Americans active in language-maintenance promotion who believed that the essential, unifying element of *italianità* was to be found in language—that is, in the mastery of standard Italian and, through language, to an association with Italian high culture.

For the series, Russo, who taught Italian at local colleges as well as through a radio program and served on the editorial staff of several Italian American newspapers, visited public schools throughout New York City where Italian was taught. He interviewed the instructors and administrators of these language programs who were themselves, to a one, Italian American. In his search for an answer to the mystery of low enrollments, Russo invariably raised the question of why comparatively few Italian American children were enrolled in the language classes. The pieces contained a discussion of this issue that most often concluded by placing the blame for low enrollments squarely on Italian immigrant parents. Indeed, taken together, the articles read like one long excoriation of immigrant parents for their failure to promote Italian language study. Russo lambasted them for complaining that Italians were not respected in this country when, according to Russo, they had yet to earn that respect. One major way to do so would have been to foster Italian language study. He berated Italian American parents for their apathy and criticized them for their inability to organize for action. Italian Americans, asserted Russo, should be ashamed of themselves for not knowing the language of their fathers, particularly when non-Italians were studying it at higher rates.[43] Russo's harsh rhetoric toward immigrant parents reveals both the degree to which language promoters were dependent on them to achieve their aims and the frustration that elite Italian Americans felt with the low esteem in which Italians were held.

Russo's articles also suggest the extent to which he and other elites felt they were in competition with other ethnic groups to become valued members of American society. Thus, in noting the increase in the numbers of students studying Italian, Russo writes that Italians should be proud that "even in this field, we can finally compete with other national groups established here."[44] This desire to achieve a more elevated status in the eyes of Americans explains why Russo took pride in the number of Americans studying the language (though he would have liked Italians to do so in greater numbers). Their interest meant that they were "drawn by the fascination of the language of Dante, of our culture, of our civilization."[45] Russo's rhetoric clearly reveals a proto-Fascist bent regarding the importance and meaning of Italian language promotion. As he noted, language "is the most efficacious method, actually the only one for a complete propaganda of *italianità* within the American element, because the language and the literature of a people are the most genuine expressions of the soul of that people."[46]

As the series extended, Russo became increasingly upset with the results of his interviews that revealed the relative indifference of Italian immigrant parents to language-maintenance efforts. He offered more reasons why parents should be interested—the practical value of knowing the language of a large immigrant community, for example. However, his central emphasis on the need to earn the respect of Americans by gaining greater self-respect through study of the "language of Dante" and all that it represented predominates.[47]

Russo's emphasis on the possibilities for Italian language study to elevate the esteem of Italian Americans within their own communities as well as in the larger society was echoed by the appeals of other Italian Americans and those organizations interested in language promotion. In 1932, Giuseppe Prezzolini, head of the Fascist-dominated Casa Italiana, placed a request to Italian American organizations in *Il Progresso Italo-Americano*, then under the leadership of noted Fascist sympathizer Generoso Pope to establish scholarships for the study of Italian. Prezzolini wrote that although Italian Americans had managed to produce a class of professionals, they would never achieve the respect accorded the "higher classes of the United States" if they failed to highlight their culture, what he refers to as "our great heritage."[48] Implicit in the view that the promotion of standard Italian would enhance the prestige of Italian Americans was the idea that the use of Italian dialects evoked the image of the unlettered, working-class immigrant. A greater knowledge of standard Italian among the second generation would connect Italians in the popular American mind with Italian cultural and scientific achievements rather than with Italian immigrant working-class culture. A corollary to this point was that second-generation children would be able to get to know themselves as Italians by learning standard Italian and reading the works of the Italian greats. Americans in turn, would get to know the "real" Italians, the descendants of Dante, rather than those of immigrant workers.[49]

Italian language promoters of all stripes stressed the potential for the Italian language to preserve the Italian family. In a letter reprinted in Italian newspapers urging parents to enroll their children in the public school classes, a representative of Casa Italiana overstated this point to dramatic effect. Describing it as the language of the "hearth," he wrote, "the families that have neglected to teach their children the language of the hearth have seen incomprehensible tragedies, divisions, ruin, countless follies."[50] In this same vein, Covello, rather disingenuously given his stated agenda, suggested in a radio broadcast aimed at Italian immigrants that the Americanization of their children could be forestalled or avoided altogether if the children were taught Italian.[51] In a letter to the New York City associate superintendent of high schools written prior to the introduction of Italian as a modern language option, the Education Committee of OSIA, composed of Covello, Cosenza, and then Justice Salvatore Cotillo, expressed similar concerns for intergenerational harmony along with the possibilities for Italian language instruction to facilitate the adjustment of both the first and second generation.[52] Italian language instruction was also viewed as a vehicle for the reproduction of community leaders who would facilitate the Americanization process of the first generation while enhancing the prestige of the larger Italian American community as educated elites. The same letter from OSIA's Education Committee referenced previously goes on to note that "the ultimate aim of these efforts is to produce leaders," adults who could straddle both worlds and interpret each to the other. "The study of Italian," according to Covello, "means more to the Italo-American community than the mere acquiring of proficiency in the Italian language. The whole question of leadership is, in a measure, involved"; leadership that, presumably, would place young

Italian Americans in a position to serve their communities by helping them to assimilate into the larger American society.[53]

An Alternative Model of Language and Italian American Identity

In addition to those who enrolled their children in Italian classes in the public schools at the junior high and high school levels, other parents opted to have their grade school–aged children learn Italian through the parochial primary school programs that were directly sponsored by the Italian government. Italian parishes in the United States were strongly allied with Italy's Fascist government. The church in Rome found in Mussolini a bulwark against Communism. Italian priests in the United States saw their alliance with Fascist Italy as a way to buttress their own position within the Irish-dominated American Catholic hierarchy.[54] It is not surprising then that parish schools were identified as the best medium to promote Italian language study and Fascist cultural propaganda, although the Italian government continued to promote the study of Italian in public schools and through private organizations such as the Dante Alighieri Society.[55] As an agent for the Fascist government in the United States reported in 1933: "Our purpose is to shape within a decade a large Italian-American cohort, made up of citizens loyal to the United States but aware and proud of our language, our culture, and our civilization to such an extent that will bequeath this tradition on to their children. . . . The first and main step is to spread our language."[56] Somewhat incongruously, the Fascist government saw no conflict in the second generation maintaining a dual identity as both Italians and Italian Americans. This policy, however, was unique to the immigrants living within the United States. In other parts of the world with large Italian communities, the Italian government encouraged immigrants to retain their Italian citizenship and resist assimilation into the host society.[57]

With the rise of Fascism, Italian language classes became a major arena for propaganda that linked language maintenance, cultural nationalism, and the preservation of the Italian family to Fascism. The greatness of ancient Rome along with the glories of Italian culture and civilization were closely tied to the Fascist regime and its heightened form of nationalism. According to a study of Chicago parochial schools, "the texts and 'Program' were organized, in our contemporary parlance, to give minority children an overdose of self-esteem."[58] Italian parochial schools in the United States received substantial resources from the Italian government, including textbooks, funds, free or discounted trips to Italy, and after 1934, even some teachers. These were carefully screened in Italy and dispatched to the United States where they taught Italian to Italian American children in the *doposcuole* (after school) as well as to workers in the *dopolavoro* (after work) clubs held in Catholic parish schools. The most promising young students were sent to Fascist summer camps in Italy where they could enjoy a visit with Mussolini.[59]

These parochial schools did attract students. According to a report to the Italian Ministero degli Esteri by the Italian general consul in New York, Gaetano Vecchiotti, as late as the 1940–41 school year, Italian American children in New York state (though it is safe to assume most were in New York City) had the option of attending one of 18 parochial schools offering 90 classes to a total of 7,140 students. The Italian government also operated 24 *doposcuola* programs offering 51 classes to an additional 1,717 students. In the tristate area of New York, New Jersey, and Connecticut in that year, just under eighteen thousand students were learning Italian in Fascist-sponsored programs. Although figures for other years are not available, Vecchiotti's report comments on the role of the growing anti-Italian sentiment in the country in shutting down these programs, suggesting that in the 1930s the enrollment figures may have been significantly higher.[60]

In his study of Fascism and the United States, John Diggins suggests that Italian parents enrolled their children in these Italian government–sponsored language classes to combat the perceived Americanization of their children and their rejection of Old World traditions. According to Diggins, Italian immigrant parents sought family loyalty by having their children learn Italian "before they were 'corrupted' by the bright lights and bland conformity of American life."[61] Under Fascism, the Italian language was closely associated with both maintaining family cohesion and Italian nationalism tinged with populist overtones. Learning Italian in the context of the *doposcuole* and parish schools had less to do with fitting into American society and more to do with asserting an Italian identity. In contrast, Italian American leaders acted in the belief that knowledge of standard Italian would produce Italians with the ultimate goal of creating Italian Americans in much the same way that Americanizers believed that simply by learning English, immigrants would be transformed into Americans.

The difference in the venues for Italian language instruction is also significant. The willingness of Covello and others to participate in the American educational system stood in marked contrast to the suspicion with which many Italian immigrants viewed American schools. They correctly identified the public schools as agents of assimilation that challenged traditional values and authority.[62] The attempt to transform Italian American identity through the American public schools signaled a desire for greater integration into American society on a par with other immigrant groups. Some members of the Italian immigrant elite felt keenly their devalued outsider status. Russo, for example, likened Italian language promoters to a vanguard army that needed the help of the larger immigrant community to overcome domination by other more prestigious languages taught in the schools.[63] The *prominenti* had much to gain from an enhancement of the status of the group. An elevation in the position of Italian Americans would reflect most positively on them both within the Italian American community as well as within the larger society.

But how do we account for the majority of Italian parents who chose not to enroll their children in either the Fascist parochial primary school programs or the public school classes in Italian? The attempt to create new Italian American identities on the part of both the Italian government and the Americanizers ignored the obvious fact that immigrant families rarely used standard Italian in the home and that most immigrant parents could not even speak it though they may have been able to understand it. Some parents questioned the value and purpose of studying Italian. According to the observations of the *prominenti*, including Covello, many families felt satisfied with their children's knowledge of the local dialect spoken in the home, however imperfect, and saw no reason to have them learn standard Italian. Contrary to the claims of both Americanizers and Fascists, it was not necessarily in the best interests of the family for a child to know standard Italian. An essay written for one of Covello's classes at DeWitt Clinton High School by an Italian American girl inadvertently suggested the rift that knowledge of standard Italian could create in an immigrant home. She wrote that her parents insisted always on her speaking Italian in the home. Only later—presumably through Covello's language class—did she realize that her parents had taught her a combination of their dialect and Italianized English. She wrote that she laughed at the memory.[64]

Attitudes about dialect and other forms of immigrant speech varied among the *prominenti*. Covello never demeaned immigrant parents for speaking in dialect, although he wrote about the shame his students felt (and perhaps he himself had as a child of immigrants) at their parents' use of dialects that clearly reflected their position as uneducated immigrants largely from Italy's degraded South. Others, however, had no compunction about humiliating parents and their children who used the dialect even as they were trying to encourage the study of standard Italian in the schools. In one of his articles for the *Bolletino*, Russo noted that the classes were important for Italian American kids because outside of the classroom, they only heard dialect spoken. He went on to write, "And what dialect! And what an accent! A real disaster, one of the greatest difficulties that Italian-American students have to overcome for the proper pronunciation of the Italian language."[65] Italian and Italian American elites also expressed disapproval and condescension for the mixture of Italian and English that became the idiom of immigrants in the New World. Prezzolini offered his opinion on the subject in an article entitled "The Language of the 'Giobba,'" a term Italian immigrants used for job that expressed both the disdain and the recognition of material necessity associated with work. Prezzolini recalls the "horror which is experienced by every good Italian, who delights in his language and possesses a certain culture," upon becoming aware of the jumble of English and Italian spoken by New York's laboring Italians. However, he goes on to note that over time, his main criticism was not so much the use of this idiom as "its restriction and its coarseness. It is a language almost completely limited to the mechanical world." Prezzolini charged the Italian teacher not with correcting the words of their immigrant students, but with enhancing their "spiritual world," which would naturally lead to an enriched vocabulary.[66] Prezzolini's relatively benign view of the dialect was less common than that expressed by Franco Ciarlantini, a member of the Fascist Italian Parliament, who wrote in a 1930 article for an English language journal that the "Italo-Americans are engaged in spreading among the English-speaking population a horrible notion of our language, an impossible mixture of dialects, and their children hardly speak a word of Italian."[67] In an article entitled *"La Lingua Italo-Americana 'La Prima Santa di America,'"* an Italian observer described the Italian American idiom as "a barbaric language that makes one shudder and laugh."[68]

Whether in rejecting Italian language instruction for their children Italian immigrants were actively rejecting any attempts to create a unified Italian American identity at the expense of local cultural and linguistic identities or whether they simply had less concern with or belief in the possibility of transcending local identities is unclear. Certainly, a host of reasons exist to explain why many chose not to encourage their children to enroll in the language classes. In schools where Italian American students did not constitute a large percentage of the school body, there may have been difficulty in finding the required sixty students to enroll. Low enrollments may, in part, have reflected the position of Italian American students within the public school system. Because Italian American students were often steered into the vocational or industrial rather than the academic track in junior high and high school based on the long-standing perception that they did not excel academically, they may not have had the option of taking foreign language classes, nor was Italian offered in the commercial high schools.[69]

That the language classes fared very differently among Italian Americans depending on the school suggests that other factors were at play. One principal speculated that enrollment in Italian classes at a neighboring high school might have been low because the school forbade students in the bottom quarter of the entering class from selecting a language course.[70] As late as 1935, some students encountered resistance when trying to select Italian in particular as a foreign language. A concerned parent wrote to the editor of *Il Progresso Italo-Americano* that although his son wanted to take Italian as a modern language upon entering New Utrecht High, he was under pressure from school administrators to take Spanish instead, a language that was already well-ensconced in the curriculum.[71] In a 1936 statement to the New York City Board of Education, Bonaschi, then a member of the board, referred to "recent ground rumblings" from "those in our school system who either fail or refuse to recognize the ineluctable force played upon children in their choice of languages by their racial backgrounds," a reference to sentiment against introducing Italian into the public schools.[72] This resistance from school administrators also manifested in less funding for Italian as compared with other modern language programs that resulted in less training for teachers and higher teacher-to-student ratios. In a report on the state of the subject in the senior high schools in 1936, Bonaschi referred to Italian as "the educational foundling of New York City." Even by 1936, just two years shy of the high point of Italian study in New York's public schools, the language was only offered in eighteen of the city's forty-three senior high schools despite the fact that it was the only modern language demonstrating a substantial increase in enrollments.[73]

Beyond the structural impediments to accessing Italian language instruction in the public schools, there are psychological issues to consider. Ethnic self-hatred should not be overlooked as a possible explanation for low enrollments. As Covello argued, Italian American students suffered from low self-esteem born of their position as a minority population. Identifying with the Italian language required an ability to identify oneself publicly, in school, as Italian American, something that many students may have shied away from.[74] Furthermore, far from bridging the gap between the generations, some children may have resisted learning Italian out of a fear of shaming their dialect-speaking parents. Although some parents certainly took pride in their children's ability to speak standard Italian, given the premium placed on knowledge of the national language and the devaluation of the dialects, many parents may have been threatened by the idea that their children might exceed them in this area.

The belief that Italian-American students were not that interested in Italian language classes may have been overstated by the community's leaders. The individual efforts of some students who, for example, organized Italian language groups in schools where the courses were not available or personally requested that the language classes be offered in their schools, indicates that interest was high among at least some Italian American students.[75] Overall, girls demonstrated more of an interest in and facility with Italian than boys. Indeed, it may be that most Italian instructors were women.[76] Finally, it is important to keep in mind that although the numbers were relatively low compared with students of other languages and the sheer number of Italian American students in New York, the study of Italian realized impressive growth. For example, in a four-year period between 1932 and 1936 enrollment increased by 145 percent.[77]

In any case, as Jonathan Zimmerman has argued, generally low enrollments in "native" European language classes in the public schools (a phenomenon that was not unique to Italians though perhaps was more pronounced with them) did not necessarily reflect apathy or a rejection of ethnicity by European immigrants and their children, but rather a different understanding and expression of ethnicity that precluded standard versions of national languages that were rarely spoken in the home. Different meanings were attached to language; some elites saw the elevation of Italian as a means to integrate more successfully into mainstream American society and to enhance their own status and power, but the average Italian pursued a path, perhaps consciously but perhaps not, that served to maintain the community's insularity and diversity. The fact that many immigrant organizations put more energy into other less divisive means of affirming and strengthening ethnic identity, such as elaborate banquets and religious feasts, suggests another understanding of what it meant to be Italian in America.[78]

The attempted Americanization of the immigrants and their children, as envisaged by Covello and his cohort, may have been a losing battle in this period regardless of the means employed. The extent and depth of Fascism's hold on Italian communities across the United States in this period was substantial. As Rudolph Vecoli has observed, "rather than speak of the Americanization of the Little Italies during the interwar years, it would be more accurate, then, to speak of their Fascistization."[79] The parochial programs that glorified the cultural and scientific accomplishments of Italy, including its language, within the context of a fervent Italian nationalism, would have had a natural advantage within the community. Although the Fascist language programs also required the negation of localized identities, they did so in the service of promoting a greater Italian identity rather than a diluted and hybridized Italian American identity.

An anecdote from Covello's autobiography suggests the different meanings that standard Italian may have held for the average immigrant and how those meanings may have influenced decisions about whether and where to have children study Italian. Covello describes a scene during one of his door-to-door campaigns to convince Italian parents to enroll their children in the language classes of the public schools. When asked whether he would like his son to study Italian, one father responded: "'Naturally we prefer him to study our own language. But *real* Italian. Italian as you speak it, Signor Maestro—the Italian of our great men, of Garibaldi.'"[80] Italian in this immigrant's eyes was the language of the famed Italian patriot and friend of the common man. Although both Covello and his cohort along with the Fascist promoters of Italian were attempting to refashion immigrant identity through the promotion of Italian language study, it may have been this populist understanding of Italian culture and language that resonated most strongly with the average immigrant, one that was perhaps better expressed within the context of the Fascist-sponsored language classes in local Catholic parishes than within American(izing) schools.

SIX

Language, Italian American Identity, and the Limits of Cultural Pluralism in the World War II Years

No Italian spoken for the duration of the war.
(Typical sign posted in Italian storefronts.)

In 1940, while America was nervously watching events unfold in Europe, an Italian American trumpeter from New Orleans was creating a sensation over the airwaves. Along with the big band sounds of Glen Miller and Benny Goodman's swing, Americans listened to Louis Prima sing the praises of "Angelina, the waitress at the local pizzeria." "Angelina" sold millions of copies and with it, Prima formally began his career as a performer of lighthearted depictions of Italian American life.[1] This song, like many of Prima's so-called novelty hits performed during the war years and beyond, was distinguished by its use of Italian, dialect, and his characterization of Italian American speaking styles. He incorporated a kind of Italian American scat into some of his songs, stringing together Italian-sounding nonsense with familiar Italian words, using food names like "zucchini" and "macaroni" along with lesser known Italian words without forming any clear meaning. Song titles such as "Bacia Galupe Made Love on the Stoop," "Josephine, Please No Lean on the Bell," and "Please No Squeeza da Banana" incorporated playful references to Italian American speech and stereotypes.

While Prima's distinctively Italian American lyrics and persona were captivating American audiences, the U.S. government was scrutinizing Italian Americans for signs of disloyalty beginning with Italy's entry into the war in June of 1940. The Italian language was a particular focus of government concern. The records of the Federal Bureau of Investigation (FBI), for example, reveal that the use of the Italian language was a marker of potential disloyalty during the World War II era. While the war generated suspicion against Italian Americans and the Italian language, it also gave rise to new opportunities for Italian Americans to use their knowledge of Italian, albeit under very controlled circumstances. As part of the war effort, the Office of Strategic Services (OSS) recruited Italian American men to join a Special Intelligence (SI) unit and to form military Operational Groups (OGs) for missions behind enemy lines in Italy. These were elite units whose members were carefully screened. The ability to speak Italian like a native was a major requirement for selection. Within this context, Italian became a vehicle for individual Italian Americans to express their patriotism.

What is the significance of the mixed reactions to the Italian language during the World War II years that these three examples suggest? How can we reconcile the widespread popularity of Prima's Italian language songs and the military's willingness to use the language skills of Italian American soldiers with government suspicion directed against Italian language speakers by the FBI and others? Looking at the position of the Italian language during the war years provides insight into the importance of this period both for Italian Americans and as part of the larger history of America's relationship to its ethnic minorities. Highlighting the single issue of language within a specific historical context allows us to see how the formation of ethnic identity occurs in the interplay between host society and immigrants/ethnics. The contests surrounding the Italian language reveal that the wartime situation created specific parameters that limited the development and expression of Italian American identity, but the war also created new opportunities for its expression. It reminds us of the power the host society can wield in shaping ethnic identity, in this case through the historically determined meanings attached to the Italian language.

In the context of the Second World War, an examination of language and ethnic identity also offers insight into the changing nature of American cultural pluralism. Some have seen the war as a pivotal moment in the history of white ethnics in the United States, the time when they entered the American mainstream. The Nazi threat caused Americans to grapple with their own forms of intolerance and to ultimately embrace white ethnics while excluding blacks and other racial minorities. American film, fiction, advertising, and government propaganda aggressively promoted a multicultural vision of America designed to unite the disparate elements of U.S.

society behind the war and reflected a genuine reappraisal of the national values. In Gary Gerstle's words, "For ethnic workers the war was the historic moment when they felt fully accepted as Americans." Some have discussed this acceptance in terms of the attainment of "whiteness."[2] For their part, ethnics welcomed the chance to be a part of the nation on a more equal footing. Yet Gerstle and others have also noted that the cultural pluralism promoted during the war years was not that of Horace Kallen, who envisioned an America composed of distinctive ethnocultural groups. Instead, ethnics were given new opportunities in the World War II era to enter the mainstream, but as individuals rather than as groups. The rhetoric of cultural pluralism during the war years then obscured an essentially assimilationist message.[3] Efforts at national unity such as New York City's 1942 I am an American Day, for example, encouraged ethnic groups to submerge their cultural differences to create an unequivocally American identity rather than a national identity based on the nation's diversity.[4] The example of Italian Americans confirms that although the war created opportunities for individuals to join the mainstream, expressions of group distinctiveness such as language were discouraged. The issue of whether or not immigrants and ethnics themselves embraced an American identity during the war remains debatable. The sharp rise in the naturalization rates of white ethnics including Italian Americans during the war years, for example, can be seen as a demonstration of loyalty during a time of international crisis when the appearance of disloyalty could have potentially dire consequences rather than as a true expression of patriotism. For a time, becoming a citizen was the only way for an Italian American to avoid being designated an enemy alien, as Italian American community leaders who facilitated the naturalization process well understood.[5]

Finally, a focus on language using the Italian American example during wartime provides a necessary caution regarding the ability of ethnics to "choose" their identities, that is, to freely decide what aspects to adopt or highlight as part of their ethnic identity.[6] It is commonly understood that during the period of mass migration southern and eastern European immigrants were under enormous pressure to assimilate. However, the experience of Italian Americans during the war years serves as an important reminder that the choices immigrants and ethnics made in forming an identity were circumscribed well beyond the initial years of blatant nativist sentiment. The war may have presented Italian Americans with a new opportunity to join the mainstream, but the degree to which they felt free to foster and express their cultural distinctiveness within a newly unified American society is questionable.

This chapter first examines the actions of the FBI and other government agencies to reveal the limitations within which Italian American identity could be expressed during the war years and beyond as well as the response of Italian Americans, largely of the immigrant generation. The military's willingness to make use of second-generation Italian Americans' facility with Italian provides a counterexample of how Italian and the soldiers who spoke it were received. The divisions within the government as to whether immigrant languages represented a strength to be exploited or a threat to be guarded against—a debate that also spilled over into civilian discourse—are also briefly considered. Through these examples, we can see how Italian American identity in this period was constructed by Italian Americans through their perception of a sometimes hostile, sometimes welcoming American culture, an identity shaped in part by an American war effort that sought to use its national and linguistic diversity for its own ends. The findings suggest that Italian Americans were not uncritically accepted into American society nor was it a matter of ethnics abandoning their own cultures to conform to the newly articulated vision of Americanism. Rather, a new Italian American ethnic identity was forged during the war years under the pressure of historical events and conditions. The chapter concludes by revisiting the figure of Louis Prima, who embodied the possibilities as well as the limitations of the cultural pluralism of the postwar era and what it meant for Italian Americans and their language.

"Don't Speak the Enemy's Language"

Although American intolerance of immigrant languages and preference for English was hardly new, popular suspicion of particular foreign languages was renewed and heightened during the war years. As a government poster from the time illustrates, Japanese, Italian, and German were each considered "the enemy's language" and should not be spoken.[7]

Like Japanese and German Americans, Italian American loyalty to the United States was questioned as fears of a fifth column spread, particularly after the bombing of Pearl Harbor in 1941 precipitated the United States' official entry into the war. The government toyed briefly with the notion of placing Italians with nonresident status in internment camps, just as it had Japanese Americans. Due in part to the logistical difficulties of rounding up such a large and widely dispersed population, along with their growing political power on the east coast in particular, the government opted to require ten thousand alien resident Italians living on the west coast to move away from the designated prohibited zone following Pearl Harbor. This area encompassed much of Monterey and Pittsburg; within San Francisco Bay, almost all of Richmond, El Cerrito, half of Berkeley and Oakland, and all of Alameda. Over fifty thousand more Italian Americans in California lived under curfew. Between December 1941 and June 1942, over 1,500 Italians including some Italian Americans were arrested on suspicion of aiding the enemy. Many of those first interned were connected to Italian language media such as newspaper editors and radio broadcasters. Also included in this group were Italian language teachers. Internees were detained by the Immigration and Naturalization Service at various sites throughout the country. (Ironically, Ellis Island served as one of the detention centers.) Following hearings, some three hundred to four hundred of these enemy aliens were placed in the custody of the U.S. Army, which dispersed them to internment sections of military bases throughout the country.[8]

Although very few Italian Americans were interned and curfews were imposed only in California, beginning in 1941 some six hundred thousand nonresident Italian Americans across the country were labeled "enemy aliens" and forced to register with the government. They were required to carry a "Certificate of Identification" at all times "as a protection."[9] Their movements were proscribed and they were banned from possessing certain items including cameras, flashlights, firearms, and shortwave radios, all of which were considered evidence of potential treasonous activity.[10] Even though the restrictions that bound them were fairly benign, especially when compared with those imposed on Japanese Americans, over 120,000 of whom were forcibly interned, losing their belongings, their livelihoods, their rights, and in some cases their lives, enemy alien status had serious consequences for Italian Americans.[11] The consequences included employment discrimination and anti-Italian sentiment generally. As a columnist for *Collier's* in 1940 noted, taking issue with the rising anti-Italian sentiment of the time, "you would think from some of the talk in circulation that our Italians were getting ready to carve up our government and hand it to Mussolini on a spaghetti-with-meatballs platter."[12] Although the U.S. government lifted the designation of enemy alien within less than a year, at the time, Italian immigrants and their children feared the prospect of internment—the logical next step to enemy alien designation.[13] Moreover, they resented the injustice of being singled out as unpatriotic solely on the basis of nationality.[14]

Enemy alien status undoubtedly contributed to the profound psychological tensions individual Italian Americans experienced at the time. Italian American authors have written movingly of the terrible conflict that the war created for their families who felt they were being asked to make an impossible choice between their adopted country and their country of origin where many still had close relatives. In *Unto the Sons*, Gay Talese describes his father's double life as he strove to reconcile this conflict. By day, he acted the part of patriot, giving a rousing pro-Allies speech at the local Rotary Club and engaging in other public acts of support for the American war effort, but at home in the evenings, he agonized over the fate of relatives in the Italian army and those still living in his native village.[15] In her memoir, the poet Diane di Prima describes the scene when her family gathered at the port to bid farewell to her uncle, who opted to return to Italy before the imminent outbreak of war between the two countries rather than risk the American draft and the possibility of having to fight against relatives in Italy: "Now the War was very close and Giuseppe had decided to 'go home,' to return to Sicily. He was leaving with all his family. The word that was used was that the family was being 'divided.' . . . Cousins wept, and wondered if they would next see each other across battle lines."[16] Di Prima's parents' anxiety about the war ran so high that, in an effort to shield their daughter, they restricted her access to newspapers and the radio. In her words, "my parents decided that since we were Italian we were on both sides of the war, and there could be no good news."[17]

In this wartime atmosphere of suspicion and anxiety, it was the very foreignness of Italians that made them suspect, and the use of the Italian language that had connoted racial separateness earlier in the century was a key signifier of difference. The distrust engendered by the use of Italian can be found in Martin Dies's 1940 book, *The Trojan Horse in America*, in which he warned of possible fifth column activity within the United States. In a chapter entitled "Mussolini's Trojan Horse in America," Dies, who would become a major figure in the House Un-American Activities Committee hearings, wrote that in some respects Mussolini's "Trojan Horse" was more dangerous than Hitler's because it received less attention in the press due to the inscrutability of the Italian language: "For the most part, it is concealed behind the barrier of the Italian language. To the extent that one Trojan Horse is more secret than another, it is also the most dangerous."[18] Even though Dies discussed the threat of a German fifth column as well, the German language seems not to have obscured the German threat or marked German Americans to the degree that Italian did for Italian Americans. Although the use of national languages by immigrant groups from other Axis nations was also cause for concern during the war, there are reasons why Italian may have been more a more stigmatized language. Unlike German immigrants, for example, Italian Americans were still a fairly recent immigrant group at the time, one that was less integrated into American life. Italian Americans accounted for the largest number of foreign-born immigrants in the United States and had the highest rates of non-English speakers.[19] Language was also more of a marker of foreignness for Italian Americans than for Japanese Americans who were more readily identifiable by physical features.

The use and promotion of the Italian language figured largely into the FBI's monitoring of Italian Americans during the war years. Italian American homes were searched for contraband items related to the use of the Italian language including newspapers, letters, or other documents written in Italian, and shortwave radios. The government's concern with subversive activity from this group ran so high that even the 140 Italian Americans living in Alaska were not spared the scrutiny of the FBI.[20] There was no formal policy regarding Italian or any other enemy alien language usage, but the FBI— and by extension the government—viewed the use and promotion of the Italian language whether in the home, in print, on the airwaves, or within organized settings as evidence of potential disloyalty, just as they equated the use of English with greater patriotism.

Agents of the FBI were especially pleased to note the shift from the use of Italian to English in Italian American newspapers and social organizations. An agent reporting on the Italian American community of Buffalo, New York, noted, "in the past year *Il Corriere Italiano* has printed its first sheet entirely in English," but, he continued, "its editorials and local news as well as most advertisements are printed in the Italian language."[21] A report from an agent in Cincinnati stated that the local Sons of Italy posed no threat to security because "it is a completely loyal organization. . . . At the present time the meetings are held and all conversation carried on in English, whereas prior to the entrance of the United States into war all conversation at the meetings was carried on in the Italian language."[22] Many of the FBI reports were limited to statements that seemed to clear the local Italian American community of wrongdoing by simply noting that no Italian language newspapers, radio broadcasts, or schools were found.[23]

Indeed, FBI files reveal that the use of the language itself in any context, independent of any direct Fascist connections, was basis enough for suspicion and further investigation. This is clear from the extent of the distrust of anything written in Italian or anyone who spoke it. Spot checks on the 121

Italian aliens living in Oklahoma City in 1942 led to the seizure of weapons, cameras, and other contraband including "a number of letters and documents written in Italian, which will be translated for any information."[24] Correspondence to and from Italy was highly suspect even in the absence of any other evidence of disloyalty. A Mr. Bertaldo of Oklahoma City was required to assure agents that neither he nor his wife had any relatives in Italy and that they had not received any correspondence from there for several years.[25] Although enemy aliens were not prohibited from speaking their native languages or reading foreign language newspapers, immigrants believed this to be so to such an extent that the U.S. Department of Justice was compelled to address the issue in a publication entitled "Questions and Answers on Regulations Concerning Aliens of Enemy Nationalities."[26]

In addition to conducting raids, FBI officials sought information from Italian American informants such as Joe Franzetti who reassured agents in Austin, Texas, regarding certain individuals, "Italian is not spoken in the homes of the above and they are all loyal."[27] Another Italian American resident of San Antonio, "Confidential Informant SA #224," informed FBI agents that "the Druid Club and the Christopher Columbus Italian Society respectively, changed their by-laws to require all meetings to be conducted in English." Agents were further heartened to learn that the "Italian language newspaper, *La Voce della Patria,* discontinued publication prior to Pearl Harbor."[28] The attitude of some FBI agents toward the meaning of language is evident in comments equating the intelligence of the respondent with his or her ability to speak English, echoing the association between English and intellect prevalent earlier in the century. An alien named Compani, according to one agent, "appeared to be very ignorant, and could speak very little English."[29] The same agent writes that a Mr. Giacobbi "appeared to be very ignorant and could not speak English fluently."[30] On the other hand, Joe Passo stood out because he "has never been arrested, and speaks good English."[31]

The FBI's actions were carried out in a time of pervasive linguistic chauvinism. In a 1944 *New York Times* article entitled "Italian Remains Greek to Yanks," the reporter noted that even after a year in Italy, many American soldiers had not acquired even a rudimentary knowledge of Italian. The reason for this according to the reporter was "not linguistic at all but psychological and it is expressed by the attitude, 'Aw, let'em learn English.'" The author interpreted the unwillingness to learn another language as evidence of "a basic indifference and contempt" for anything foreign.[32] Some days later, an editorialist for the same newspaper sought to excuse the GIs for their unwillingness to learn another language by claiming that the example of high level diplomacy had shown that, thanks to interpreters, it was unnecessary to bother learning other languages. After all, the editorialist noted, Churchill had an easier time reaching an understanding with Stalin without knowing Russian than he had with de Gaulle, despite Churchill's knowledge of French.[33] The general distrust of foreign languages could only have contributed to the assumption that apparently guided the FBI's investigations of Italian Americans, namely, that any evidence of foreign language usage was suspect.

The government's focus on the subversive potential of the Italian language was not entirely without basis. As the language-maintenance efforts in New York reveal, the promotion of the Italian language and culture both at home and abroad were major elements of Mussolini's brand of Fascism, and cultural organizations that fostered Italian language study were often closely linked to the Italian government. Many Italian language newspapers, including the four with the largest circulations, expressed pro-Fascist sympathies prior to the war.[34] Generoso Pope, longtime Fascist sympathizer and publisher of the nationally distributed *Il Progresso Italo-Americano*, was accused of making anti-Fascist declamations only in the English section of the newspaper, but he continued defending Italy's actions in the Italian section. Only when confronted with this charge in 1941 did Pope fully reject Fascism in both the Italian and English sections of his newspaper.[35]

Fervent Italian American anti-Fascists such as labor leader Luigi Antonini accused certain New York City broadcasters of using "sweet double meaning expressions," an allusion to veiled Fascist support, while ostensibly promoting the sale of war bonds over the radio.[36] Although major figures in the community embraced Mussolini and his policies, a number of prominent Italian American public figures spoke out consistently against Fascism and sometimes took action. In 1925, New York State's Grand Lodge of Order of the Sons of Italy (OSIA), led by La Guardia and State Senator Salvatore Cotillo, was troubled enough by the national OSIA's Supreme Venerable Giovanni M. Di Silvestro's close ties with Fascist Italy and his public statements of support that the New York branch split off from the national organization. The local lodge only rejoined the national in 1943, after Mussolini's fall.[37] However, the point here is not to determine whether the government overreacted to the potential threat represented by Italian Americans, but rather that government actions and the climate they created led to a further stigmatization of Italian Americans and the Italian language.

Italian Americans quickly grasped the need to prove their linguistic and thus patriotic loyalty, as the "No Italian Spoken for the Duration of the War" signs in shop windows demonstrated.[38] In Indianapolis, the local branch of OSIA officially changed its name from the Società Italiane di Mutuo Beneficenze Umberto to Victory Benefit Association, severing its ties to OSIA in the process.[39] In certain instances, name changes may have been made in response to specific government requests. For example, the Office of War Information (OWI), the government's main propaganda organ, wrote to Italian organizations with names that contained Fascist overtones, such as certain lodges of OSIA, to request that they Americanize their names.[40]

Individual Italian Americans were quick to realize that the Italian language was a liability, with some going as far as denying any knowledge of it. A Mrs. Passini of Oklahoma City insisted to FBI agents conducting a spot check that she could not understand Italian. Later, agents were informed by an Italian American neighbor that "Mrs. Passini could translate and understand Italian fluently."[41] The importance American society placed on learning English and its relationship to patriotism was not lost on Italian Americans. Nunzio Rossi, also of Oklahoma City, reported to agents that not only had he not received any Italian publications or literature of any kind since coming to the United States, but he also had tried to read American newspapers to learn the language. Some of the aliens interviewed had learned this lesson much earlier as evidenced by their Americanized names: Pauline Mitchell, interviewed by the FBI, turned out to be Pauline Miceli; Frank Campbell was the name Francesco Carnovale had been using when the FBI came to visit him.[42]

The message conveyed to Italian Americans through the actions of the FBI and the pervasive attitudes that informed them was clear: the use of the Italian language was incompatible with being or becoming a loyal American during the war years. This message was reinforced by other arms of the government, although with some ambivalence. The OWI and the Foreign Nationalities Branch (FNB) of the OSS were also involved in monitoring Italian language usage, but there were internal divisions in each agency as to whether foreign language usage represented a danger to the war effort or a resource to be exploited.

Italian as well as German language radio was a particular concern of the government during the war years. The fear that broadcasters were secretly signaling enemy vessels in the seas under the cover of a foreign language was prevalent. The Foreign Language Division within the Office of Facts and Figures, both established in 1941, merged into the OWI in June 1942 to monitor foreign language media and disseminate pro-U.S. information.[43]

As a result of the pressure implicit in this surveillance of radio broadcasts, some radio stations that offered Italian programming began prohibiting the use of the Italian language for any broadcasts, regardless of how innocuous their content. Thus, Mr. Litteri, a grocer in Washington, D.C., who had a half-hour program on WINX every Sunday through which he advertised grocery items and Italian records, was forbidden to speak Italian by the station and required to make all announcements in English.[44]

Italian Americans had sixty-five radio stations of their own offering programming in Italian that served over four million Italian Americans. The largest of these—mainly stations in big cities such as New York's WBNX, WHOM, and WOV—were targeted by the Foreign Language Broadcasters Wartime Control Commission, established by the Foreign Language Division, which used the Federal Communications Commission to threaten stations suspected of Fascist leanings with the suspension of their licenses unless particular broadcasters or programs were removed from the air. Over time, this illegal practice, together with the withdrawal of support by advertisers and criticism by non-Italian listeners, had the effect of diminishing the number and extent of Italian (and German) language broadcasts.[45]

There were some voices of opposition to government efforts to mute or control the foreign language media. As one *New York Times* editorialist noted, the language itself was not the problem but rather how it is used.[46] Even within OWI, some lamented the demise of foreign language programming, claiming that these radio stations and programs provided the best means for the government to reach ethnic audiences and encourage their participation in the war effort.[47] Indeed, the government, through the OWI, tried to reach ethnic audiences with programs such as *Uncle Sam Speaks in Italian* and others. Of the four Italian language radio program broadcasts in St. Louis in 1943, three were programs issued directly from OWI. The fourth was *The Neapolitan Serenade*, a music segment that included a short message by an Italian-speaking announcer, which, according to the station manager who closely monitored the program, was usually "very patriotically American" without "any pro-Fascist leaning."[48]

In another attempt to take advantage of Italian language media to promote American war aims, the OWI, led by Alan Cranston, tried to exert its influence on Italian language newspapers as well radio with press releases in Italian. In letters to the publishers of Italian newspapers, Cranston questioned why OWI's Italian language press releases had not been incorporated into the newspapers and urged the inclusion of this information.[49] Other branches of state and federal government were involved in the regulation and control of foreign language newspapers. California, for example, beginning in 1943, required foreign language newspapers to submit English translations of their articles to the local district attorney.[50]

The federal agency most involved in monitoring the foreign language media was the FNB, which collected detailed information on the Italian American press, including English summaries of articles, descriptions of the political orientation and readership of each newspaper, and what letters to the editors revealed about Italian American popular opinion of the war, Mussolini, and Fascism.[51] Like the OWI, the FNB was split over whether the agency should devote most of its resources to monitoring immigrants or winning them over to the side of the Allies through their own languages. Ultimately, this was a division between those who were able to separate, in this case, the Italian language from its association with Fascism, and those who could not.[52]

Cranston and the OWI attempted to draw the distinction between the Italian language itself, wherever it was spoken or written, and its use to support the Fascist cause. In a speech to the anti-Fascist Mazzini Society, Cranston acknowledged the special importance of the Italian language to his listeners: "it is the legitimate and fitting desire of America—and I am sure that you share in this desire—that the beautiful language of Dante, which has been made to serve fascist propaganda and treason, shall henceforth be used more and more to express the ideals of Italian humanism, to interpret the ideals of democracy, to be the instrument of your economic and cultural uplifting in the American land, to facilitate your contributions to American victory and speed the liberation of Italy."[53] In this excerpt, Cranston acknowledges the relationship of language to the Italian identity of his literate and literary listeners while attempting to separate that language from its Fascist associations.

Leaders within the Italian American community also tried to break the connection in the American mind between the Italian language and Fascism by using the Italian language to demonstrate the commitment of Italian Americans to the war effort. For example, Italian American educational leaders in New York City sponsored an essay contest for Italian language students, asking them to write on the subject of war bonds and stamps. Cranston was invited to attend the awards ceremony in honor of the six hundred–plus students who competed in the contest.[54]

These examples of the Cranston-led OWI and the FNB suggest an alternative approach to Italian immigrants/ethnics and the Italian language that was open to the government and the wider American society but that ultimately did not prevail. The use of the Italian language did not have to be equated with potential disloyalty. Italian and Fascism were not inseparable, they were only interpreted as such by the FBI and the American public at large. That they were so linked necessarily created limitations for the expression of Italian American identity.

Italian in the Service of America

While Italian homes were searched for evidence of Italian language usage and the Italian language media scrutinized, Italian American civilians and enlisted men were given an unusual opportunity: to put their native fluency in Italian and their general knowledge of Italian ways and manners in the service of the government. Within this limited context, the ability to speak Italian created an opportunity for Italian Americans to demonstrate their loyalty to the United States. In 1942, the OSS began a nationwide recruiting campaign for Italian American civilians to join a separate Italian unit of the SI. As part of its recruitment campaign, the OSS broadened its contacts with Italian American anti-Fascist organizations and labor groups and brought in Girolamo Valenti, editor of a New York anti-Fascist weekly, to assist with recruitment.[55] The Italian section of the SI took part in intelligence gathering missions in North Africa as well as throughout Italy. It played a significant role in the planning and execution of the invasion of Sicily in the summer of 1943 with the help of Sicilian Americans who spoke Sicilian, and later in assisting the efforts of the anti-Fascist resistance in northern Italy. In addition to gathering intelligence on the ground, the Italian Section of the SI conducted counterintelligence work, line infiltration, and psychological warfare.[56]

Prior to their missions overseas, the Italian Section of the SI was involved in recruiting Italian American soldiers for special military OGs. From April 20 to May 14, 1943, over two thousand Italian American soldiers from the various divisions of the Second and Third Armies were interviewed by the OSS. The goal was to recruit Italian American soldiers with knowledge of Italian into separate OGs that would conduct military operations and assist local resistance efforts.[57] Italian secret intelligence agents trained new recruits in special operations and intelligence collection through OSS schools in Maryland and Virginia. Recruits were chosen according to ethnicity, and fluency in Italian was a major criterion for selection. Because these Italian American OGs were military rather than intelligence gathering units, recruits were chosen on the basis of their physical qualifications rather than any special mental aptitude. What distinguished them from other soldiers, however, was their intimate knowledge of the Italian language and dialects. One author explained the thinking behind the formation of Italian American OGs this way: "Almost all of the men would have learned the foreign language in the home, not in high school or college. They would speak the language more like the natives. They would know not only the spoken languages but also the facial expression and body language which are part of oral communication. In the case of Italians, the American [*sic*] say: if you tie their hands, they cannot speak."[58] Although the volunteers were not told the exact nature of their missions, they were informed that they involved "extra hazardous duty behind enemy lines." Nevertheless, there do not seem to have been any difficulties in attracting the necessary recruits. Company A of the OSS—the Italian OGs—came to include 17 officers and 126 enlisted men divided into four separate groups under one field-service headquarters.[59]

The OGs were sent throughout Italy, including Sardinia, Sicily, and, toward the end of the war, northern Italy. The missions that they conducted were varied. In some instances, soldiers were placed behind enemy lines in full uniform, and in others, they were given clothing that would allow them to blend in with the local population. Upon parachuting behind enemy lines in Italy, their varied objectives included coordinating resistance efforts by supplying money, arms, medical equipment, and such to local guerilla groups, serving as "nuclei" in planning and executing attacks, carrying out their own operations against the enemy, gathering intelligence, rescuing Allied airmen, and more. The reports on OG missions contain numerous testaments to the effectiveness and importance to the war effort of the Italian American OGs, particularly with regard to their language capabilities. A report on one mission carried out by the OGs notes, "their language facility, in addition to their highly specialized training, proved of particular value."[60] Two Italian American officers from Operation Sardinia were singled out for their language skills: "Both proved invaluable as interpreters and contributed immensely to establishing good will with the officers and men of the Italian Army."[61] The ability of the Italian American OGs to speak Italian like natives seems to have been key to their success and accounts in large part for their ability to penetrate so far behind enemy lines.

It is unclear if government use of Italian American recruits for their special linguistic skills during the war was widely known within Italian American communities. In a 1975 interview conducted as part of an oral history of International Ladies' Garment Workers' Union workers, one Italian American man noted that the use of Italian Americans in the OSS was the only positive in an otherwise hostile, anti-Italian wartime environment.[62] How he knew of the Italian OGs—through public channels or privately garnered information—is unclear. Whether or not the program was publicized, word of the effort likely made its way into Italian American neighborhoods soon after the war ended if not before.

The army was a vehicle to enter into mainstream American life in other ways as well. For example, Italian American civilians had to go through the military if they wanted to use their language skills on behalf of the war effort. Even translators in civil service jobs such as censors for the post office were recruited and placed through the army.[63] Indeed, Covello came to see the war effort as almost a godsend for Italian American youth who were trapped between two cultures, unable to fully identify with either, and as a result subject to low self-esteem and alienation. In a speech to the United Nationalities Council in March 1943, Covello noted that although the war had had the effect of demeaning all things Italian and lessening even further the influence of Italian parents on their children, the possibility of entering the military held out a chance for these young men (and perhaps through them, their female relations)[64] to forge a more direct identification with America than any other prior experience had allowed for them. According to Covello, the decision of young Italian Americans to enter the military before they were drafted was "based on a very conscious effort on the part of this youth to acquire status, recognition, dignity, equality—attributes that characterize one's full membership in the American nation."[65] During the war, the military achieved what years of Italian language promotion in the public schools by Covello and others had failed to do, namely, to enable Italian American youth to hold their heads up in mainstream American society.

The option of using the military to gain greater acceptance and a greater sense of identification with American society did not exist, however, for first-generation Italian American men who were beyond the draft age. Instead, Covello and other *prominenti* strongly encouraged older Italian Americans to learn English and become citizens. The two were related: to become a citizen, one had to pass an English language test. In a letter to radio station WBNX, which offered Italian language programming, Covello insisted on the need to urge Italian immigrants to learn English and take citizenship classes in evening elementary schools through on-air announcements.[66] Encouraging immigrant parents to learn English and Americanize was nothing new for Covello and other promoters of intercultural education. Just as Italian American children needed to learn Italian to communicate better with their parents, Covello and his supporters argued that parents needed to learn the language of their children, English. However, the war and particularly the designation of Italian nationals as enemy aliens undoubtedly lent a different character and a far greater urgency to this call.

The Second World War offered an opportunity, primarily to second-generation Italian Americans, to use Italian to demonstrate their patriotism. In so doing, they could secure a stronger foothold within the country, but there was a catch. Through military service, whether in the OGs or in regular units, Italian American youth were able to enter the American mainstream, but they had to do so single file, as individuals rather than as members of an ethnic group.

Louis Prima and the Limits of *Italianità* in the Postwar Era

Italian Americans exhibited diverging responses to the confused messages of this era regarding the Italian language. As the records of the FBI reveal, many Italian Americans seem to have understood the need to downplay their attachment to their language(s) and necessarily restricted its use in the public sphere. Others eagerly seized the opportunity that the military presented to use Italian to prove their worth as Americans. Louis Prima's popularity among Italian American audiences suggests a continued attachment to the language and a willingness to assert an Italian American identity, however limited.

Initially, Prima was most successful with Italian American audiences, particularly though not exclusively with young people, who responded immediately to his first hit, "Angelina." Prima's brother described the Italian American response to the music and the man: "It struck a nerve. Wherever he went people would come up to him on stage and give him big pizzas and Italian candies. They loved him for singing those Italian songs. There'd be pretty girls and their mothers wearing black, with the dark shawls and all. It was crazy."[67] A reporter for *Variety* reviewing a show in Boston wrote that Prima's act consisted of "scattered dialect wisecracks . . . unquestionably a sock layout . . . [Prima] takes many a whack at the trumpet, sings, shouts, and carries on, letting fly . . . many a fast crack in Italo [*sic*] that by no means escapes the audience." The audience was so taken with him that after four choruses, Prima "finally had to throw them out."[68]

Prima's lyrics represent, at best, an approximation of the language of his Italian American listeners that could border on caricature set to his interpretation of jazz, that distinctly American musical form. Yet his songs reflect an insider's familiarity with the language and sensibility of Italian Americans.

The title (and refrain) of the song "For Mari-Yootch (I Walka da Pooch)"[69] suggests Prima's appeal for Italian American audiences. "Mari-Yootch" is an anglicized spelling of the southern Italian diminutive for Maria. The use of the diminutive as a form of endearment would have been very familiar to Prima's Italian American audience. Performed by an outsider, the attempt to replicate the rhythm and syntax of Italian immigrant speech in the song could easily come across as offensive, but Prima's clear identification with Italian America makes his interpretation of the song a sympathetic one.

Prima also enjoyed an astounding degree of crossover success with younger non-Italian audiences. By the end of the war, he was breaking box office records and topping the pop charts for weeks on end. Even in middle America, Prima's music was driving American teenagers wild. A non-Italian fan from Lancaster, Ohio, wrote in a letter to the editor of *Life Magazine*: "With the possible exception of versatile Lionel Hampton, no other bands have caused such widespread acclaim from central Ohio's jazz-crazy juveniles as have Louis Prima and Benny Goodman. Prima's rendition of 'Please No Squeeza da Banana' sent thousands of us into ecstasy and smashed box-office records."[70] Despite his popularity, however, Prima, too experienced the limits of asserting a publicly Italian American identity. His novelty songs caused some alarm in the war years. In Britain, for example, Prima's "Papa Nicolini," which favorably depicted an Italian immigrant merchant, was banned because of its potential to induce sympathy toward an enemy nation.[71] According to Prima's widow, there was some opposition in the United States to playing Prima's music on the radio during the war.[72]

Perhaps even more ominous were the strong reactions his lyrics and performance style elicited in some individuals. Prima's popularity owed much to his extravagant showmanship. Growing up in New Orleans in the early years of jazz, Prima was heavily influenced by Louis Armstrong, who also hailed from the Big Easy. (Prima's speaking and singing voice are both reminiscent of Armstrong's.) In his early years, Prima had earned a reputation as a serious jazz musician of some note. His early mix of Dixieland and swing made him a star in New York City music circles within six months of his arrival there in 1935. Some critics interpreted his move to novelty songs as evidence of "selling out," but his biographer contends that Prima was merely following in the New Orleans tradition of "playing to the crowd."[73]

Some non–Italian American music observers, however, were put off by Prima's stage antics and indecipherable lyrics. As one contemporary New York disc jockey noted, "the Italianisms obviously mean something hilarious to dancers from New York's Little Italy to San Francisco's North Beach, but Prima's affected accents leave a non-comprende group cold."[74] Another critic was far more harsh in his assessment, referring to Prima as "a buffoon" whose act consisted "solely of repeating the same questionable Italian jokes, wild-arm-and-leg waving, and screeching of idiotic lyrics, jitterbugging with girls from the audience."[75]

He antagonized the censors and undoubtedly some listeners with his song from the early 1940s, *"Felicia No Capricia"* [*sic*] (Felicia Doesn't Understand), which some thought contained lewd references. La Guardia, New York City's Italian American mayor, had to reassure the censors on the innocuous content of the song. In a similar vein, three students from Phillips Exeter Academy in New Hampshire felt compelled to write *Life Magazine* to express their "extreme disgust" at an article on Louis Prima that referred to the female fans who regularly threw themselves at the charismatic Prima, who is said to have had a strong sexual stage presence. The three wrote: "How any self-respecting female could lower herself to such an extent . . . merely to touch him is utterly incomprehensible to us."[76]

The loathing expressed by critics such as these students suggests a lingering degree of racial prejudice toward southern Italians. Indeed, Prima was, on occasion, mistaken for black by both whites and African Americans. The first time he was scheduled to appear at one of the jazz clubs on Fifty-Second Street in New York, he was barred from playing by the white owner who thought Prima was black.[77] According to the performer Sammy Davis Jr., Prima, a third-generation Italian American of Sicilian ancestry with dark skin, kinky hair, and broad features, was taken to be African American or at least someone of mixed ancestry at a performance he gave at Harlem's legendary Apollo Theater.[78] Prima himself further contributed to the confusion over his racial origins by openly crossing the color line as the only white bandleader of his time who performed regularly at major black clubs throughout the country.[79]

Prima's experience growing up in New Orleans undoubtedly influenced his own feelings about race. New Orleans' Italian Americans, who in 1910 numbered over 150,000, mixed freely with the city's black population in the early years of the twentieth century, much to the consternation of native whites. Unlike native whites who distanced themselves from the work and leisure activities of blacks, Italian Americans joined blacks in the sugarcane fields as well as in the jazz clubs. Indeed, Italian American musicians figure into the history of jazz; names such as Sharkey Bonano were as well-known to New Orleans jazz fans as Louis Armstrong. Italian Americans and African Americans had in common poverty, low levels of education, and a largely oral tradition, all of which drew both groups to the jazz form and its venues. They also shared, though not nearly to the same extent, the persecution and prejudice of New Orleans whites: it was in New Orleans in 1890 that eleven Sicilians were lynched, the largest mass lynching in the country.[80]

Besides having a racially questionable outward appearance, Prima clearly identified as Italian American at a time when perceptions of Italian Americans as not fully white that had developed in the era of mass migration lingered. The accusations of lewdness in his lyrics and performing style recall white fears of black sexuality. In his person, performance style, and in his use of the Italian language, Prima embodied Italian American difference as well as the potential danger Italian Americans represented during World War II. A 1945 *Life Magazine* spread on Prima suggests just how threatening his Italianness was at the time and particularly his incorporation of Italian lyrics into his songs. The caption to a photo of Prima jitterbugging to "Please No Squeeza Da Bananas" with a young girl makes a point of noting that "Italian dialect numbers like this did not become popular until after Italy joined the Allies."[81] It is telling that in an article otherwise wholly devoid of political content, the author felt compelled to make this qualification. The implication is that it would have been somehow inappropriate—perhaps disloyal—of mainstream Americans to embrace Prima and the Italian Americans he represented along with their language prior to Italy's joining the United States and the Allies.

At the same time, Prima represented the new possibility then becoming available to Italian Americans of finding widespread acceptance within the American mainstream while still retaining some sense of ethnic identification. Prima's biographer claims that the novelty songs provided "a healthy outlet" for Italian Americans, "one that allowed for a certain amount of sentimentality coupled with self-parody." This in an era when anti-Italian stereotypes reduced them to "loud and arrogant buffoons . . . or . . . crass underworld mob chieftains."[82] However, Prima's novelty songs served another function, on a much wider scale. Much like Farfariello's performances, Prima's songs, whether recorded or performed live, created a context within which Italian Americans could express a collective, in-group association made possible by the familiarity with the language Prima used, a language that only Italian Americans could fully appreciate. What was even more exciting about Prima for Italian Americans was that his performances were not limited to local ethnic theaters where only other Italians would be likely to see them; they were broadcast across the airwaves and performed at major venues nationwide, all in a period when Italian Americans and their language were questioned. Although his songs made use of stereotypes, they were performed by someone who self-consciously identified as Italian American and that gave them quite a different character. Not surprisingly, long after

Prima had faded from the national consciousness, he remained a favorite with Italian American audiences who remembered him from his heyday in the 1940s and later in the clubs of Las Vegas.

To the wider American audience, Prima's music and persona for the most part meshed with the most benign stereotypes of Italians as a pleasure-loving if somewhat vulgar people who could easily be included within the melting pot. Indeed, the popularity of Italian novelty songs well into the 1950s suggests the degree to which the American public continued to embrace this two-dimensional version of *italianità*. Other Italian Americans as well as non-Italians also had big hits with songs that used Italianized lyrics or references. In 1950, Irish American singer Rosemary Clooney's rendition of "Come On-a My House" topped the charts and made her a star. The song, written by an Armenian American, was performed by Irish American Clooney using an Italian American accent because, she claims, "it was the only kind of accent I knew. Thanks to all the guys in Tony's band who had always taken me to meet their families on the road, I was very up on Italian accents."[83] Though probably true, the success of Prima with Italian American and wider audiences was undoubtedly not far from her—or the record company's—mind. Anticipating a hit, Prima, whose career had cooled by the early 1950s, had tried to get the recording rights to the song, claiming, "but it's for me, it's an Italian song."[84] Clooney went on to record other Italianized songs such as "Mambo Italiano," "That's a Nice, Don't Fight," and "Botcha Me," proving the appeal of this genre for middle America, although not necessarily for Italian Americans.[85]

The popularity of these songs with a wider American audience, beginning with Prima and followed by Clooney and others, may have been due in part to the way they diffused any sense of threat posed by a formerly foreign population that suddenly found itself on the fast track to entering the American mainstream as a result of wartime pressures to assimilate and the concomitant desire on the part of the second generation to fit in. Even though Louis Prima and his audience celebrated and perpetuated a particular vision of *italianità*, it was a limited one that, independent of the occasional opaqueness of Italian American dialect used in the songs, was entirely non-threatening and even embraced popular stereotypes of Italian Americans.

• • •

Certainly Italian Americans entered the mainstream during and after the war to a greater degree than they had ever before. The military, as Covello recognized, inadvertently served to integrate Italian Americans into American life, as did the enhanced opportunities for mobility made possible by the GI bill and a changing wartime economy. Suburbanization, which led to the dispersion of tightly knit urban ethnic neighborhoods, and the decline in the immigrant generation also played their parts.[86] That Italian Americans entered the mainstream to a greater degree than ever before during this period in socioeconomic terms is indisputable, but how their integration into American life played out in terms of the formation and expression of ethnic identity is another question.

Even though the decline in the number of Italian language speakers was underway before the war began, reflecting a common pattern among ethnic groups,[87] the war contributed to the decreasing use of the Italian language. It hastened the demise of Italian and with it a major although not necessarily essential expression of Italian American ethnic identity. The trend toward a more positive identification with the Italian language, begun with the work of Covello and others in the preceding decades, was reversed. By the time the United States entered the war, Italian language instruction had been eliminated from two-thirds of the high schools and colleges where it had previously been taught. Enrollment in the remaining programs entered a period of decline from which they would never recover. Coinciding with the drop in Italian language instruction was a 40 percent reduction in the number of Italian language periodicals between 1942 and 1948 along with a decrease in the number of Italian radio broadcasts during the war years.[88]

Wartime America accepted Italian Americans to a greater degree than before, but it did so within clearly circumscribed limits. The new American cultural pluralism, ostensibly based on an appreciation of the unique cultural contribution of all ethnic groups, in practice discouraged certain overt expressions of ethnicity including language. A 1938 article in *Life Magazine* on the young Joe DiMaggio reveals quite clearly what America's immigrants and ethnics had to do in exchange for full acceptance. The author gushed, "although he learned Italian at first, Joe, now twenty-four, speaks English without an accent, and is otherwise adapted to most United States mores. . . ." The article went on to note approvingly that Joe preferred chow mein to spaghetti and did not "reek of garlic." By the war's end, such expectations had not been substantially altered.[89] In this climate, Italian Americans had little motivation to speak Italian or pass it on to future generations and good reason to abandon it.

Epilogue

In June 2007, proposed legislation that would have constituted the most sweeping change in immigration policy in decades died in the Senate after a pitched battle between supporters and opponents of the bill. The clamor for immigration reform has been fueled by a heightened concern for security in the post-9/11 era that has drawn particular attention to securing the national borders. The economic dislocations and uncertainty caused by globalization constitute another source for the sense of urgency attached to passing new immigration legislation. However, much of the debate around the proposed legislation reflected familiar fears of the country becoming overrun with immigrants who would threaten the American way of life by failing to assimilate. Now as in years past, some of that fear was expressed in discussions of the meaning and place of English in American society.

The various versions of the immigration bill attempted to secure the borders against illegal immigrants, allow some illegal immigrants already in the country to obtain citizenship, and change the criteria for new immigrants to enter the country. In May 2006 and again in June 2007, legislators introduced amendments to allay the fears of those who feel that the continued flow of immigrants into the country poses a cultural threat. These amendments would have designated English as the national language, denied the right to obtain government services in any other language, and required some proficiency in English for citizenship. Supporters of these measures claimed that they would merely acknowledge the crucial role of English in the national culture. Critics saw it as fostering an atmosphere of linguistic and cultural intolerance and anti-immigrant sentiment more generally.

Efforts at the local level to address illegal immigration in the absence of any acceptable federal action have included similar language provisions such as the Hazelton, Pennsylvania, ordinance that, among other measures, would make English the official language. Nor is this impulse to legislate language a new one. Since the early 1980s when the English-only movement led by "U.S. English" came on the scene, dozens of measures to declare English the official language have been proposed in Congress and in a number of states. Just as the measures involving border security and how to deal with illegal migrants already in the country are largely aimed at Hispanic migrants and Mexicans in particular, language measures are primarily a response to the Spanish-speaking immigrants in the country. The popular sentiment behind the desire to legislate the role of the English language in American life is encapsulated in the statement of a seventy-one-year-old man, living in an upper-middle-class Colorado suburb, in response to the immigration situation: "Portugal is Portugal because of the Portuguese language; Spain is Spanish; France is—God knows—France is French; Germany is Germany, all because of language. . . . That, to me, is the thing that holds, that builds a country."[1] In the United States today, as in years past, the association between language usage and nationality is pervasive.

Even though many of those who favor making English the national or official language claim that this does not imply any animosity toward immigrant languages, America's more recent history with linguistic minorities suggests otherwise, especially when contrasted with the linguistic histories of other nations. Language policy scholar James Crawford draws a telling comparison between the United States and Australia, another nation of immigrants. Although English is the official language of Australia, a designation that is actually stronger than "national" language, that country also fosters the preservation of immigrant languages and promotes non-English languages among English speakers. As Crawford notes regarding the difference between the two countries, "Australia doesn't have an English-only movement. . . . They don't use language as a lightning rod for expressing your views on immigration. Language has not become a major symbolic dividing line."[2]

That dividing line rests on a couple of false assumptions in addition to the notion that language and nation are coterminous. One is that the predominance of English is being threatened by the large influx of immigrants in recent decades and by Spanish-speaking immigrants in particular. As a number of studies demonstrate, this is just not so. Although there are pockets with large immigrant populations where non-English languages are more commonly used than in other parts of the country, the overwhelming majority of the population speaks English exclusively. Today as in the past, foreign language groups typically become monolingual in English within a generation.[3] A corollary to this mistaken proposition that is not always openly voiced but is never far from the surface is the belief that today's immigrants are not learning English as quickly or as willingly as did the immigrants from the turn-of-the-twentieth century. In actuality, there are not nearly enough English as a Second Language classes to meet the demand.[4] Many Americans also mistakenly believe that the children of Spanish-speaking immigrants in particular are retaining their languages to a much greater extent than those in the past at the expense of learning English.[5] This thinking in part reflects the mythologizing of the ancestors by white ethnics in the 1970s that continues to inform public policy and politics.[6] It is also a reflection of how little many Americans know of their own history. In the introductory level history course that I teach on immigration, ethnicity, and race in the United States, students are often surprised to discover that the traditional narrative of immigration in America that they absorb in elementary and secondary school as well as through popular culture contrasts so forcefully with what they learn in college. For them as for Americans generally, the story of immigration in America remains that of a selfless nation, symbolized by the Statue of Liberty, welcoming the poor, huddled masses at Ellis Island. Early immigrants expressed their gratitude by assimilating rapidly and thoroughly to American life and by achieving the dream of upward mobility for the second generation, if not for themselves, in the form of home ownership, education, and white collar employment.

Like many Americans, many of my students draw a sharp distinction between the migrants of the last Age of Migration and the migrants of recent decades. They assume that the Poles, Russian Jews, Italians, and others—who in many cases were their ancestors—assimilated easily and without resistance. An oft-cited example of their acquiescence in becoming Americans was their ready acquisition of the English language. A central complaint about contemporary migrants is not only that they fail to learn English quickly or at all, but that they demand special linguistic accommodation. Just as students grapple with the idea that at the turn of the twentieth century, U.S. businesses exploited cheap, unskilled immigrant labor and that many questioned the "whiteness" of the new immigrants, they are surprised to learn that Americans back then complained at great length about the failure of immigrants to learn English and their insistence on speaking their own languages.

Significant differences exist in how immigrants and their languages are viewed today. These differences help us to understand the reaction against immigrant languages and the defense of English. In recent years, the ethos of multiculturalism and the general celebration of diversity in America have created a climate of greater tolerance for the use of non-English languages.

Today, native-born Americans in Queens, New York, study Mandarin to communicate with their Chinese neighbors; French is undergoing a revival in Maine where, even as recently as the 1960s, the descendants of French-Canadian immigrants were stigmatized for speaking their language; and, for the first time in the history of the nation, two Hispanic surnames—Garcia and Rodriguez—are among the top ten most common nationwide, with Martinez only narrowly losing out to Wilson for the #10 slot. This may be the first time "non-Anglo" names have made the list.[7] The contemporary linguistic landscape differs markedly from the one southern Italians and other earlier immigrants inhabited. Nevertheless, just as the rise of multi-culturalism engendered a severe backlash across campuses and in the media throughout the 1980s and 1990s, the greater receptivity to immigrant languages has coexisted with more forceful calls to protect and promote the use of English to the exclusion of other languages.

The linguistic chauvinism behind English-only efforts may have a material as well as an ideological basis. When the government and societal institutions accommodate non–English-speaking immigrants, some monolingual English speakers may perceive this as a loss of an economic advantage that even the least educated can claim over those with limited facility in English. Conversely, English monolinguals may feel at a competitive disadvantage in a society that recognizes the benefits of knowing more than one language.[8] Whatever motivates those who have been seeking to legislate the clear advantage that English has always enjoyed over all other languages spoken in the United States, the perspectives of the other side of this issue are more elusive. A look at immigrant literary production offers an alternative view.

Poet Vincenzo Ancona expresses the linguistic predicament of the immigrant. A fisherman and a farmer from Trapani in Sicily, Ancona emigrated to the United States in 1956. He lived in Bensonhurst, Brooklyn. For years, he worked in a broom factory and later in a jewelry shop. His dialect poetry, which he began writing in Sicily after World War II, was celebrated in his homeland and in Canada, as well as in the United States, where he performed in cities along the east coast, including Philadelphia, Buffalo, Trenton, and New York. He was also known for his sculptures made of telephone wire, which were exhibited in the Museum of American Folk Art in a 1988 exhibition entitled "City Folk: Ethnic Traditions in the Metropolitan Area." Once he retired, in 1979, after twenty-three years in the United States, he began spending half of each year in Sicily until his death in 2000. Like countless immigrants today and in the past, Ancona struggled with the English language. His obituary in the *New York Times* contains a translation of a fragment of a poem he wrote:

> Immigrants, illegal aliens and tourists
> Have found a place in this country.
> In this great land you can find every blessing
> Even if thorns at times will prick your hands.[9]

Ancona never learned much English, but he appreciated what America offered.

In *"Maladittu la lingua!"* (Damned Language!), the title poem of his 1990 collection, Ancona explores the frustration and shame he experienced due to his limited ability to speak English:

> *S'un mi la 'nsignu sugnu ruvinatu,*
> *sta lingua 'nglisi c'un sacciu parrari.*
> *Quantu malifiguri c'aiu pruvatu,*
> *sparti di chiddi ancora ch' è pruvari.*
> *Pi la me lingua sugnu un avvucatu,*
> *ma cu li mura pozzu ragiunari*
> *picchi sta maliditta lingua 'nglisi*
> *è fatta di papocchi e mali 'ntisi.*

> If I do not learn English soon, I'll be ruined.
> Damn this language I don't know how to speak!
> So much embarrassment have I endured,
> not mentioning what else may be in store.
> In my own language I'm a Cicero,
> but I feel like I'm speaking to the wall
> when I speak English; this accursed tongue
> is made of scribblings, ciphers—it's all wrong![10]

Ancona articulates his linguistic maladjustment through the use of two powerful linguistic tools: poetry and cursing. Through the use of poetry, Ancona places himself within the ranks of those who know how to effectively wield language. By cursing, an ancient and powerful use of language from his culture of origin, he neutralizes the power of the English language to silence him. Within the context of the poem, the English language loses the power to minimize him as an immigrant. Ancona dignifies the languages of the immigrants along with their perceptions of America and its sometimes-maddening language. Here, he becomes a spokesperson for those immigrants who, while living and participating in the creation of the culture we call American, still inhabit its linguistic and cultural margins. Almost twenty years later, the voices of those who speak languages other than English remain less likely to be heard.

I began this book with my childhood impressions of the languages of my family life that were illuminated for me on that initial visit to Italy. From silent child-observer witnessing the permutations of language that I experienced from the inside of the immigrant world, but at its periphery, I have returned to the subject as a historian seeking to place my family's small story within a bigger frame. Indeed, the story of their lives and their languages is embedded within the larger history of the United States as an immigrant nation. Much more remains to be said and written, in many languages.

Notes

Introduction

Epigraph: Leonard Covello, "Language Usage in Italian Families," Covello Papers, box 20, folder 30: 4, Balch Institute Collections, Historical Society of Pennsylvania.

1. Eva Hoffman, *Lost in Translation: A Life in a New Language* (New York: E. P. Dutton, 1989), 106.

2. Quoted in Italian in Paolo A. Giordano, "Emigrants, Expatriates, and Exiles: Italian Writing in the United States," in *Beyond the Margins: Further Writings in Italian Americana*, ed. Anthony J. Tamburri (Madison, N.J.: Fairleigh Dickinson University Press, 1997), 231. The translation is mine.

3. Richard Rodriguez, *Hunger of Memory: The Education of Richard Rodriguez* (Boston: David R. Godine, 1981), 13.

4. Hoffman, *Lost in Translation*, 121.

5. See, for example, Jim Rutenberg, "Bush Enters Anthem Fight on Language," *New York Times*, April 29, 2006, late edition; "Major Immigration Surgery," editorial, *New York Times*, May 20, 2005; "Press One for English," editorial, New York Times, May 20, 2006.

6. Rosean Duenas González with Ildiko Melis, eds., *Language Ideologies: Critical Perspectives on the Official English Movement*, vol. 1 (Mahwah, N.J.: Lawrence Erlbaum Associates Inc.; Urbana, Ill.: National Council of Teachers of English, 2001), xxx–xxxii.

7. On how language and accents reinforce difference in the United States, see Rosina Lippi-Green, *English with an Accent: Language, Ideology, and Discrimination in the United States* (London: Routledge, 1997).

8. For an example of the position that Spanish speakers pose a threat to the country, see Samuel P. Huntington, *Who Are We? The Challenges to America's National Identity* (New York: Simon & Schuster, 2004).

9. Robert McCrum, William Cran, and Robert MacNeil, *The Story of English* (New York: Elisabeth Sifton Books—Viking, 1986), 239–42; Shirley Brice Heath, "English in Our Language Heritage," in *Language in the USA*, ed. Charles A. Ferguson and Shirley Brice Heath (Cambridge: Cambridge University Press, 1981), 6; Jill Lepore, *A is for American: Letters and Other Characters in the Newly United States* (New York: Alfred A. Knopf, 2002), 5–6: Marc Shell, "Babel in America; or, The Politics of Language Diversity in the United States," *Critical Inquiry* 20 (Autumn 1993): 108; Dennis Baron, "Federal English," in *Language Loyalties: A Source Book on the Official English Controversy*, ed. James Crawford (Chicago: University of Chicago

Press, 1992), 37–38. See also in *Language Loyalties:* Shirley Brice Heath, "Why No Official Tongue?" 26–28; John Adams, "Proposal for an American Language Academy," 31–32; Noah Webster, "Declaration of Linguistic Independence," 33–35. For more detailed accounts of the intersection of language and politics in early America, see Julie Tetel Andresen, *Linguistics in America 1769–1924: A Critical History* (London: Routledge, 1990), chap. 1; David Simpson, *The Politics of American English, 1776–1850* (New York: Oxford University Press, 1986); Michael P. Kramer, *Imagining Language in America: From the Revolution to the Civil War* (Princeton, N.J.: Princeton University Press, 1992).

10. Lepore, *A is for American*, 28; J. L. Dillard, *Toward a Social History of American English* (New York: Mouton, 1985), 96; Shell, "Babel in America," 105.

11. Orm Overland, ed., *Not English Only: Redefining 'American' in American Studies* (Amsterdam: Vu University Press, 2001); Werner Sollors, ed., *Multilingual America: Transnationalism, Ethnicity, and the Languages of American Literature* (New York: New York University Press, 1998). Sollors comments specifically on the absence of attention to language in the rhetoric of multiculturalists on p. 4. See also Werner Sollors and Marc Shell, eds., *The Multilingual Anthology of American Literature: A Reader of Original Texts with English Translations* (New York: New York University Press, 2000) and Marc Shell, ed., *American Babel: Literatures of the United States from Abnaki to Zuni* (Cambridge, Mass.: Harvard University Press, 2002).

12. Although there are studies of immigrants and language that go beyond the traditional treatment of the subject, they are written mainly by scholars working in other areas of history or from different disciplines. David A. Gerber is an immigration historian who has explored language more broadly particularly in his most recent work on immigrant correspondence, which argues for the use of letters to access immigrant consciousness through an analysis of transformations in language usage. David A. Gerber, *Authors of Their Own Lives: The Personal Correspondence of British Immigrants to North America in the Nineteenth Century* (New York: New York University Press, 2006); Gerber, "'You See I Speak Very Well Englisch': Literacy and the Transformed Self as Reflected in Immigrant Personal Correspondence," *Journal of American Ethnic History* 12, no. 2 (Winter 1993): 56–62; Gerber, "The Immigrant Letter Between Positivism and Populism: The Uses of Immigrant Personal Correspondence," *Journal of American Ethnic History* 16 (Summer 1997): 3–32; Gerber, "Acts of Deceiving and Withholding in Immigrant Letters: Personal Identity and Self-Presentation in Personal Correspondence," *Journal of Social History* 39, no. 2 (Winter 2005); "Epistolary Ethics: Personal Correspondence and the Culture of Emigration in the Nineteenth Century," *Journal of American Ethnic History* 19 (Summer 2000): 3–23.

13. On the cultural/linguistic turn in the study of history, see, for example, Lynn Hunt, ed., *The New Cultural History* (Berkeley: University of California Press, 1989); Victoria E. Bonnell and Lynn Hunt, eds., *Beyond the Cultural Turn: New Directions in the Study of Society and Culture* (Berkeley: University of California Press, 1999); William H. Sewell Jr., "Whatever Happened to the 'Social' in Social History?" in *Schools of Thought: Twenty-Five Years of Interpretive Social Science*, eds. Joan W. Scott and Debra Keates (Princeton, N.J.: Princeton University Press, 2001), 209–26. On

the need for more historical inquiry into language, see the introduction to Peter Burke and Roy Porter, eds., *The Social History of Language* (Cambridge: Cambridge University Press, 1987), 1–17; Roy Porter, "Introduction," in *Language, Self, and Society*, ed. Peter Burke and Roy Porter (Cambridge, UK: Polity Press, 1991), 1–20. On the need to better theorize the study of language and history, see Tony Crowley, *Language in History: Theories and Texts*, The Politics of Language Series, (London: Routledge, 1996), 1–3.

14. A number of collections by sociolinguists take language and ethnic identity as their focus: William B. Gudykunst, ed., *Language and Ethnic Identity* (Clevedon, UK: Multilingual Matters Ltd, 1988); James R. Dow, ed., *Language and Ethnicity* (Amsterdam: John Benjamin Publishing Co., 1991); Winston A. Van Horne and Thomas V. Tonneson, eds., *Ethnicity and Language* (Madison: University of Wisconsin System Institute on Race and Ethnicity, 1987). Much of Joshua A. Fishman's work deals with this subject. For a complete bibliography, see Ofelia García, Rakhmiel Peltz, and Harold Schiffman, with Gella Schweid Fishman, *Language Loyalty, Continuity and Change: Joshua A. Fishman's Contributions to International Sociolinguistics* (Clevedon, UK: Multilingual Matters, 2007). For a summary of the different disciplinary perspectives on language and ethnicity, see Joshua A. Fishman, ed., *The Handbook of Language and Ethnicity* (Oxford: Oxford University Press, 1999).

15. The number of recent collections of letters by immigrants is indicative of the interest in subjectivity, but they do not involve an examination of language in immigrant life per se. In his review of one such collection (Walter D. Kamphoefner, Wolfgang Helbich, and Ulrike Sommer, eds., *News from the Land of Freedom: German Immigrants Write Home*, trans. Susan Carter Vogel [Ithaca, N.Y.: Cornell University Press, 1991]), Gerber considers how letters can be analyzed rather than used merely for anecdotal evidence or "color." See Gerber, "'You See I Speak Very Well Englisch." See also his "The Immigrant Letter Between Positivism and Populism." Lacan is closely associated with language and subjectivity. For a succinct explanation of his position, see Madan Sarup, *An Introductory Guide to Post-Structuralism and Postmodernism* (1988; repr., Athens: University of Georgia Press, 1993), 10–12. See also Lev Vygotsky, *Thought and Language*, trans. and ed. Alex Kozulin, rev. ed. (1934; repr., Cambridge, Mass.: MIT Press, 1992); Benjamin L. Whorf, *Language, Thought and Reality: Selected Writings*, ed. John B. Carroll (Cambridge, Mass.: Technology Press of Massachusetts Institute of Technology, 1956); John Arthur Lucy, *Language Diversity and Thought* (Cambridge: University of Cambridge Press, 1992).

16. Nancy C. Carnevale, "Lingua/Lenga'/Language: The 'Language Question' in the Life and Work of an Italian American Woman," *Frontiers: A Journal of Women's Studies* 27, no. 2 (2006): 3–33. There is a growing recognition within the field of Italian American studies of the critical importance of language to understanding Italian immigrant/ethnic life and cultural production. See, for example, Edvige Giunta, *Writing with an Accent: Contemporary Italian American Women Authors* (New York: Palgrave, 2002); Maria Laurino, *Were You Always Italian? Ancestors and Other Icons of Italian America* (New York: W. W. Norton, 2001), 100–120; Robert Viscusi, *Buried Caesars and Other Secrets of Italian American Writing* (Albany: State University

188 • NOTES TO PAGES 6-8

of New York, 2006); Pellegrino D'Acierno, "Introduction," in *The Italian American Heritage: A Companion to Literature and Arts*, ed. George Leonard, Garland Reference Library of the Humanities (New York: Garland Publishing, Inc., 1999), xlvii–lii; Gloria Nardini, *Che Bella Figura: The Power of Performance in an Italian Ladies' Club in Chicago* (Albany: State University of New York Press, 1999); Nardini, "Italian Patterns in the American Collandia Ladies' Club: How Do Women Make Bella Figura," in *Ethnolinguistic Chicago: Language and Literacy in the City's Neighborhoods* (Mahwah, N.J.: Lawrence Erlbaum Associates, 2004), 251–74; Dominic Candeloro, Fred L. Gardaphé, and Paolo A. Giordano, eds., *Italian Ethnics: Their Languages, Literature and Lives: Proceedings of the 20th Annual Conference of the American Italian Historical Association* (Staten Island, N.Y.: The Association, 1990). The linguist Robert Di Pietro began calling attention to the role of language in Italian American life and the need for more studies in the 1970s. See, for example, "Language as a Marker of Italian Ethnicity," *Studi Emigrazione* 42 (1976): 202–17.

17. As an example of a history of colonial America that focuses on immigration, see David Hackett Fisher, *Albion's Seed: Four British Folkways in America* (New York: Oxford University Press, 1991). For examples of cultural histories of U.S. immigration, see Matthew Frye Jacobson, *Special Sorrows: The Diasporic Imagination of Irish, Polish, and Jewish Immigrants in the United States* (Berkeley: University of California Press, 2002); Robert A. Orsi, *The Madonna of 115th Street: Faith and Community in Italian Harlem, 1880–1950* (New Haven, Conn.: Yale University Press, 1985).

18. Rudolf J. Vecoli, "Comment: We Study the Present to Understand the Past," *Journal of American Ethnic History* 18, no. 4 (Summer 1999): 115–25, 122. On the need for immigration scholars to pay more attention to language, see also Donna Gabaccia, *From the Other Side: Women, Gender and Immigrant Life in the U.S., 1820–1990* (Bloomington: Indiana University Press, 1994), 182.

19. For a sociolinguistic study of the Italian language(s) in America, see Lawrence Biondi, *The Italian American Child: His Sociolinguistic Acculturation* (Washington, D.C.: Georgetown University School of Language, 1975). Hermann W. Haller has written extensively on this subject. I cite his work throughout.

20. S. Gal, "Language and Political Economy," *Annual Review of Anthropology* 18 (1989): 345–67; J. J. Gumperz, *Discourse Strategies* (Cambridge: Cambridge University Press, 1982); Richard Bauman and J. Sherzer, *Explorations in the Ethnography of Speaking* (Cambridge: Cambridge University Press, 1974); Dell Hymes, *Foundations in Sociolinguistics: An Ethnographic Approach* (Philadelphia: University of Pennsylvania Press, 1974). Gal notes the connection between work in the ethnography of speaking with Foucault's notions of how power is consolidated and wielded through control of language (352).

21. Pierre Bourdieu, *Outline of a Theory of Practice*, trans. Richard Nice (Cambridge: Cambridge University Press, 1977); Bourdieu, *Language and Symbolic Power*, ed. John B. Thompson, trans. Gino Raymond and Matthew Adamson (Cambridge, Mass.: Harvard University Press, 1991). See also Norman Fairclough, *Language and Power* (London: Longman Group UK Limited, 1989); Lippi-Green, *English with an Accent*, 64–72.

22. Alejandro Portes and Rubén G. Rumbaut, *Immigrant America: A Portrait* (Berkeley: University of California Press, 1990), 183. On the rapidity of language loss in the United States in particular, see Stanley Lieberson, Guy Dalto, Mary Ellen Johnson, "The Course of Mother-Tongue Diversity in Nations," *American Journal of Sociology* 84, no. 1 (July 1975): 34–61.

23. Ana Celia Zentella, *Growing Up Bilingual: Puerto Rican Children in New York* (Cambridge, Mass.: Blackwell, 1997), 13.

24. On language ideologies, see Bambi B. Schieffelin, Kathryn A. Woolard, and Paul V. Kroskrity, *Language Ideologies: Practice and Theory* (New York: Oxford University Press, 1998); Paul V. Kroskrity, ed., *Regimes of Language: Ideologies, Polities, and Identities* (Santa Fe, N.Mex.: School of American Research Press; Oxford, UK: J. Currey, 2000); Kathryn A. Woolard and Bambi B. Schieffelin, "Language Ideology," *Annual Review of Anthropology* 23 (1994): 55–82. S. Gal's often cited study of an Austrian village in which German, the prized language, comes to overtake a devalued Hungarian, illustrates the way languages can acquire different valuations by their speakers and how this influences language usage. S. Gal, *Language Shift: Social Determinants of Linguistic Change in Bilingual Austria* (New York: Academic Press, 1979). Some of Bakhtin's insights on language are relevant here: the concept of heteroglossia that calls attention to language in society as multivocal, the power differentials inherent in and derived from language use and hence its ideological functioning, and the contextual or dialogic nature of language learning. See Mikhail Bakhtin, "Discourse in the Novel," in *The Dialogic Imagination: Four Essays*, ed. Michael Holquist, trans. Caryl Emerson and Michael Holquist (Austin: University of Texas Press, 1982). For a recent anthropological study of Spanish language speakers that uses the concept of language ideologies and Bakhtin's ideas on language, see Norma Gonzalez, *I Am My Language: Discourses of Women and Children in the Borderlands* (Tucson: University of Arizona Press, 2001).

25. For an overview of performance and language, see Richard Bauman and Charles L. Briggs, "Poetics and Performance as Critical Perspectives on Language and Social Life," *Annual Review in Anthropology* 19 (1990): 59–88. Oral historians have drawn attention to the performative aspect of the interview, yet language per se is rarely highlighted in this literature. For an exception, see Antonio T. Diaz Royo, "Maneuvers and Transformations in Ethnobiographies of Puerto Rican Migrants," *International Journal of Oral History*, 4, no. 1 (February 1983): 19–28. For just a few examples from the interdisciplinary work on language and gender, see Susan Gal, "Between Speech and Silence: The Problematics of Research on Language and Gender," in *Gender at the Crossroads of Knowledge: Feminist Anthropology in the Postmodern Era*, ed. Micaela di Leonardo (Berkeley: University of California Press, 1991), 175–203; Judith Butler, *Gender Trouble: Feminism and the Subversion of Identity* (New York: Routledge, 1990); Joan W. Scott, "On Language, Gender, and Working-Class History," in *Gender and the Politics of History* (New York: Columbia University Press, 1988), 53–67.

26. Joshua Fishman, *Language and Ethnicity in Minority Sociolinguistic Perspective* (Clevedon, UK: Multilingual Matters, Ltd., 1989), 7; Fishman, *Language Loyalty*

in the United States (The Hague, Netherlands: Mouton, 1966); Einar Haugen, *The Norwegian Language in America: A Study in Bilingual Behavior*, 2nd ed. (1953; repr., Bloomington: Indiana University Press, 1969). On the relativism of language in ethnicity, see for example, Harold Haartman, *Language in Ethnicity: A View of Basic Ecological Relations* (Berlin: Mouton de Gruyter, 1986). For a general treatment of bilingualism, see Ellen Bialystok and Kenji Hakuta, *In Other Words: The Science and Psychology of Second-Language Acquisition* (New York: Basic Books, 1994).

27. Fishman, ed., *Handbook of Language and Ethnicity*, 160.

28. John Edwards, *Language, Society and Identity* (Oxford, UK: Basil Blackwell Ltd., 1985). For an overview of the interdisciplinary literature on the relationship between language and identity, see John E. Joseph, *Language and Identity: Ethnic, National, Religious* (New York: Palgrave MacMillan, 2004).

29. See the introduction by Otto Kernberg in Jacqueline Amati-Mehler, Simona Argentieri, and Jorge Canestri: *The Babel of the Unconscious: Mother Tongue and Foreign Languages in the Psychoanalytic Dimension*, trans. Jill Whitelaw-Cucco (Madison, Conn.: International Universities Press, Inc., 1993).

30. Amati-Mehler, et al., *Babel of the Unconscious*, vii. For a review of classic psychoanalytic and linguistic theories of language and how they may be applied to immigrants, see Leon Grinberg and Rebecca Grinberg, *Psychoanalytic Perspectives on Migration and Exile* (New Haven, Conn.: Yale University Press, 1989), chap. 11.

31. The classic interpretation of assimilation remains Milton Gordon's *Assimilation in American Life: The Role of Race, Religion, and National Origins* (New York: Oxford University Press, 1964). The literature on assimilation is voluminous. For reviews of the evolution of theories of assimilation, see Russell A. Kazal, "Revisiting Assimilation: The Rise, Fall, and Reappraisal of a Concept in American Ethnic History," *American Historical Review* (April 1995): 437–71; Michael R. Olneck, "Assimilation and American National Identity," in *A Companion to American Immigration*, ed. Reed Ueda, Blackwell Companions to American History Series (Oxford, UK: Blackwell Publishing, 2006), 202–24. I use Kazal's definition of assimilation, which he takes from Harold J. Abramson. Per Kazal, *assimilation* refers "to processes that result in greater homogeneity within a society" (438). Americanization is a form of assimilation through which immigrants and their children come to self-identify as American (440). For a recent reinterpretation of the assimilation model, see Richard Alba and Victor Nee, *Remaking the American Mainstream: Assimilation and Contemporary Immigration* (Cambridge, Mass.: Harvard University Press, 2003).

32. I am referring here to the largely sociological literature that emphasizes the lessening of ethnicity with each generation. Richard D. Alba, *Italian Americans: Into the Twilight of Ethnicity* (Englewood Cliffs, N.J.: Prentice-Hall, 1985); Alba, *Ethnic Identity: The Transformation of White America* (New Haven, Conn.: Yale University Press, 1990); Herbert J. Gans, "Symbolic Ethnicity: The Future of Ethnic Groups and Cultures in America," *On the Making of Americans: Essays in Honor of David Riesman*, ed. Herbert J. Gans and David Riesman (Philadelphia: University of Pennsylvania Press, 1979): 193–220; James Crispino, *The Assimila-*

tion of an Ethnic Group: The Italian Case (Staten Island, N.Y.: Center for Migration Studies, 1980). For the theory of the resurgence of the third generation, see Marcus Lee Hansen, "The Third Generation in America," *Commentary* 14 (1952): 492–500. For sociolinguistic perspectives, see Fishman, *Language and Ethnicity*; Calvin Veltman, *Language Shift in the United States* (Berlin: Mouton Publishers, 1983).

33. Alejandro Portes and Rubén G. Rumbaut, *Legacies: The Story of the Second Generation* (Berkeley: University of California Press, 2001), chap. 6.

34. Rubén G. Rumbaut, "Assimilation and Its Discontents: Ironies and Paradoxes," *The Handbook of International Migration: The American Experience*, eds. Charles Hirschman, Philip Kasinitz, and Josh DeWind (New York: Russell Sage Foundation, 1999), 183–85, 190–91; Alejandro Portes and Rubén G. Rumbaut, *Immigrant America: A Portrait*, 2nd ed. (Berkeley: University of California Press, 1996), chap. 6.

35. Benjamin H. Bailey, *Language, Race, and Negotiation of Identity: A Study of Dominican Americans* (New York: LFB Scholarly Publishing LLC, 2002).

36. Sociological studies of language loss and language maintenance generally do not take into account the common phenomenon of mixed languages or dialect use. On the interethnic linguistic environment, Italians in Ybor City, Florida, for example, spoke a mix of Italian, Sicilian, English, and Spanish. Gary R. Mormino and George E. Pozzetta, *The Immigrant World of Ybor City: Italians and Their Latin Neighbors in Tampa, 1885–1985* (Urbana, Ill.: University of Illinois Press, 1987), 6. In Arizona during the early 1900s, Italians encouraged their children to learn Spanish rather than English, due to the greater affinity they felt for Mexican culture. Phylis Cancilla Martinelli, "Examining the Relationships of Italians and Mexicans in a 'Mexican Camp' and a 'White Man's Camp': Mexicans and Euro Latins in the Arizona Copper Industry: 1900–1930," in *Italian Immigrants Go West: The Impact of Locale on Ethnicity*, eds. Janet E. Worrall, Carol Bonomo Albright, and Elvira G. DiFabio (Cambridge, Mass.: American Italian Historical Association, 2003), 58.

37. On code-switching, see for example, S. Gal, *Language Shift*, 9–10, 21; Gumperz, *Discourse Strategies*. On hybridity and "linguistic multivocality" in a post-colonial context, see Homi Bhabha, *The Location of Culture* (London: Routledge, 1994).

38. For recent scholarship highlighting Italian transnationalism, see, for example, Linda Reeder, *Widows in White: Migration and the Transformation of Rural Women, Sicily: 1880–1928* (Toronto: University of Toronto Press, 2003); Donna Gabaccia and Franca Iacovetta, eds., *Women, Gender and Transnational Lives: Italian Workers of the World* (Toronto: University of Toronto Press, 2002); Carol Lynn McKibben, *Beyond Cannery Row: Sicilian Women, Immigration, and Community in Monterey, California, 1915–1999* (Urbana and Chicago: University of Illinois Press, 2006).

39. David E. López: "Social and Linguistic Aspects of Assimilation Today," *The Handbook of International Migration: The American Experience*, eds. Charles Hirschman, Philip Kasinitz, and Josh DeWind (New York: Russell Sage Founda-

tion, 1999), 214. Overall, López's findings confirm the generational pattern of language loss.

40. J. L.Dillard, *Toward a Social History of American English*, 103–4; David L. Gold, "The Speech and Writing of Jews," in *Language in the U.S.A.*, ed. Charles A. Ferguson and Shirley Brice Heath (Cambridge: Cambridge University Press, 1981), 284.

41. Benjamin Harshav, *The Meaning of Yiddish* (Berkeley: California University Press, 1990), xiii.

42. Hermann W. Haller, "Italian in New York," *The Multilingual Apple: Languages in New York City*, ed. Ofelia Garcia and Joshua Fishman, Contributions to the Sociology of Language 77 (Berlin: Mouton de Gruyter, 1997), 137.

43. Kazal's summary of the literature on assimilation considers changing understandings of ethnic identity, "Revisiting Assimilation."

44. See, for example, James R. Barrett and David R. Roediger, "Inbetween Peoples: Race, Nationality and the 'New Immigrant' Working Class," *Journal of American Ethnic History* 16, no. 3 (Spring 1997), 3–44; David R. Roediger, *Working Towards Whiteness: How America's Immigrants Became White: The Strange Journey from Ellis Island to the Suburbs* (New York: Basic Books, 2005); Matthew Frye Jacobson, *Whiteness of a Different Color: European Immigrants and the Alchemy of Race* (Cambridge, Mass.: Harvard University Press, 1998); Gary Gerstle, *American Crucible: Race and Nation in the Twentieth Century* (Princeton, N.J.: Princeton University Press, 2001).

45. Katharine W. Jones, *Accent on Privilege: English Identities and Anglophilia in the U.S.* (Philadelphia: Temple University Press, 2001); Lippi-Green, *English with an Accent*. On language more generally as constitutive of racial identities, see Etienne Balibar, "The Nation Form: History and Ideology," in Etienne Balibar, Immanuel Maurice Wallerstein, and Chris Turner, *Race, Nation, Class: Ambiguous Identities* (New York: Verso, 1991), 86–106.

46. For examples of works treating Italian emigration as a diaspora, see Pasquale Verdicchio, *Bound by Distance: Rethinking Nationalism through the Italian Diaspora* (Madison, N.J.: Fairleigh Dickinson University Press, 1997); Donna Gabaccia, *Italy's Many Diasporas* (Seattle: University of Washington Press, 2000). For a comparison between Italians in Argentina and Italians in New York, see Samuel L. Baily, *Immigrants in the Lands of Promise: Italians in Buenos Aires and New York City, 1870-1914* (Ithaca, N.Y.: Cornell University Press, 1999).

47. Deborah Cameron, *Feminism and Linguistic Theory*, 2nd ed. (1985; repr., New York: St. Martin's Press, 1992); William Labov, *Sociolinguistic Patterns* (Philadelphia: University of Pennsylvania Press, 1972): 243–44, 301–4; R. T. Lakoff, *Language and Women's Place* (New York: Harper and Row, 1975).

48. Yole Correa-Zoli, "The Language of Italian Americans," in Ferguson and Heath, eds, *Language in the U.S.A.* 239–56; Francis Grosjean, *Life with Two Languages: An Introduction to Bilingualism* (Cambridge, Mass.: Harvard University Press, 1982), 55.

49. For example, a 1911 government report notes that the percentages of southern Italians in New York City's garment industry who claimed an ability to speak

English was lower than males of other immigrant groups in every age category. Even males who arrived in the United States prior to age 14 scored lower than immigrants from other groups who arrived at a comparably young age. As was also the case with literacy levels, southern Italian women had even lower rates of English fluency than men did. U.S. House of Representatives, "Immigrants in Industries," *Reports of the Immigration Commission*, 61st Congress, 2d sess., 1910, Vol. 11, pt. 6 (Washington, D.C.: Government Printing Office, 1911), 400–403. This lag in learning English persisted. The United States Census of 1930 and 1940 ranks Italians last in English language fluency. Leonard Covello, *The Social Background of the Italo-American School Child* (Totowa, N.J.: Rowman and Littlefield, 1972), 279n2.

50. Although his research supports the generational model of assimilation, Alba notes that the Italian respondents in his study were more likely than others of European ancestry to maintain the mother tongue. In addition, "knowledge of mother-tongue words and phrases among those who can no longer speak the language . . . is markedly greater among the Italians than among other groups." Alba, *Ethnic Identity*, 118. On the latter phenomenon, see also Richard Gambino, *Blood of My Blood: The Dilemma of Italian-Americans* (1974; repr., New York: Guernica Editions, 2003).

51. Donna Gabaccia notes the conundrum of immigration historians who can only insert their subjects into the narrative of American history by subjugating them. Donna Gabaccia, "Liberty, Coercion, and the Making of Immigration Historians," *Journal of American History* 84, no. 2 (September 1997): 570–75.

Chapter One: The Italian Languages in Italy and America

Epigraph: Quoted in Jonathan Steinberg, "The Historian and the *Questione Della Lingua*," in *The Social History of Language*, ed. Peter Burke and Roy Porter (Cambridge: Cambridge University Press, 1987), 199. The phrase is an adaptation of the maxim cited by the Yiddish linguist Max Weinreich in "Der yivo un di problemen fun undzer tsayt," *Yivo-bleter* 25, no. 1 (1945): 13. Linguists agree that there is no real difference between a dialect and a language other than the status that languages are accorded as a result of the political, cultural, and/or economic position of the nation or area that uses it and the concomitant popular acceptance of the "correct" language. See, for example, Martin Maiden, *A Linguistic History of Italian* (London: Longman Group Limited, 1995), 3–4.

1. Tullio De Mauro, "Linguistic Variety and Linguistic Minorities," in *Italian Cultural Studies: An Introduction*, ed. David Forgacs and Robert Lumley (New York: Oxford University Press, 1996), 97; De Mauro, *Storia linguistica dell'Italia unita*, vol. 1 (Rome-Bari: Editori Laterza, 1976), 17–18; De Mauro and Mario Lodi, *Lingua e dialetti* (Rome: Editori Riuniti, 1993), 21–22. De Mauro's *Storia linguistica* remains the major source for the social history of the Italian language and so I rely heavily on it here as do a number of the other authors I cite.

2. De Mauro, *Storia linguistica*, 16–19; Francesco Bruni, *L'italiano: Elementi di Storia della lingua e della cultura* (Torino: UTET, 1984), 5; Antonio Gramsci, *Gli intellectuali e l'organizzazione della cultura*, vol. 2, *Quaderni del Carcere* (1949; repr.,

Turin: Einaudi, 1966), 22; De Mauro, "Linguistic Variety," 95, 97; Maiden, *Linguistic History of Italian*, 6. Bruni notes that it is not possible to speak of dialects in Italy until the establishment of a standard language variety because the dialects exist only in relation to the standard form. Bruni, *L'italiano: Elementi di Storia*, 24.

3. De Mauro, *Lingua e dialetti*, 26–27; Maiden, *Linguistic History of Italian*, 7; Bruni, *L'italiano: Elementi di Storia*, 60. For a more detailed discussion of the rise and consolidation of Florentine as the language of Italy during the Renaissance, see Bruni, *L'italiano: Elementi di Storia*, 43–80.

4. Howard Moss, "Language and Italian National Identity," in *The Politics of Italian National Identity: A Multidisciplinary Perspective*, ed. Gino Bedani and Bruce Haddock (Cardiff, UK: University of Wales Press, 2000), 99–100; Maiden, *Linguistic History of Italian*, 8; Bruno Migliorini, *The Italian Language*, abridged and recast by T. Gwynfor Griffith (London: Faber & Faber, 1966), 407; Francesco Bruni, ed., *L'Italiano nelle regioni: Lingua nazionale e identita regionali* (Torino: UTET, 1992), xxxi–xxxii.

5. Gino Bedani, "Introduction," in Bedani and Haddock, eds, *Politics of Italian National Identity*, 4–5.

6. De Mauro, *Storia linguistica*, 46; Moss, "Language and Italian National Identity," 101–3. The quote is from Hermann W. Haller, *The Other Italy: The Literary Canon in Dialect* (Toronto: University of Toronto Press, 1999), 13.

7. De Mauro, *Storia linguistica*, 89. Bruni argues that Manzoni also appreciated the value of the dialects and did not want to do away with them. See Bruni, *L'italiano: Elementi di Storia*, 41. For further discussion of the Manzoni-Ascoli debate, see De Mauro, *Storia linguistica*, 46–50; Bruni, *L'italiano: Elementi di Storia*, 140–46; Migliorni, *The Italian Language*, 415–17; Maiden, *Linguistic History of Italian*, 9.

8. Moss, "Language and Italian National Identity," 109. Moss notes that the tolerance for the dialects evinced in the 1948 constitution was based on the implicit assumption that the dialects would eventually give way to standard Italian.

9. Maiden, *Linguistic History of Italian*, 8; Moss, "Language and Italian National Identity," 100; Migliorini, *The Italian Language*, 407. Other European nations had similar issues with language. For example, as late as the mid-nineteenth century, fully half of the population of France did not understand French. What distinguishes Italy is the greater degree of the problem. Peter Ives, *Language and Hegemony in Gramsci* (London: Pluto Press, 2004), 37.

10. De Mauro, *Storia linguistica*, 51–53, 63, 77–78, 105–9, 117–24; De Mauro and Lodi, *Lingua e dialetti*, 32; Bruni, *L'Italiano: Elementi di storia*, 146–61; Migliorini, *The Italian Language*, 455–56; Maiden, *Linguistic History of Italian*, 9–10.

11. De Mauro, *Storia linguistica*, 56, 60–63; Rudolph J. Vecoli, "The Italian Immigrant Press and the Construction of Social Reality, 1850–1920," in *Print Culture in a Diverse America*, ed. James P. Danky and Wayne A. Wiegand (Urbana: University of Illinois Press, 1998), 17–18. On female literacy in Sicily, see Linda Reeder, "Women in the Classroom: Mass Migration, Literacy and the Nationalization of Sicilian Women at the Turn of the Century," *Journal of Social History* 32, no. 1 (Fall 1998): 101–24.

12. De Mauro and Lodi, *Lingua e dialetti*, 8.

13. Moss, "Language and Italian National Identity," 100.

14. De Mauro, *Storia linguistica*, 102. For more on the role of the schools in the diffusion of standard Italian, see Francesco Bruni, *L'italiano: Elementi di storia*, 146–53.

15. Giulio Lepschy, *Mother Tongues and Other Reflections on the Italian Language* (Toronto: University of Toronto Press, 2002), 20, 44.

16. Moss, "Language and Italian National Identity," 104–7; Gabriella Klein, *La Politica linguistica del Fascismo* (Bologna, Italy: Societa Editrice Il Mulino, 1986). The linguist Haller also notes the "dialettophobia" of the Fascist years. See Hermann W. Haller, *Una lingua perduta e Ritrovata: L'Italiano degli italo-americani* (Firenze: La Nuova Italia, 1993), 23–24. Alessandra Stanley, "Italy is Speechless: Movies Lose their Voices," *New York Times*, September 16, 1998.

17. Ives, *Language and Hegemony*, 83–100.

18. On the positive reappraisal of the dialects by the Italian Left, see De Mauro and Lodi, *Lingua e dialetti*, 7; Moss, "Language and the Italian National Identity," 116. On Italian hip hop, see, for example, Tony Mitchell, "Questions of style: Notes on Italian Hip Hop," *Popular Music* 14, no. 3 (1995): 333–48; Pierfrancesco Pacoda, *Potere alla parola: Antologia del rapitaliano* (Milano: Giangiacomo Feltrinelli Editore, 1996).

19. Benedict Anderson, *Imagined Communities: Reflections on the Origin and Spread of Nationalism*, rev. ed. (London: Verso, 1991), chap. 5; Hugh Seton-Watson, *Nations and States: An Enquiry into the Origins of Nations and the Politics of Nationalism* (Boulder, Colo.: Westview Press, 1977).

20. Stephen G. Alter, *Darwinism and the Linguistic Image: Language, Race, and Natural Theology in the Nineteenth Century* (Baltimore: Johns Hopkins University Press, 1999), 2–3; Edward G. Gray, *New World Babel: Languages and Nations in Early America* (Princeton, N.J.: Princeton University Press, 1999), 4–5. Maurice Olendar, *The Languages of Paradise: Race, Religion, and Philology in the Nineteenth Century*, trans. Arthur Goldhammer (Cambridge, Mass.: Harvard University Press, 1992).

21. Jane Schneider, ed., "Introduction," in *Italy's "Southern Question": Orientalism in One Country* (Oxford: Berg, 1998), 4–6. The quote is taken from Nelson Moe, *The View from Vesuvius: Italian Culture and the Southern Question* (Berkeley: University of California Press, 2002), 2, 37.

22. Mary Gibson, "Biology or Environment? Race and Southern 'Deviancy' in the Writings of Italian Criminologists, 1880–1920," in Schneider, ed., *Italy's "Southern Question,"* 99–116. See also Gibson's monograph, *Born to Crime: Cesare Lombroso and the Origins of Biological Criminology* (Westport, Conn.: Praeger, 2002), chap. 5; Verdicchio, *Bound by Distance*, 21–29; Peter D'Agostino, "Craniums, Criminals, and the 'Cursed Race': Italian Anthropology in American Racial Thought, 1861–1924," *Comparative Studies in Society and History* 44, no. 2 (April 2002): 323; Cesare Lombroso, *In Calabria (1862–1897)* (Catania, Italy: Giannotta editore, 1898).

23. Enrico Ferri, *The Positive School of Criminology*, trans. Ernest Untermann (Chicago: Charles H. Kerr & Company, 1908), 64–68.

24. The quotations are Niceforo's as they appear in Leonard Covello, *The Social Background of the Italo-American School Child* (Totowa, N.J.: Rowman and Littlefield, 1972), 25. Alfredo Niceforo, *L'Italia barbara contemporanea* (Milan-Palermo: Remo Sandron, 1898).

25. Gibson, "Biology or Environment,'" 114. Niceforo, for example, is cited in the entry on Italians in volume 5 of the influential 1911 report on immigration that influenced the restriction legislation of the 1920s. U.S. House of Representatives, "A Dictionary of Races or Peoples," *Reports of the Immigration Commission*, 61st Cong., 3rd sess., 1910 (Washington, D.C.: Government Printing Office, 1911), 82. On the challenges to Italian anthropological thought and its influence on American racialist thought, see D'Agostino, "Craniums, Criminals, and the 'Cursed Race.'"

26. In her introduction to *Italy's "Southern Question,"* Schneider notes two influential works that participate in the traditional North-South discourse: Edward Banfield, *The Moral Basis of a Backward Society* (New York: Free Press, 1958); Robert D. Putnam, *Making Democracy Work: Civic Traditions in Modern Italy* (Princeton, N.J.: Princeton University Press, 1993). See also Jonathan Morris, "Challenging *Meridionalismo*: Constructing a New History for Southern Italy," in *The New History of the Italian South*, ed. Robert Lumley and Jonathan Morris (Devon, UK: University of Exeter Press, 1997), 9–11. For more on the way stereotypes of the South insert themselves into modern scholarship as well as popular understanding of the South today, see in the same collection, Gabriella Gribaudi, "Images of the South: The *Mezziogiorno* as seen by Insiders and Outsiders," 106–10.

27. John Dickie, *Darkest Italy: The Nation and Stereotypes of the Mezzogiorno, 1860–1900* (New York: St. Martin's Press, 1999), 1, 13, 146–47.

28. Moe, *The View from Vesuvius*, 38.

29. Morris, "Challenging *Meridionalismo*," 5–7; Schneider, "Introduction," 1–23; John A. Davis, "Casting Off the 'Southern Problem': Or the Peculiarities of the South Reconsidered," in *Italy's "Southern Question,"* 205–12; Edward Said, *Orientalism* (1978; repr., New York: Vintage Books, 1979).

30. Pasquale Verdicchio, *Bound by Distance: Rethinking Nationalism Through the Italian Diaspora* (Madison, N.J.: Fairleigh Dickinson University Press, 1997), 50–51. The term is also a reference to the preponderance of illegal immigrants who work as street vendors and are generally reviled by Italians. Graziella Parati, *Mediterranean Crossroads: Migration Literature in Italy* (Madison, N.J.: Fairleigh Dickinson University Press; London: Associated University Presses, 1999), 20.

31. Verdicchio, *Bound by Distance*, 28. In *De Vulgari Eloquentia*, Dante dismisses all fourteen of the then extant dialects in Italy as suitable for a literary language. Despite the history of the devaluation of southern dialects, Sicilian achieved considerable prestige for a time. During the reign of Fredrick II in the first half of the thirteenth century, Sicilian became recognized as an important literary language. However, the defeat of the Sicilians by the Angevins in the battle at Benevento in 1266 marked the beginning of the decline of Sicily and its language. Gaetano Cipolla, "U sicilianu è na lingua o un dialettu?/Is Sicilian a Language?" *Arba Sicula* 25, nos. 1 and 2 (2004): 138–75.

32. On the role of urbanism in the history of Italian, see De Mauro, *Storia*

linguistica, 71–78, 87. For the statistic on illiteracy, see p. 100. The quote is from Haller, *Una lingua perduta*, 159. The translation is mine.

33. Maiden, *A Linguistic History of Italian*, 230.

34. Moss, "Language and Italian National Identity," 116.

35. Steinberg, "The Historian and the *Questione della lingua*," 204–5.

36. De Mauro, *Storia linguistica*, 21; Maiden, *A Linguistic History of Italian*, 234–35; Haller, *The Other Italy*, 11.

37. Francesco Bruni, ed., *L'Italiano nelle regioni: Lingua nazionale e identita regionali* (Torino: UTET, 1992). For a collection of essays in English on the Italian dialects from a linguistic perspective, see Martin Maiden and Mair Parry, eds., *The Dialects of Italy* (London: Routledge, 1997). See also Anna Laura Lepohy and Arturo Tosi, eds., *Multilingualism in Italy Past and Present* (Oxford, UK: Legenda, 2002).

38. Maiden, *A Linguistic History of Italian*, 5; De Mauro and Lodi, *Lingua e dialetti*, 14. On Manzoni, see Moss, "Language and Italian National Identity," 101–3.

39. Haller, *Una lingua perduta*, 29.

40. For the percentage of contemporary Italian dialect speakers, see De Mauro and Lodi, *Lingua e dialetti*, 6; Maiden, *A Linguistic History of Italian*, 10. On the effects of the marginalization of the South on language practices, see De Mauro and Lodi, *Lingua e dialetti*, 5–6; Migliorini, *The Italian Language*, 457; Hermann W. Haller, "Italian in New York," in *The Multilingual Apple: Languages in New York City*, eds. Ofelia Garcia and Joshua Fishman, Contributions to the Sociology of Language 77, ed. Joshua Fishman (Berlin: Mouton de Gruyter, 1997), 122.

41. See, for example, De Mauro and Lodi, *Lingua e dialetti*, 9; Haller, *Una lingua perduta*, 27.

42. Herbert Vaughn, "Italian and Its Dialects as Spoken in the United States," *American Speech* 1, no. 8 (May 1926):431.

43. Bruni, *L'Italiano: Elementi di Storia*, 137. The translation is mine. On Freud and dialect usage, see Jacqueline Amati-Mehler, Simone Argentieri, and Jorge Canestri, *The Babel of the Unconscious: Mother Tongue and Foreign Languages in the Psychoanalytic Dimension*, trans. Jill Whitelaw-Cuocco (Madison, Conn.: International Universities Press, Inc., 1993), 21.

44. Migliorini, *The Italian Language*, 457; Haller, *Una lingua perduta*, 6.

45. De Mauro and Lodi, *Lingua e dialetti*, 31.

46. De Mauro, *Storia linguistica*, 48; De Mauro and Lodi, *Lingua e dialetti*, 3.

47. See, for example, Marie J. Concistre, "Adult Education in a Local Area: A Study of a Decade in the Life and Education of the Adult Italian Immigrant in East Harlem, New York City" (PhD diss., New York University, 1943), 331.

48. De Mauro, *Storia linguistica*, 32, 45.

49. Sydel Silverman, *Three Bells of Civilization: The Life of an Italian Hill Town* (New York: Columbia University Press, 1975), 5, 37.

50. Haller, *Una lingua perduta*, 129.

51. Donna Gabaccia, *From Sicily to Elizabeth Street: Housing and Social Change among Italian Immigrants, 1880–1930* (Albany: State University of New York Press, 1984); Donald Tricarico, *The Italians of Greenwich Village: The Social Structure and Transformation of an Ethnic Community* (Staten Island, N.Y.: Center for Migration Studies, 1984), 5–7; Haller, "Italian in New York," 124. The degree to which Ital-

ian regions of origin and corresponding dialects determined the organization of Italian neighborhoods was remarked upon in a number of early studies of Italian immigrant women, particularly of homeworkers in New York City's garment industry. Amy A. Bernardy, "L'emigrazione delle donne e dei fanciulli italiani nella North Atlantic Division (Stati Uniti d'America)," *Bolletino D'Emigrazione* 1 (1909): 36; Elizabeth C. Watson, "Homework in the Tenements," *The Survey,* February 4, 1911, 775; Mabel Hurd Willett, *The Employment of Women in the Clothing Trade* (New York: Columbia University Press, 1902) 260–62.

52. Haller, "Italian in New York," 122.

53. Herbert Vaughn, "Italian Dialects in the United States II," *American Speech* 11, no. 1 (October 1926): 118. Tosi claims that trilingualism is a distinguishing feature of Italians living in English-speaking countries even though most Italians did not have mastery of standard Italian. Arturo Tosi, "Italian in English-Speaking Countries," in *Language and Society in a Changing Italy,* Multilingual Matters 117 (Clevedon, UK: Multilingual Matters Ltd, 2001), 224–25.

54. This phenomenon was not limited to Italians in the United States. Studies of the Italian languages abroad have noted similar developments in Canada, Australia, and England as well as in non-English speaking countries. See Tosi, *Language and Society in a Changing Italy* and his *L'italiano d'oltremare: la lingua delle comunità italiane nei paesi anglofoni* (Firenze: Giunti, 1991). For a study of Italians in Australia, see Camilla Bettoni, *Italian in North Queensland: Changes in the Speech of First and Second Generation Bilinguals* (Townsville: James Cooke University of North Queensland, 1981). On the Argentine case, see Michael La Sorte, *La Merica: Images of Italian Greenhorn Experience* (Philadelphia: Temple University Press, 1985), 161. Samuel L. Baily notes that Italians in Argentina made a smoother linguistic transition than those who emigrated to New York. See *Immigrants in the Lands of Promise: Italians in Buenos Aires and New York City, 1870–1914* (Ithaca, N.Y.: Cornell University Press, 1999), 75, 220–21.

55. This form of Italian immigrant speech has been referred to as "Italglish" (denoting its similarity to other hybrid immigrant languages such as Yinglish and Spanglish) and more recently as "Italo-Americanese." Haller uses "Italian-American proper" to distinguish the creole from its different variations. See Hermann W. Haller, "Between Standard Italian and Creole: An Interim Report on Language Patterns in an Italian-American Community," *Word* 32, no. 3 (December 1981): 184. "Italglish" is used by Michael La Sorte in his *La Merica.* The following discussion of the Italian American dialects relies heavily on his chapter 5, one of the few detailed treatments of the subject. For a more formal linguistic analysis of Italian American speech in 1980s New York City, see Haller, *Una lingua perduta,* chap. 1. Emelise Aleandri coined "Italo-Americanese"; see her *Italian-American Immigrant Theatre in New York City* (New York: Arcadia Tempus Publishing Group, Inc., 1999). For the 1860 date, see La Sorte, *La Merica,* 159.

56. La Sorte, *La Merica,* 163. Haller notes greater use of dialect by Italian women than men, a finding that is consistent with much though not all of the sociolinguistic literature on women and language. See Haller, *Una lingua perduta,* 29.

57. Haller, "Between Standard Italian and Creole," 183.

58. Ibid., 184.

59. On regional variations of the Italian American dialects, see H. L. Mencken,

The American Language: An Inquiry into the Development of English in the United States (New York: Alfred A. Knopf, 1936), 644. Haller notes differences in vocabulary between, for example, Sicilians, Pugliese, and Calabrese. See "Between Standard Italian and Creole," 189. On the Flatbush expression, see Arthur Livingston, "La Merica Sanemagogna," *Romanic Review* 9 (1918): 214. Livingston notes several variant meanings of this expression, including "to fail in business" and "to be done for." The exclamation "Flabussce!" could mean "Good night!" or "It's all over!"

60. La Sorte, *La Merica*, 160. For more detailed discussion and some disagreement over the linguistic fine points of the Italian immigrant idiom, see Livingston, "La Merica Sanemagogna"; Haller, "Between Standard Italian and Creole"; Alberto Menarini, "'L'Italo Americano degli Stati Uniti," *Lingua Nostra* 18 (October–December 1939):154–55; Tosi, *Language and Society in a Changing Italy*.

61. The example of a calque is taken from Haller, "Italian in New York," 128. On the use of the Italian American dialect when the Italian equivalent is well-known see La Sorte, *La Merica*, 167.

62. Anthony Turano, "The Speech of Little Italy," *American Mercury* 26 (July 1932): 357–58.

63. Example from La Sorte, *La Merica*, 165. See also Menarini, "'L'Italo Americano degli Stati Uniti," 154–55.

64. On the influence of Neapolitan, see Livingston, "La Merica Sanemagonga," 214; La Sorte, *La Merica*, 168. For non-Italian influences see La Sorte, *La Merica*, 165; Livingston, "La Merica Sanemagonga," 212.

65. La Sorte, *La Merica*, 168–69.

66. Ibid., 162.

67. La Sorte, *La Merica*, 180; Migliorini, *The Italian Language*, 448; Livingston, "La Merica Sanemagonga," 215, De Mauro, *Storia linguistica*, 56.

68. Leon Grinberg and Rebecca Grinberg, *Psychoanalytic Perspectives on Migration and Exile* (New Haven, Conn.: Yale University Press, 1989), 109–10; Nobuko Yoshizawa Meaders, "The Transcultural Self," in *Immigrant Experiences: Personal Narrative and Psychological Analysis*, ed. Paul H. Elovitz and Charlotte Kalin (London: Associated University Press, 1997), 49; Robert A. Orsi, *The Madonna of 115th Street: Family and Community in Italian Harlem, 1880–1950, 2nd ed.* (1985; repr., New Haven, Conn.: Yale University Press, 2002) 111; Orsi, "The Fault of Memory: 'Southern Italy' in the Imagination of Immigrants and the Lives of Their Children in Italian Harlem, 1920–1945," *Journal of Family History* 15, no. 1 (1990): 134.

69. I suggest possible explanations for why southern Italians learned English at lower rates than other immigrant groups at various points in the text. Obvious reasons include their lack of formal schooling in Italy that resulted in high rates of illiteracy and may have made them resistant to learning English through classes aimed at immigrants. In New York City, Italian immigrants enrolled in these classes at significantly lower rates than other immigrants did. See Bernardy, "L'emigrazione delle donne e dei fanciulli italiani," 95–96. Their high rates of repatriation meant that for the early immigrants, there was little incentive to learn English. Dino Cinel, *The National Integration of Italian Return Migration, 1870–1929* (New York: Cambridge University Press, 1991); Betty Boyd Caroli, *Italian Repatriation from the United States, 1900–1914* (New York: Center for Migration Studies,

1973). Covello notes that even once settled in America, the marked tendency of Italians to live among their own provided little motivation to learn English. Leonard Covello, *The Social Background of the Italo-American School Child* (Totowa, N.J.: Rowman and Littlefield, 1972), 279. Given that many Italian women of the immigrant generation worked at home, it is not surprising that they learned English at even slower rates. On the reasons for homework among Italian immigrant women, see Nancy C. Carnevale, "Culture of Work: Italian Immigrant Women Homeworkers in the New York City Garment Industry, 1890–1914," in *A Coat of Many Colors: Immigration, Globalization and Reform in New York City's Garment Industry*, ed. Daniel Soyer (New York: Fordham University Press, 2005), 141–68.

70. Vecoli, "Italian Immigrant Press," 19; George E. Pozzetta, "The Italian Immigrant Press of New York City: The Early Years, 1880–1915," *Journal of Ethnic Studies* 1, no. 3 (Fall 1973): 33; Robert E. Parks, *The Immigrant Press and Its Control* (New York: Harper & Brothers Publishers, 1922; St. Clair Shores, Mich.: Scholarly Press, 1970), 304. Citation is to the Scholarly Press edition.

71. Joshua Fishman, V. Nahirny, J. Hoffman, and R. Hayden, *Language Loyalty in the United States* (The Hague, Netherlands: Mouton, 1966), 52–60; Vecoli, "The Italian Immigrant Press," 19; Park, *The Immigrant Press*, 304. Circulation figures underrepresent readership because it was common for people to read to each other.

72. Livingston, "La Merica Sanemagonga," 212. For more examples and discussion, see La Sorte, *La Merica*, 175–76.

73. Livingston, "La Merica Sanemagonga," 212.

74. Pozzetta, "The Italian Immigrant Press," 35.

75. Park, *The Immigrant Press*, 12, 55.

76. Bénédicte Deschamps, "De la presse 'coloniale' á la presse italo-americaine: le parcours de six periodiques italiens aux États-Unis, 1910–1935" (Ph.D. diss., University of Paris 7, Denis Diderot, 1996), 230; Fishman et al., *Language Loyalty*, 63.

77. Vecoli, "The Italian Immigrant Press," 17–19; Carlo M. Cipolla, *Literacy and Development in the West* (Middlesex, England: Penguin Books, 1969), 95, 106. On the poor quality of much Italian American journalism, see Deschamps, "De la presse 'coloniale' á la presse italo-americaine," 405; Haller, *Una lingua perduta*, 89–101; Alberto Menarini, "L'Italo-Americano degli Stati Uniti," *Lingua Nostra* 1 (October–December, 1989): 157.

78. Sisca Papers, Immigration History Research Center, box 1, folder 3, 16 Ottobre 1934; The translation is mine.

79. Pozzetta, "The Italian Immigrant Press," 33–34.

80. For an English language introduction to Italian dialect poetry, see Haller, *The Other Italy.*

Chapter Two: Linguistic Boundaries in American History

Epigraph: Quoted in Frank M. Grittner, "Public Policies and Ethnic Influences upon Foreign Language Study in the Public Schools," in *Ethnicity and Language*, ed. Winston A. Van Horne and Thomas V. Tonnesen (Milwaukee: University of Wisconsin System Institute on Race and Ethnicity, 1987), 195.

1. Ruth Spack, *America's Second Tongue: American Indian Education and the Ownership of English, 1600–1900* (Lincoln: University of Nebraska Press, 2002).

2. Ibid., 7.

3. Nancy Faires Conklin and Margaret A. Lourie, *A Host of Tongues: Language Communities in the United States* (New York: The Free Press, 1983), 68.

4. Edward G. Gray, *New World Babel: Languages and Nations in Early America* (Princeton, N.J.: Princeton University Press, 1999), 4–5; Spack, *America's Second Tongue*, 3; Jane Kamensky, *Governing the Tongue: The Politics of Speech in Early New England* (Oxford: Oxford University Press, 1997), 48–55; Julie Tetel Andresen, *Linguistics in America 1769–1924: A Critical History* (London and New York: Routledge, 1990), 83–119. Greenblatt notes a wide range of reactions to Native languages including an association with savagery as early as the sixteenth century. See Stephen J. Greenblatt, "Learning to Curse: Aspects of Linguistic Colonialism in the Sixteenth Century," in *First Images of America: The Impact of the New World on the Old*, ed. Fred Chiappelli, Michael J. B. Allen, and Robert L. Benson (Berkeley: University of California Press, 1976). The French Jesuits, in contrast to the British colonists, sought to learn Native American languages to convert Native Americans to Catholicism. Gray, *New World Babel*, 32–35. For more on the impressions of early colonists regarding Native languages, see Edward G. Gray and Norman Fiering, eds., *The Language Encounter in the Americas, 1492–1800*, European Expansion and Global Interaction Series (New York: Berghahn Books, 2000).

5. John Reyhner, "Policies toward American Indian Languages: A Historical Sketch," in *Language Loyalties*, 43–44; Spack, *America's Second Tongue*, 3–4, 13–42.

6. Conklin and Lourie, *A Host of Tongues*, 24–26; Ronald Schmidt Sr., *Language Policy and Identity Politics in the United States* (Philadelphia: Temple University Press, 2000), 108; Shell, "Babel in America," 105.

7. On slaveholders' resistance to slaves achieving literacy, see, for example, Cornelius, *When I Read My Title Clear: Literacy, Slavery, and Religion in the Antebellum South* (Columbia: University of South Carolina Press, 1991). The quote is from Schmidt, *Language Policy*, 108.

8. Conklin and Lourie, *A Host of Tongues*, 25; J. L. Dillard, *Towards a Social History of American English* (New York: Mouton, 1985), 123; Philip D. Morgan, "British Encounters with Africans and African Americans, circa 1699–1780," in *Strangers Within the Realm: Cultural Margins of the First British Empire*, ed. Bernard Bailyn and Philip Morgan (Chapel Hill: University of North Carolina Press, 1991), 203–7.

9. Shirley Brice Heath, "English in our Language Heritage" in *Language in the USA*, ed. Charles A. Ferguson and Shirley Brice Heath (Cambridge, UK; New York; Melbourne: 1981), 11; Heath, "Why No Official Tongue?" in *Language Loyalties: A Source Book on the Official English Controversy*, ed. James Crawford (Chicago and London: University of Chicago Press, 1992), 21–23; Shell, "Babel in America," 105–6. Shell suggests that Jefferson's sympathy for French and Spanish might have been motivated by expansionist considerations. Andresen, *Linguistics in America*, 25.

10. Heath, "Why No Official Tongue?" 24, 30; John Adams, "Proposal for an American Language Academy," *Language Loyalties*, 31–33. Andresen, *Linguistics in America*, 35. For detailed discussions of why the idea of a language academy was rejected, see Heath, "A National Language Academy? Debate in the New Nation," *Linguistics. An International Review* 189 (1977): 9–43; Dennis Baron, *Grammar and*

Good Taste: Reforming the American Language (New Haven, Conn.: Yale University Press, 1982), 99–118.

11. Dennis Baron, "Federal English," *Language Loyalties*, 37; Baron, *Grammar and Good Taste*, 26; Simpson, *The Politics of American English*, 36; Andresen, *Linguistics in America*, 35.

12. Shell, "Babel in America," 109–10; Heath, "English in our Language Heritage," 10; Heath notes that "critical documents" were issued during the Revolutionary era in French and German when deemed necessary to drum up support for independence. See Heath, "Why No Official Tongue?" 23. The quotes are taken from an excerpt of the letter written by Benjamin Franklin, reproduced in Crawford, ed., *Language Loyalties*, 19.

13. This story is the basis of the Muhlenberg legend according to which Congress, during or shortly after the Revolutionary War, voted to abolish English and replace it with German as the national language. According to the legend, the measure did not pass due to Pennsylvania Congressman Muhlenberg, who was also the Speaker of the House. Although of German origins, he voted against the measure. See Heinz Kloss, *American Bilingual Tradition* (Washington, D.C.: Center for Applied Linguistics, 1998), 28; Heath, "English in our Language Heritage," 9. Another version of the story situates the incident within the Pennsylvania congress. See Shell, "Babel in America," 110. The significance of the legend lies not in its veracity; the very existence of the story is itself telling.

14. Simpson, *Politics of American English*, 40–46; Noah Webster, "Declaration of Linguistic Independence," 33–36; Andresen, *Linguistics in America*, 29–34; Shell, "Babel in America," 112–13; John Howe, *Language and Political Meaning in Revolutionary America* (Amherst: University of Massachusetts Press, 2004), chap. 3. For a discussion of the influences on Webster's ideas regarding language, see V. S. Bynack, "Noah Webster's Linguistic Thought and the Idea of an American National Culture," in *Language and the History of Thought*, ed. Nancy Struever (Rochester, N.Y.: University of Rochester Press, 1995), 204–19.

15. Baron, *Grammar and Good Taste*, 3; the quote is on p. 213. Shell notes that an interest in proper elocution and pronunciation is evident even in the early nineteenth century. See Shell, "Babel in America," 115n53. Conquergood discusses the elocution movement in the eighteenth and nineteenth centuries from the vantage point of workers and slaves as the "performativity of whiteness naturalized." Dwight Conquergood, "Rethinking Elocution: The Trope of the Talking Book and Other Figures of Speech," *Text and Performance Quarterly* 20, no. 4 (October 2000): 325–41.

16. Kloss, *American Bilingual Tradition*, 29–31, 60; Heath, "Why no Official Tongue?" 22.

17. Kloss, *American Bilingual Tradition*, 67, 76; Heath, "Why no Official Tongue?" 12–13. The quote appears in Heath, on p. 13; see also Carolyn Toth, *German-English Bilingual Schools in America: The Cincinnati Tradition in Historical Context* (New York: Peter Lang, 1990).

18. Heath, "Why no Official Tongue?" 12–14; Kloss, *American Bilingual Tradition*, 69.

19. Heath, "Why no Official Tongue?" 12–14; Kloss, *American Bilingual Tradition*,

69, 71–73; Conklin and Lourie, *A Host of Tongues*, 29–31. For the text of the *Meyer v. Nebraska* ruling, see Crawford, ed., *Language Loyalties*, 235–37.

20. Richard Y. Bourhis and David E. Marshall, "The United States and Canada," in Fishman, ed., *The Handbook of Language and Ethnicity*, 248; Carl Wittke, *German-Americans and the World War* (Columbus: The Ohio State Archeological and Historical Society, 1936); Kloss, *American Bilingual Tradition*, 52–61; John Higham, *Strangers in the Land: Patterns of American Nativism, 1860–1925* (New Brunswick, N.J.: Rutgers University Press, 1992), 208–9; Grittner, "Public Policies and Ethnic Influences," 191–95. Recent scholarship argues that German culture was already waning prior to World War I. See Peter Conolly-Smith, *Translating America: an Immigrant Press Visualizes American Popular Culture, 1895–1918* (Washington, D.C.: Smithsonian Books, 2004); Russell A. Kazal, *Becoming Old Stock: The Paradox of German-American Identity* (Princeton, N.J.: Princeton University Press, 2004).

21. Conklin and Lourie, *A Host of Tongues*, 67; Kloss, *American Bilingual Tradition*, 129–34; Schmidt, *Language Policy and Identity Politics*, 101, 114. Crawford, ed., *Language Loyalties*, 11; Shell, "Babel in America," 106, 111n40; U.S. Commission on Civil Rights, "Language Rights and New Mexico Statehood," in Crawford, ed., *Language Loyalties*, 62; Carlos Kevin Blanton, *The Strange Career of Bi-lingual Education in Texas, 1836–1981* (College Station, Tex: Texas A&M University Press, 2004).

22. James Crawford, *Hold Your Tongue: Bilingualism and the Politics of "English Only"* (Boston: Addison Wesley Publishing Company, 1993), 49–51.

23. Heath, "English in our Language Heritage," 10.

24. Conklin and Lourie, *A Host of Tongues*, 68. Though the 1906 law was aimed in large part at limiting immigrant political influence and corruption at the polls, that knowledge of English was used for this purpose is significant. See Reed Ueda, "Naturalization and Citizenship," in *Dimensions of Ethnicity*, ed. Stephan Thernstrom, Ann Orlov, and Oscar Handlin (Cambridge, Mass.: Belknap Press of Harvard University Press, 1982), 106–54.

25. Immigration and Naturalization Service, *1975 Annual Report: Immigration and Naturalization Service* (Washington, D.C.: Government Printing Office, 1976), 62–64, table 13, reprinted in *Harvard Encyclopedia of American Ethnic Groups*, ed. Stephen Thernstrom (Cambridge, Mass.: Belknap Press, 1980), 1048; Virginia Yans-McLaughlin and Marjorie Lightman, *Ellis Island and the Peopling of America* (New York: New Press, 1997), 10.

26. Ann Douglas, *Terrible Honesty: Mongrel Manhattan in the 1920's* (New York: Farrar, Straus and Giroux, 1995), 304.

27. Ross is quoted in Barbara Miller Solomon, *Ancestors and Immigrants: A Changing New England Tradition* (Cambridge, Mass.: Harvard University Press, 1956), 167. Even earlier in the nineteenth century, prior to the arrival of the new immigrants, ethnologists and others were distinguishing between degrees of whiteness. Writing in 1854, the widely respected ethnologist, Josiah Clark Nott, included southern and eastern Europeans as well as Nordics (or one branch of their descendants, the Anglo Saxons) within the Caucasian race. However, he differentiated between the "strictly-*white* races" that is Anglo-Saxons, vs. "the *dark*-skinned races" that included not only blacks, but most southern Europeans including Italians. See William H. Tucker, *The Science and Politics of Racial Research* (Urbana, Ill.: University

of Illinois Press, 1994), 21. For a popular, contemporary work on racialist thought, see Madison Grant, *The Passing of the Great Race* (1918; repr., New York: Arno Press, 1970). See also Lothrop Stoddard, *The Rising Tide of Color Against White World Supremacy* (New York: Charles A. Scribner's Sons, 1920). For the history of eugenics and scientific thought regarding racial difference, see, in addition to Tucker, *Science and Politics of Racial Research*, Audrey Smedley, *Race in North America: Origin and Evolution of a Worldview* (Boulder, Colo.: Westview Press, Inc., 1993).

28. John R. Commons, *Race and Immigrants in America* (Chautauqua, N.Y.: Chautauqua Press, 1907; New York: Augustus M. Kelley Publishers, 1967), 12.

29. Calling attention to the role of the courts in determining and reproducing racial classifications during the era of mass migration, recent scholarship confirms the instability of racial categories and the ramifications of such categorization. Peggy Pascoe, "Miscegenation Law, Court Cases and Ideologies of 'Race' in Twentieth Century America," *Journal of American History* 83, no. 1 (June 1996): 44–69; Roger M. Smith, *Civic Ideals: Conflicting Visions of Citizenship in U.S. History* (New Haven, Conn.: Yale University Press, 1997), 441–48; James Barrett and David Roediger, "Inbetween Peoples: Race, Nationality and the 'New Immigrant' Working Class," *Journal of American Ethnic History* 16, no. 3 (1997): 10; Ian F. Haney Lopez, *White By Law* (New York: New York University Press, 1997).

30. Matthew Frye Jacobson, *Whiteness of a Different Color: European Immigrants and the Alchemy of Race* (Cambridge, Mass.: Harvard University Press, 1994), 8. In *White on Arrival: Italians, Race, Color, and Power in Chicago, 1890–1945* (Oxford: Oxford University Press, 2004), Thomas Guglielmo attempts to explain how southern Italians could be considered both legally white and yet racially distinct from native-born Americans. His answer is to draw a distinction between race and color. Although southern Italians were considered racially distinct from the American "stock" by a wide segment of society, Guglielmo contends that their *color*—that is, their whiteness—was never challenged in a "sustained or systematic" way. This distinction, though logical, assumes that racial thought and categories in the late nineteenth century and early decades of the twentieth century were coherent and consistent. In any case, although their color may not have been challenged in a "sustained or systematic" manner, it was widely questioned as his own evidence demonstrates. For a similar critique of Guglielmo's thesis, see David R. Roediger, *Working Toward Whiteness: How America's Immigrants Become White. The Strange Journey from Ellis Island to the Suburbs* (New York: Basic Books, 2005): 110–19.

31. For more on the racially ambiguous position occupied by southern Italians in particular, see Robert Orsi, "The Religious Boundaries of an In between People: Street *Feste* and the Problem of the Dark-Skinned Other in Italian Harlem, 1920–1990," *American Quarterly* 44, no. 3 (1997), 313–47; Joseph Conesco, *Imagining Italians: The Clash of Romance and Race in American Perceptions, 1880–1910* (Albany: State University of New York Press, 2003); David A. J. Richards, *Italian American: The Racializing of an Ethnic Identity* (New York: New York University Press, 1999); Roediger, *Working Toward Whiteness*, 45–47, 51; Jennifer Guglielmo and Salvatore Salerno, eds., *Are Italians White? How Race is Made in America* (New York: Routledge, 2003). For general critiques of the "whiteness studies" literature, see Eric Arnesen, "Whiteness and the Historians' Imagination," *International*

Labor and Working-Class History 60 (Fall 2001): 3–32; Peter Kolchin, "Whiteness Studies: The New History of Race in America," *Journal of American History*, 89, no. 1 (2002): 154–73. Unless otherwise indicated, I use the term *race* throughout this chapter as it was used at the time, as a loosely defined concept that differentiated between European groups though not necessarily on the basis of color.

32. Barrett and Roediger, "Inbetween Peoples," 6; Jacobsen, "Whiteness of a Different Color," 41–42, 69; Gerstle, *American Crucible*.

33. Matthew Guterl notes that color took precedence over race beginning in the 1920s. *The Color of Race in America: 1900–1940* (Cambridge, Mass.: Harvard University Press, 2001). Mae Ngai argues that the restrictive immigration legislation of the 1920s created a legal basis for racializing the national origins of non-Europeans. *Impossible Subjects: Illegal Aliens and the Making of Modern America* (Princeton, N.J.: Princeton University Press, 2004); Ngai, "The Architecture of Race in American Immigration Law: An Examination of the Immigration Act of 1924," *Journal of American History* 86, no. 1 (June 1999): 67–92.

34. Stephen G. Alter, *William Dwight Whitney and the Science of Language* (Baltimore, Md.: Johns Hopkins University Press, 2005), 14–15; Alter, *Darwinism and the Linguistic Image: Language, Race, and Natural Theology in the Nineteenth Century* (Baltimore, Md.: Johns Hopkins University Press, 1999), 8–9.

35. Stocking, *Victorian Anthropology*, 24; Alter, *Darwinism and the Linguistic Image*, 31–32.

36. It was a linguist—Friedrich Max Muller—who coined the current spelling of Aryan and propagated the idea that Aryans were the original ancestors of [civilized] Europeans. Stocking notes that comparative philology was established in Britain earlier, but the discipline has been most consistently associated with Germans, Muller in particular. George Stocking Jr., *Victorian Anthropology* (New York: Free Press, 1987), 56, 59. For more on comparative philology, see Maurice Olender, *The Languages of Paradise: Race, Religion, and Philology in the Nineteenth Century* (Cambridge, Mass.: Harvard University Press, 1992). Although Herder is credited with first drawing the link between language and nationality, the eighteenth-century French philosopher Etienne Bonnot de Condillac set the stage for the idea of the *volksgeist* further elaborated by Herder. According to Condillac, "everything confirms that each language expresses the character of the people who speak it." Hans Aarsleff, *From Locke to Saussure: Essays on the Study of Language and Intellectual History* (Minneapolis: University of Minnesota Press, 1982), 30, 195–96; Olender, *Languages of Paradise*, 5. See also, Shell, "Babel in America," 116–17. The quote is from Reginald Horsman, *Race and Manifest Destiny: The Origins of American Racial Anglo-Saxonism* (Cambridge, Mass.: Harvard University Press, 1981), 35.

37. Stocking, *Victorian Anthropology*, 58

38. Amy L. Fairchild, *Science at the Borders: Immigrant Medical Inspection and the Shaping of the Modern Industrial Labor Force* (Baltimore, Md.: Johns Hopkins University Press, 2003), 193–94.

39. Thomas Gossett, *Race: The History of an Idea in America* (Dallas, Tex.: Southern Methodist University Press, 1963), chap. 6; Thomas G. Dyer, *Theodore Roosevelt and the Idea of Race* (Baton Rouge: Louisiana State University Press, 1980), 59–60, 37–38; George Stocking, *Race, Culture, and Evolution: Essays in the History of Anthropology* (New York: Free Press, 1968), 63–64.

40. The first quote appears in Harry P. Fairchild, *Race and Nationality as Factors in American Life* (New York: Ronald Press, 1947), 29–30. On the artificiality of separating race from culture in this period, see, for example, Waltraud Ernst, "Introduction: Historical and Contemporary Perspectives on Race, Science and Medicine," in *Race, Science and Medicine, 1700–1960*, ed. Waltraud Ernst and Bernard Harris (London: Routledge, 1999), 1–28. The last quote is from Pascoe, "Miscegenation Law," 48.

41. Gossett, *Race*, 128, 132–34. Gossett notes that Anglo-Saxon was taught at universities as late as 1925. On colonial interest in Anglo-Saxon languages, see Andresen, *Linguistics in America*, 29–56.

42. Henry Cabot Lodge, *Speeches and Addresses 1884–1909* (Boston: Houghton Mifflin Company, 1909), 253.

43. Lodge, *Speeches and Addresses*, 254.

44. Ibid., 255.

45. Ibid., 259.

46. Ibid., 261.

47. Ibid., 262.

48. Dyer, *Theodore Roosevelt and the Idea of Race*, 67. For more on Roosevelt's racialist thought, see Gary Gerstle, "Theodore Roosevelt and the Divided Character of American Nationalism," *Journal of American History* 86, no. 3 (December 1999): 1280–1307, 1296.

49. Quoted in Dyer, *Theodore Roosevelt and the Idea of Race*, 134.

50. Guterl, *Color of Race*, 42–43.

51. Henry Pratt Fairchild, *Race and Nationality as Factors in American Life* (New York: Ronald Press Company, 1947), 29.

52. Ruth Benedict, *Race: Science and Politics* (New York: Modern Age Books, 1940), 14.

53. Grant, *Passing of the Great Race*, 241.

54. Margaret Mead, "Intelligence Tests of Italian and American Children" (master's thesis, Columbia University, 1924). Margaret Mead Collection, I1, Library of Congress. The association between low intelligence, illiteracy, and immigrants in the popular mind was strengthened by the use of intelligence tests to classify soldiers during World War I. Italians, blacks, and Slavs performed poorly on both tests for soldiers who were literate in English and those who were nonliterate in English, as well as tests for the non-English speaking. For a contemporary analysis of the World War I intelligence tests that supports the idea of innate racial differences, see Carl C. Brigham, *A Study of American Intelligence* (Princeton, N.J.: Princeton University Press, 1923). See also Ellen Bialystok and Kenji Hakuta, *In Other Words: The Science and Psychology of Second Language Acquisition* (New York: Basic Books, 1995), 17–22.

55. The image of Italian children as particularly slow learners was already commonly accepted by the 1920s. Even in the early 1900s, public school teachers and administrators in New York and elsewhere expected Italian children to perform poorly; as a result, many were steered toward commercial or technical education. Paula S. Fass, *Outside in: Minorities and the Transformation of American Education* (New York: Oxford University Press, 1989), 37–38, 46–48; Tucker, *Science and Politics of Racial Research*, 80–85. For more on the low expectations of Italian

schoolchildren, see, for example, Selma C. Berrol, "School Days on the Old East Side: The Italian and Jewish Experience," *Education and the Immigrant*, ed. George E. Pozzetta (New York: Garland Publishing, 1991), 29, 38–39; Edward Alsworth Ross, *The Old World in the New: The Significance of Past and Present Immigration to the American People* (New York: The Century Company, 1914), 114.

56. Margaret Mead, "Group Intelligence Tests and Linguistic Disability Among Italian Children," *School and Society* 25, no. 642 (April 16, 1927): 465–68, Margaret Mead Collection, I1, Library of Congress; "The Methodology of Racial Testing," *American Journal of Sociology* 31, no. 5 (March, 1926): 657–67.

57. Clifford Kirkpatrick, *Intelligence and Immigration* (Baltimore: Williams & Wilkins Co., 1926), chap. 4; the quote is on p. 104.

58. J. Herskovits, *Franz Boas: The Science of Man in the Making* (New York: Scribner's Sons, 1953), 78–81; Smedley, *Race in North America*, 276–78; Marshall Hyatt, *Franz Boas, Social Activist: The Dynamics of Ethnicity* (Westport, Conn.: Greenwood Press, 1990), 105–18. For a mixed review of Boas and the culturalist challenge to racialist thinking, see Pascoe, "Miscegenation Law."

59. Franz Boas, "Race and Nationality," *International Conciliation: Special Bulletin*, Covello Papers, box 53, folder 6, Balch Institute for Ethnic Studies, Philadelphia.

60. U.S. House of Representatives, "A Dictionary of Races or Peoples," 3, 4. For a discussion of Brinton, a linguist who worked on aboriginal languages in North and South America, and his hierarchical views that privileged the language of the "Aryan stock," see Andreson, *Linguistics in America*, 197–204.

61. U.S. House of Representatives, "A Dictionary of Races or Peoples," 57.

62. Ibid., 55.

63. Oscar Handlin, *Race and Nationality in American Life* (Boston: Little, Brown: 1957), 121.

64. For a history of immigration law, including the Literacy Test and restrictions on Chinese immigrants, see E. P. Hutchinson, *Legislative History of American Immigration Policy, 1798–1965* (Philadelphia: University of Pennsylvania Press, 1981).

65. Jacobson, *Whiteness of a Different Color*, 77; Dyer, *Theodore Roosevelt and the Idea of Race*, 59–60; Solomon, *Ancestors and Immigrants*, chap. 5.

66. Arnold H. Leibowitz, "The Official Character of Language in the United States: Literacy Requirements for Immigration, Citizenship, and Entrance into American Life," *Aztlan* 15, no. 1 (1984): 31.

67. These laws were modeled on those aimed at blacks in the South. See Leibowitz, "Official Character of Language," 38.

68. "The Literacy Test," editorial, *New York Times*, 25 January 1922, Finley Papers, Special Collections, New York Public Library (hereafter, Finley Papers), box 154. "'The Only Sure Guide,'" editorial, *New York Times*, 10 March 1922, Finley Papers, box 154.

69. "A Real 'Americanization' Law," editorial, *New York Times*, 29 April 1923, Finley Papers, box 154.

70. "The School Test," editorial, *New York Times*, 18 October 1923, Finley Papers, box 154.

71. William C. Smith, letter to John Finley, 3 December 1929, Finley Papers, box 66.

72. "The Illiteracy Committee," editorial, *New York Times*, 18 November 1929, Finley Papers, box 155. "Illiteracy," editorial, *New York Times*, 14 October 1921, Finley Papers, box 154. Cora W. Stewart, letter to John H. Finley, 14 August 1930, Finley Papers, box 66. Frank Pierrepont Graves, letter to John Finley, 22 May 1930, Finley Papers, box 66. "Wiping Out Illiteracy," editorial, *New York Times*, 7 May 1929, Finley Papers, box 155.

73. Elizabeth A. Woodward, letter to John H. Finley, 4 September 1930, Finley Papers, box 66.

74. Higham, *Strangers in the Land*, 101; Betty Boyd Caroli, "The United States, Italy and the Literacy Act," *Studi Emigrazione* 13 (March 1976): 3.

75. Solomon, *Ancestors and Immigrants*, 87.

76. U.S. House of Representatives, *Restriction of Immigration: Hearing before the House Committee on Immigration and Naturalization*, on H.R. 558 by U.S. Congress, House Committee on Immigration and Naturalization, 64th Cong., 2d sess., 1916, 38.

77. U.S. House of Representatives, *Restriction of Immigration*, 11.

78. Senator Nelson of Minnesota to the U.S. Congress, *Congressional Record*, 64th Cong., 2nd sess., (12 December 1916) 54, pt. 1:225.

79. Robert A. Carlson, *The Quest for Conformity: Americanization through Education* (New York: John Wiley & Sons, 1975), 8. In contrast to the nativism on the home front, two recent studies argue that the experience of ethnics in the U.S. military during World War I was largely positive and facilitated their entry into American society. See Nancy Gentile Ford, *Americans All: Foreign-born Soldiers in World War I* (College Station: Texas A&M University, 2001); Christopher M. Sterba, *Good Americans: Italian and Jewish Immigrants during the First World War* (New York: Oxford University Press, 2003).

80. The role of English language instruction in the Americanization movement has been examined, but my focus here is on the racial construction of the immigrant through language.

81. U.S. Department of Labor, Bureau of Naturalization, *Educational Summary*, n.d., Records of the Immigration and Naturalization Service (INS), National Archives (NA), Record Group (RG) 85, entry 152, box 4.

82. For the involvement of the Bureau of Naturalization in the public schools in its effort to naturalize aliens, see Ueda, "Naturalization and Citizenship," 140–41. Despite the involvement of the bureau and its persistent attempts to receive congressional approval to oversee Americanization efforts nationwide, the Americanization movement was largely decentralized and operated through local school systems, businesses, and unions. See John F. McClymer, "The Americanization Movement and the Education of the Foreign-Born Adult, 1914–1925," *American Education and the European Immigrant: 1840-1940*, ed. Bernard J. Weiss (Urbana: University of Illinois Press, 1982), 96–116. The other major federal agency involved in Americanization efforts was the Office of Education. For its role in English language instruction of foreigners, see Frank Van Nuys, *Americanizing the West: Race, Immigrants, and Citizenship, 1890-1930* (Lawrence: University Press of Kansas, 2002).

83. R. Campbell, "Letter to All Chief Examiners," 27 October 1916, INS, NA, RG

85, entry 152, box 1. Commissioner of Naturalization, "To All Chief Examiners," 24 October 1916, INS, NA, RG 85, entry 152, box 1.

84. Richard K. Campbell, "Memorandum to Superintendents of Schools cooperating last year," 27 October 1916, INS, NA, RG 85, entry 152, box 5.

85. Harry Downer, *Chats with Possible Americans* (1918; repr., Davenport, Iowa: Friendly House Drookery, 1924), 100.

86. U.S. Department of Labor, Naturalization Service, *Proposed Four Minute Speech*, 18 October 1918, Records of the INS, NA, RG 85, entry 152, box 4.

87. U.S. Department of Labor, Bureau of Naturalization, n.d., *Memorandum: Campaign for Public School Work*, INS, NA, RG 85, entry 152, box 4.

88. U.S. Department of Labor, Naturalization Service, n.d., *An Appeal to Every Citizen of the United States*, INS, NA, RG 85, entry 152, box 4.

89. Ibid.

90. Ibid.

91. Richard K. Campbell, letter to H. E. Jenkins, 9 February 1916, INS, NA, RG 85, entry 152, box 1. On the professionalization of adult education, see Carlson, *The Quest for Conformity*, 8.

92. Notes for "The Proper Education of the Alien," National Education Association Convention, Madison Square Garden, New York, 5 July 1916, Finley Papers, box 116. *Twenty-Seventh Annual Report of the Superintendent of Schools for the Year Ending July 31, 1925*, New York City Board of Education, Special Collections, Milbank Memorial Library, Teacher's College, Columbia University.

93. Dwight Braman, letter, *New York Times*, 7 May 1923, Finley Papers, box 154.

94. New York City Board of Education, *The First Fifty Years: A Brief Review of Progress 1898–1948, Fiftieth Annual Report of the Superintendent of Schools* (1948), 68.

95. Katrina Irving, *Immigrant Mothers: Narratives of Race and Maternity, 1890–1925* (Urbana: University of Illinois Press, 2000), 70–75; Gabaccia, *From the Other Side*, 113.

96. McClymer, "The Americanization Movement," 109; Van Nuys, *Americanizing the West*, 122–27. On the importance Americanizers placed on immigrant women, see also George Sanchez, "Go After the Women: Americanization and the Mexican Immigrant Woman, 1915–1929," in *Unequal Sisters: An Inclusive Reader in U.S. Women's History*, ed. Vicki L. Ruiz and Ellen Carol DuBois, 2nd ed. (New York: Routledge, 1994), 250–63.

97. Richard K. Campbell, letter to City Superintendent of Schools, 17 November 1915, Records of Field Office District 2, INS, NA, RG 85, entry 152, box 1.

98. Raymond F. Crist, letter to Raymond Moley, 4 October 1918, INS, NA, RG 85, entry 152, box 3.

99. Mencken, *American Language*, 766.

100. "A Language of Diplomacy," editorial, *New York Times*, 4 September 1921, Finley Papers, box 154.

101. "The English Tongue," editorial, *New York Times*, 10 October 1923, Finley Papers, box 154. "A 'Whole Earth of One Speech,'" editorial, *New York Times*, 1 January 1930, Finley Papers, box 155. "Many Languages and One," editorial, *New*

York Times, 15 August 1936, Finley Papers, box 156. "Healing the Hurt of Babel," editorial, New York Times, 13 May 1937, Finley Papers, box 156.

102. Mencken, American Language, vii–viii, 772–77; Andresen, Linguistics in America, 1–2.

103. Robert E. Park and Herbert A. Miller, Old World Traits Transplanted (New York: Harper & Brothers Publishers, 1921), 267–68.

104. Ibid., 281.

105. Ibid., 282.

106. Ibid., 283–87.

107. Stow Persons, Ethnic Studies at Chicago, 1905-45 (Urbana: University of Illinois Press, 1987), 21–23.

108. Ellen Condliffe Lagemann, ed., Jane Addams on Education (New York: Teachers College Press, 1985), 81.

109. Ibid., 87.

110. Jane Addams, Twenty Years at Hull-House (New York: The MacMillan Company, 1910), 232. For critical appraisals of Hull House and the settlement movement in general, see Rivka Shpak Lissak, Pluralism and Progressives: Hull House and the New Immigrants, 1890-1919 (Chicago: University of Chicago Press, 1989); Ruth Hutchinson Crocker, Social Work and Social Order: The Settlement Movement in Two Industrial Cities, 1889-1930 (Urbana: University of Illinois Press, 1992); Mina Carson, Settlement Folk: Social Thought and the American Settlement Movement, 1885-1930 (Chicago: The University of Chicago Press, 1990).

111. Emory S. Bogardus, Essentials of Americanization, 3rd ed. (Los Angeles: University of Southern California Press, 1923), 346; Frank V. Thompson, Schooling of the Immigrant, vol. 1 in Americanization Studies: The Acculturation of Immigrant Groups into American Society, ed. William S. Bernard (1920; repr., Montclair, N.J.: Patterson Smith, 1971), 288–89; 327–62. For a positive appraisal of Americanizers such as Bogardus and Thompson, see Van Nuys, Americanizing the West, 118–19.

112. On the goals of adult classes for immigrants, see New York City Board of Education, Annual Report of the Superintendent of Schools for the Year Ending July 31, 1933 (1933). For the quote by Leipzig, see New York City Board of Education, Report of Public Lectures, A University for the People: Annual Report of the Supervisor of Lectures to the Board of Education for the Year 1913-1914 (1914).

113. New York City Board of Education, Report of Public Lectures, 1913-1914, 92–95; New York City Board of Education, Report of Public Lectures, A University for the People: Annual Report of the Supervisor of Lectures to the Board of Education for the Year 1911-1912 (1912), 11.

114. New York City Board of Education, The First Fifty Years, 107.

115. New York City Board of Education, Report of Public Lectures, A University for the People: Annual Report of the Supervisor of Lectures to the Board of Education for the Year 1915-1916 (1916), 8.

116. Ibid., 77. For more on Leipzig and the Public Lectures, see Stephan F. Brumberg, Going to America Going to School: The Jewish Immigrant Public School Encounter in Turn-of-the-Century New York City (New York: Praeger Publishers, 1986), 150–69.

117. Winthrop Talbot, ed., *Americanization* (New York: H. W. Wilson, 1920), 86–87.

118. McClymer, "The Americanization Movement," 103–4. In failing to register or stick with adult education programs established by the native born, immigrants were not necessarily demonstrating a lack of interest in education. The numbers of immigrants, including Italians, who participated in educational programs created within the ethnic community suggest that they may simply have been eschewing a curriculum that was narrowly focused on English and civics. Maxine S. Seller, "Success and Failure in Adult Education: The Immigrant Experience 1914–1924," *Adult Education* 28, no. 2 (1978): 85–99.

119. Oscar Durante, "To Make Americanization Painless," 10 January 1924, INS, NA, RG 85, entry 30, box 14.

120. Higham, *Strangers in the Land*, 262–63; Carlson, *Quest for Conformity*, 129–30; Gino Speranza, *Race or Nation: A Conflict of Divided Loyalties* (1925; repr., New York: Arno Press, 1975); Thomas Guglielmo, "Toward Essentialism, Toward Difference: Gino Speranza and Conceptions of Race and Italian-American Racial Identity, 1900–1925," *Mid-America* 81, no. 2 (Summer 1999): 204–5.

121. New York City Board of Education, *Courses of Study in Civics* (1918), 5.

122. Brumberg, *Going to America*, 6.

123. New York City Board of Education, *Course of Study in English* (1924), 2.

124. New York City Board of Education, *Prospectus of a Guide to the Teaching of Oral English through the Use of Phonetics* (1931), 3.

125. "Present Day English," editorial, *New York Times*, n.d. 1928, Finley Papers, box 155.

126. Fass, *Outside in*, 30, 70. New York City Board of Education, *The First Fifty Years*, 31; David K. Cohen, "Immigrants and the Schools," *Review of Educational Research* 40 (1970): 135–36.

127. Thomas Paul Bonfiglio, *Race and the Rise of Standard American* (Berlin: Mouton de Gruyter, 2002), 4.

128. In his 1943 study of Italian American school children, Irvin Childs notes, regarding the Italian immigrant, "the most conspicuous and uniform feature that sets him off from his fellow Americans is his language. He is known as the fellow who 'maka da moosic' but 'no speaka da Eng. [sic]." Irvin L. Childs, *Italian or American? The Second Generation in Conflict* (New York: Russell & Russell, 1970), 21.

129. R. M. Brinkerhoff, "Another Day of Suspense," cartoon, 1922, INS, NA, RG 85, entry 30, box 25, file 27671/80.

Chapter Three: "He could not explain things the way I tell it"

Epigraph: Quoted in Jerre Mangione and Ben Morreale, *La Storia: Five Centuries of the Italian American Experience* (New York: HarperCollins Publishers, 1993), 130.

1. La Guardia Papers, New York City Municipal Archives (hereafter, La Guardia Papers), microfilm reel #102, images #1839–40. This anecdote is also recounted

in David M. Brownstone, Irene M. Franck, and Douglass L. Brownstone, *Island of Hope, Island of Tears* (New York: Rawson, Wade Publishers, Inc., 1979), 211–12.

2. La Guardia Papers, microfilm reel #102, image #1839.

3. Alan M. Kraut, *Silent Travelers: Germs, Genes, and the "Immigrant Menace"* (New York: Basic Books, 1994), 75.

4. Treasury Department, United States Public Health Service, Miscellaneous Publication No. 18, *Manual of the Mental Examination of Aliens* (Washington, D.C.: Government Printing Office, 1918).

5. E. H. Mullan, "Mental Examination of Immigrants," *Ellis Island, Statue of Liberty, Historic Resource Study (historical component)*, vol. 3, ed. Harlan D. Unrau (Washington, D.C.: U.S. Department of the Interior/National Park Service, 1984), 857.

6. Ibid., 857.

7. Ibid., 856.

8. Ibid., 855.

9. LaGuardia Papers, microfilm #102, images #1841–42.

10. *Manual of the Mental Examination of the Alien*, 30, app. C, 17. The manual goes on to note that there were instances in which the opinion of a qualified interpreter could be valuable in assessing the mental status of the immigrant (18).

11. Ibid., 16.

12. Ibid., 16–17.

13. Ibid., 23–26, 28–29.

14. For an example of the popular understanding of the phenomenon of name changing, see Brownstone et al., *Island of Hope*, 177–78.

15. Marian L. Smith, "American Names/Declaring Independence." http://uscis .gov/graphics/aboutus/history/articles/NameEssay.html (accessed February 28, 2003). On Italians specifically, Michael La Sorte notes that name changing was a relatively rare phenomenon that was most often "an adaptive concession that some immigrants chose to make to their new environment," rather than a residual effect of the passage through Ellis Island. La Sorte, *La Merica*, 152–58; quote is from p. 158.

16. Child, *Italian or American?*, 22; Joseph G. Fucilla, *Our Italian Surnames* (Evanston, Ill.: Chandler's Inc., 1949), 236–42.

17. For examples of the defenders of Sacco and Vanzetti, see Herbert B. Ehrmann, *Commonwealth vs. Sacco and Vanzetti* (Boston: Little, Brown and Company, 1969); Osmond Fraenkel, *The Sacco-Vanzetti Case* (New York: Alfred A. Knopf, 1931); Felix Frankfurter, *The Case of Sacco and Vanzetti: A Critical Analysis for Lawyers and Laymen* (1927; repr., New York: Little, Brown & Company, Inc., 1961); Roberta Strauss Feuerlicht, *Justice Crucified: The Story of Sacco and Vanzetti* (New York: McGraw-Hill, 1977); Michael A. Musmanno, "The Sacco-Vanzetti Case," *Kansas Law Review* 11, no. 4 (May 1963): 481–525; William Young and David E. Kaiser, *Postmortem: New Evidence in the Case of Sacco and Vanzetti* (Amherst: University of Massachusetts Press, 1985). Those who question the innocence of one or both of the defendants include Francis Russell in his books *Tragedy in Dedham: The Story of the Sacco-Vanzetti Case* (1962; repr., New York: McGraw-Hill Book Company, 1971)

and *Sacco & Vanzetti: The Case Resolved* (New York: Harper & Row Publishers, 1986). See also Robert H. Montgomery, *Sacco-Vanzetti: The Murder and the Myth* (New York: The Devin-Adair Company, 1960); and David Felix, *Protest: Sacco-Vanzetti and the Intellectuals* (Bloomington: University of Indiana Press, 1962). For the political context of the case, see Paul Avrich, *Sacco and Vanzetti: The Anarchist Background* (Princeton, N.J.: Princeton University Press, 1991).

18. In a brief discussion of the role of translation in the trial, Brian Jackson claims that it was a contributing though not a decisive factor in the verdict. Topp notes that the prosecutor in Vanzetti's trial for attempted robbery in Bridgewater, harped on the inability of the Italian immigrants who testified in Vanzetti's favor to speak English. In mentioning translation, other authors imply that at the very least, it constituted another element of unfairness in the trial. Brian Jackson, *The Black Flag: A Look at the Strange Case of Sacco and Vanzetti* (Boston: Routledge & Kegan Paul, 1981), 105–6; Michael M.Topp, *The Sacco and Vanzetti Case: A Brief History with Documents* (New York: Palgrave MacMillan, 2005), 20–21; Mary Anne Trasciatti and Jerome H. Delamater, "Introduction," *Representing Sacco and Vanzetti* (New York: Palgrave MacMillan, 2005), 4; Fraenkel, *Sacco-Vanzetti Case*, 72, 191, 199, 477–78; Frankfurter, *Case of Sacco and Vanzetti*, 8.

19. *The Sacco-Vanzetti Case: Transcript of the Record of the Trial of Nicola Sacco and Bartolomeo Vanzetti in the Courts of Massachusetts and Subsequent Proceedings, 1920–1927*, 5 vols., with a supplemental volume (New York: Henry Holt, 1928).

20. Jackson, *Black Flag*, 105–6.

21. Frankfurter, *Case of Sacco and Vanzetti*, 35–36.

22. Jackson, *Black Flag*, 105–6; Frankfurter, *Case of Sacco and Vanzetti*, 8. Even though their English was limited at the time of their arrest, both men studied English while incarcerated; Vanzetti's English improved significantly. See *The Letters of Sacco and Vanzetti*, ed. Marion Denman Frankfurter and Gardner Jackson (New York: Viking Press, 1928), vii–viii.

23. *The Sacco-Vanzetti Case*, vol. 2, 1744–45.

24. *The Sacco-Vanzetti Case*, vol. 2, 1956.

25. Jackson, *Black Flag*, 105–6.

26. Frankfurter, *Case of Sacco and Vanzetti*, 97.

27. *The Sacco-Vanzetti Case*, vol. 2, 1818.

28. For beginning of cross-examination along these lines, see *The Sacco-Vanzetti Case*, vol. 2, 1867.

29. Ibid., 1967.

30. Ibid., 1778.

31. Ibid., 1785.

32. Ibid., 1698, 1956.

33. Ibid., 1117–18.

34. Ibid., 1113–14.

35. Ibid., 5191.

36. Lawrence Venuti, *The Translator's Invisibility: A History of Translation* (London: Routledge, 1995), 18–19. Venuti's solution to this problem is to reveal rather than try to erase the strangeness of the foreign language in translation.

37. "The Interpreter Service in Our Courts," Gino Speranza Papers, Special

Collections, New York Public Library (NYPL) (hereafter, Speranza Papers), box 35, folder "Gino Speranza Papers on Immigration 'I.'"

38. For more on the problems immigrants faced with court interpreters from contemporary observers, see Kate Holladay Claghorn, *The Immigrant's Day in Court* (1923; repr., Montclair, N.J.: Patterson Smith, 1971); John Horace Mariano, *The Italian Immigrant and Our Courts* (1925; repr., New York: Arno Press, 1975).

39. Dominick DeMasso Case, 13 January 1902, microfilm roll #60, 209, Transcripts of Court of General Sessions, Special Collections, John Jay College of Criminal Justice, New York City.

40. Ibid., 209.

41. DeMasso Case, 304.

42. Michalagio Russo Case, microfilm roll #200, 51, Transcripts of the Court of General Sessions, Special Collections, John Jay College of Criminal Justice, New York City.

43. Ibid., 59.

44. Ibid., 59.

45. "North Carolina vs. Jim Mazzone et al.," Speranza Papers, box 30, folder "Gino Speranza papers Legal Papers Nic-Nuz."

46. Child, *Italian or American*, 22–23.

47. Biaggio Calandra Case, microfilm roll #97, 255–56, Transcript of the Court of General Sessions, Special Collections, John Jay College of Criminal Justice, New York City.

48. Ibid., 258.

49. "Court Gives English Test," *New York Times*, June 14, 1928; Ivan Hubert Light, *Italians in America: Annotated Guide to The New York Times 1890–1940* (New York: Council of Planning Librarians, 1975).

50. Jerre Mangione, *Mount Allegro* (1942; repr., New York: Crown Publishers, Inc., 1972), 50.

51. Ibid., 51.

52. Ibid., 52.

53. Ibid., 57.

54. Ibid.

55. Ibid., 67.

56. Ibid., 65.

57. Pascal D'Angelo, *Son of Italy* (1924; repr., New York: Arno Press, 1975).

58. Olga Peragallo, *Italian-American Authors and their Contribution to American Literature* (New York: S.F. Vanni, 1949), 67.

59. D'Angelo, *Son of Italy*, 171.

60. William Boelhower, *Immigrant Autobiography in the United States* (Verona, Italy: Essedue Edizioni, 1982), 102.

61. Quoted in Luigi Fontanella, *La Parola Transfuga: Scrittori italiani in America* (Firenze, Italy: Cadmus, 2003), 58.

62. Ibid., 73. The Italian name Pasquale is usually translated as Patrick.

63. D'Angelo, *Son of Italy*, 61.

64. Ibid., 70–71

65. Ibid., 72–73. Contrary to this story, D'Angelo and others note the positive

role of the foreman or *padrone* as an interpreter for the immigrant: "Mario Lancia . . . was about forty years of age and had passed almost half of his life in America. He could read and write some English, and was the guiding spirit of the gang." (65).

66. Ibid., 70.

67. Ibid., 68.

68. Ibid., 64.

69. Ibid., 121, 132–33.

70. Ibid., 67.

71. Ibid., 83.

72. Ibid., 137.

73. Ibid., 141.

74. Ibid., 159.

75. Ibid., 185.

76. Constantine Panunzio, *The Soul of an Immigrant* (1928; repr., New York: Arno Press, 1969).

77. Peragallo, *Italian-American Authors*, 173.

78. Panunzio, *Soul of an Immigrant*, 61.

79. Ibid., 63.

80. Ibid., 76.

81. Ibid., 79.

82. Ibid., 107.

83. Ibid., 108.

84. Boelhower, *Immigrant Autobiography*, 55.

85. Jacqueline Amati-Mehler, Simona Argentieri, and Jorge Canestri, *The Babel of the Unconscious: Mother Tongue and Foreign Languages in the Psychoanalytic Dimension* (Madison, Conn.: International Universities Press, Inc., 1993), 264.

86. Fred Gardaphé, "My House Is Not Your House: Jerre Mangione and Italian-American Autobiography," in *Multicultural Autobiography: American Lives*, ed. James Robert Payne (Knoxville: University of Tennessee Press, 1992), 140; Gardaphé, *Italian Signs, American Streets: The Evolution of Italian American Narrative* (Durham, N.C.: Duke University Press, 1996), 25.

87. Marie Hall Ets, *Rosa, The Life of an Italian Immigrant* (Minneapolis: University of Minesota Press, 1970).

88. Ibid., 3–4.

89. Ets writes that Rosa "was excited" when Ets's first publication, a children's book, came out: "She wanted to help me publish other books and offered to tell me more of her stories." (6).

90. Ibid., 7 for both quotes in this paragraph. Rosa is part of a tradition of storytelling common to oral cultures. Gardaphé notes that Rosa's narrative, more so than D'Angelo's or Pannunzio's, contains elements of oral cultures. Gardaphé, *Italian Signs, American Streets*, 25. On orality, see Walter J. Ong, *Orality and Literacy: The Technologizing of the Word* (1982; repr., London: Routledge Press, 1991); Jack Goody, *The Domestication of the Savage Mind* (Cambridge: Cambridge University Press, 1977).

91. Ibid., 7 for both quotes in this paragraph.

92. Ibid., 183.

93. On the presentation of Rosa through Ets, see Gardaphé, "My House" and *Italian Signs, American Streets*, 31–32.

94. Ets, *Rosa*, 254.

95. Gardaphé, "My House," 141–46; Gardaphé, *Italian Signs, American Streets*, 36.

96. Maria Parrino, "Breaking the Silence: Autobiographies of Italian Immigrant Women," *Storia Nordamericana* 5, no. 2 (1988): 137–58.

97. Ets, *Rosa*, 27.

98. Ibid., 42.

99. Ibid.

100. Ibid., 191.

101. There are a number of late nineteenth- and early twentieth-century auto-biographies/memoirs by Italian intellectuals who either visited the United States or lived here for a time. These authors may have made observations on Italian immigrant life, but at a remove from it. For this reason, I do not consider them here.

102. Carmine Biagio Iannace, *La scoperta dell'America*, trans. by William Boelhower (West Lafayette, Ind.: Bordighera Press, 2000), 199.

103. Ibid., 1. The quotes are taken from the English translation included in the text.

104. Ibid., 36.

105. Antonio Margariti, *America! America!* 6th ed. (Salerno, Italy: Galzerano Editore, 1994), 72, 118.

106. Ibid., 118, 121, 124.

107. Ibid., 56.

108. Ibid., 67. All translations from Margariti are mine.

109. Iannace, *La scoperta*, 219.

110. Margariti, *America! America!* 82.

111. Ibid., 62.

112. Ibid., 83.

Chapter Four: The World Turned Upside Down in Farfariello's Theater of Language

Epigraph: "Italian language," Migliaccio Collection, box 7, Immigration History Research Center, Minneapolis, Minnesota (IHRC).

1. For an overview of the theater of other groups, see Maxine Schwartz Seller, ed., *Ethnic Theatre in the United States* (Westport, Conn.: Greenwood Press, 1983). On immigrant songs, many of which were performed on the variety stage, see Victor Greene, *A Singing Ambivalence: American Immigrants Between Old World and New, 1830-1930* (Kent, Ohio: Kent State University Press, 2004). For the Italian immigrant theater, see Emelise Aleandri, *Italian-American Immigrant Theatre in New York* (New York: Arcadia Tempus Publishing Group, Inc., 1999); Aleandri, "Italian American Theatre," in *Ethnic Theatre in the United States*, 237–76; Aleandri,

"A History of Italian American Theatre: 1900 to 1905" (PhD diss., City University of New York, 1983).

2. Lawrence Estavan, "The Italian in San Francisco," in *The Italian Theatre in San Francisco: Being a History of the Italian-Language Operatic, Dramatic, and Comedic Productions Presented in the San Franciso Bay Area Through the Depression*, ed. Mary Wickizer Burgess and Lawrence Estavan, Clipper Studies in the American Theatre 3 (San Francisco: Borgo Press, 1991), 55; Aleandri, *Italian-American Immigrant Theatre*, 94; Christopher Charles Newton, "Ethnicity and the New Deal: Italian Language Theatre Sponsored by the Federal Theatre Project in Boston, 1935–1939," (PhD diss., Tufts University, 1994). Newton notes that Farfariello visited Boston regularly throughout the 1930s.

3. Migliaccio was promoted as *Il re dei macchiettisti*. See "Farfariello (Edoardo Migliaccio) Il Re Dei Macchiettisti, People's Theatre, 201 Bowery, New York City," Carl Van Vechten Collection, Billy Rose Theatre Collection, Performing Arts Library, NYPL. For a more in-depth treatment of Migliaccio, see Aleandri, "A History of Italian American Theatre,"130–75.

4. For the Italian antecedents of Farfariello's theater, see Richard A. Sogliuzzo, "Notes for a History of the Italian-American Theatre of New York," *Theatre Survey: The American Journal of Theatre History* 14, no. 2 (November 1973): 68; Aleandri, *Italian-American Immigrant Theater*, 358–59; Estavan, "The Italian in San Francisco"; Hermann W. Haller, *Tra Napoli e New York: Le macchiette italo-americane di Eduardo Migliaccio* (Rome: Bulzoni Editore, 2006), 16–22.

5. Giuseppe Cautela, "The Italian Theatre in New York," *The American Mercury* 5, no. 12 (September 1927): 110. *Macchiete coloniale* translates as sketches or character studies of colonists, that is, immigrants.

6. Sogliuzzo, "Notes," 72; "Farfariello, an Italian Lauder," *Christian Science Monitor*, February 4, 1919.

7. Pietro Trifone, "L'italiano a teatro," in *Storia della lingua italiana*, vol 2., *Scritto e parlato*, ed. Luca Serianni and Pietro Trifone (Torino, Italy: Giulio Einaudi, 1994): 81–160 (see in particular pp. 117–27); Hermann W. Haller, *The Other Italy: The Literary Canon in Dialect* (Toronto: University of Toronto Press, 1999), chap. 2; Salvatore Primeggia and Joseph A. Varacalli, "Pulcinella to Farfariello to Paone to Uncle Floyd: A Socio-Historical Perspective on Southern Italian and Italian-American Comedy," *Eastern Community College Social Science Journal* 5, no.1 (1990): 45–53; Salvatore Primeggia, Pamela Primeggia, and Joseph A. Varacalli, "Uncle Floyd Vivino: A Modern Italian-American Comic," *New Jersey History* 107, no s. 3–4 (Fall/Winter 1989): 1–20.

8. For a discussion of the linguistic features of Migliaccio's material, including a glossary, see Haller, *Tra Napoli e New York*, 27–67.

9. For biographical information, see Ario Flamma, *Italiani di America* (New York: Cocce Brothers, ca. 1936), 232; "Migliaccio, 'The Tiny Butterfly' of U.S. Italian Theater, is Dead," *New York Herald Tribune*, March 29, 1946; Aleandri, "Italian-American Theater," 130–75. Quote taken from "Figure e Scene del Teatro Popolare Italiana a New York," *Il Progresso Italo-Americano*, July 6, 1942. The translation is mine.

10. Estavan, "The Italian in San Francisco," 58.

11. For how Migliaccio obtained his sobriquet, see A. Richard Sogliuzzo, "Shakespeare, Sardou, and Pulcinella: Italian-American Working-Class Theatre in New York: 1880–1940," *Theatre for Working-Class Audiences in the United States, 1830–1980*, ed. Bruce A. McConachie and Daniel Friedman (Westport, Conn.: Greenwood Press, 1985), 82; and, "Figure e Scene." For some of the locations of his performances, see Carl Van Vechten, "A Night with Farfariello," *The Theatre*, January 1919, 32; Edmund Wilson, "Alice Lloyd and Farfariello," *New Republic*, October 21, 1925, 230; Handbill from People's Theatre, n.d., Carl van Vechten Collection, Billy Rose Theatre Collection, Performing Arts Library, NYPL. Cautela notes two theaters on 14th Street. Cautela, "Italian Theatre in New York," 110.

12. James H. Dorman, "American Popular Culture and the New Immigration Ethnics: The Vaudeville Stage and the Process of Ethnic Ascription," *Amerikastudien/American Studies* 36, no. 2 (1991): 191. On the Yiddish theater, Irving Howe, *World of Our Fathers, The Journey of the East European Jews to America and the Life They Found and Made* (1976; repr., New York: Galahad Books, 1994), ch. 14; Rhonda Helfman Kaufman, *The Yiddish Theater in New York and the Immigrant Jewish Community: Theater as Secular Ritual* (Ann Arbor, Mich.: UMI, 1990); David S. Lifson, "Yiddish Theatre," in *Ethnic Theatre in the United States*; David S. Lifson, *The Yiddish Theatre in America* (New York: T. Yoseloff, 1965); Nahma Sandrow, *Vagabond Stars: A World History of Yiddish Theater* (New York: Harper & Row, 1977). On Jewish theater in English, see Harley Erdman, *Staging the Jew: The Performance of an American Ethnicity, 1860–1920* (New Brunswick, N.J.: Rutgers University Press, 1997). For mainstream variety theater, vaudeville, and related forms of popular entertainment, see, for example, Albert F. McClean Jr., *American Vaudeville as Ritual* (Lexington: University of Kentucky Press, 1965); Robert W. Snyder, *The Voice of the City: Vaudeville and Popular Culture in New York* (New York: Oxford University Press, 1989).

13. Aleandri, "Italian-American Theater," 360; Cautela, "The Italian Theatre in New York," 110–11. The nature of Italian American theater varied depending on time and place. A study of Italian language theater in St. Louis claims that Italians in that community staged primarily sentimental melodramas with the avowed goal of preserving the Italian language and culture. See Dominic J. Cunetto, "Italian Language Theatre Clubs in St. Louis, Missouri 1910 to 1950" (master's thesis, University of Florida, 1960). Italian language theater in Boston during the New Deal also had a distinct character largely due to its connection with mainstream America through the Federal Theatre Project. See Newton, "Ethnicity and the New Deal."

14. Cautela, "The Italian Theater in New York," 109; on the Yiddish theater's role in maintaining Yiddish, see Kaufman, *Yiddish Theater*, 123. On the broader role of the Yiddish theater in promulgating "the politics of nationalism and 'peoplehood,'" see Matthew Frye Jacobson, *Special Sorrows: The Diasporic Imagination of Irish, Polish, and Jewish Immigrants in the United States* (Cambridge, Mass.: Harvard University Press, 1995), 81–97.

15. Sogliuzzo, "Shakespeare, Sardou, and Pulcinella," 82; "Figure e Scene."

16. Cautela, "Italian Theatre in New York," 110; Giuseppe Cautela, "The Bowery," *The American Mercury* 9, no. 35 (November 1926): 368; Van Vechten, "A Night with Farfariello," 32.

17. Sogliuzzo, "Shakespeare, Sardou, and Pulcinella," 77; Hapgood Hutchins, "The Foreign Stage in New York, III: The Italian Theatre," *The Bookman*, August 11, 1900, 551. Italian American theatergoers resembled the early nineteenth-century audiences Lawrence Levine described in his seminal work on popular culture. Lawrence Levine, *Highbrow/Lowbrow* (Cambridge, Mass.: Harvard University Press, 1988).

18. "Farfariello, an Italian Lauder," *Christian Science Monitor*, February 4, 1919.

19. "Farfariello, an Italian Lauder."

20. Sogliuzzo, "Shakespeare, Sardou, and Pulcinella," 82. His stage name may have also been an allusion to "the character's *transformiste* performances." Giorgio Bertellini, *Southern Crossings: Italians, Cinema, and Modernity (Italy, 1861–New York, 1920)* (Ann Arbor, Mich.: UMI, 2001),525n136. I do not deal with the cross-dressing aspect of his work per se because it is not central to the language theme.

21. Van Vechten, "A Night with Farfariello," 32. Scholars have used Bakhtin's concept of "grotesque realism" to describe Farfariello's familiar, but exaggerated renderings of neighborhood types. Esther Romeyn, "Farfariello: Worlds in Between Worlds: Italian-Americans and Farfariello, Their Comic Double" (PhD diss., University of Minnesota, 1990); Bertellini, *Southern Crossings*, 535.

22. Cautela, "Italian Theatre in New York," 110.

23. Ibid.

24. "Farfariello, an Italian Lauder"; Van Vechten, "A Night with Farfariello," 32.

25. "Che Suonno," Eduardo Migliaccio Collection, box 9, IHRC. All translations in this chapter are mine.

26. "Chrley," Eduardo Migliaccio Collection, box 7, IHRC.

27. "O Cucchiere Napulitano," lyrics by A. Gigliatti, Migliaccio Collection, box 8, IHRC.

28. Guido Basso, "Sabato Santo," Migliaccio Collection, box 10, IHRC.

29. "Il Calandriello," Migliaccio Collection, box 6, IHRC.

30. For Italian anticlericalism, see Rudolph J. Vecoli, "Prelates and Peasants: Italian Immigrants and the Catholic Church," *Journal of Social History* 2, no. 3 (1969): 223–24.

31. "'a Lengua 'Taliana," Migliaccio Collection, box 7, IHRC. (It is worth noting that there are several versions of this particular song among Migliaccio's papers. See box 7.) Psychologists have noted that language acquisition is affected by the attitude the speaker has toward leaving the motherland and the mother tongue for a new country and language. Even the degree to which one maintains an accent is rooted in individual psychology. The greater the degree of attachment one maintains toward one's primary language and the homeland it represents, which is shaped in part by one's parents, the greater the likelihood that one will speak with a strong accent. Paul H. Elovitz, "Introduction," in *Immigrant Experiences: Personal Narrative and Psychological Analysis*, ed. Paul H. Elovitz and Charlotte

Kalin (London: Associated University Press, 1977), 14–15; Elovitz, "Family Secrets and Lies My Parents Told Me," 98–99.

32. "A Lengua d' 'a Dummeneca."

33. Some examples from Migliaccio's papers are "Francheschino," box 7; the various versions of "La Lingua Italiana," box 7; "Che Suonno," box 9, IHRC.

34. "Pulcinella e Colombina in America," Migliaccio Collection, box 9, IHRC.

35. Kaufman, *Yiddish Theater,* 123, 130–32; Lawrence E. Mintz, "Humor and Ethnic Stereotypes in Vaudeville and Burlesque," *Melus* 21, no. 4 (Winter 1996): 19–28.

36. "Italian language," Migliaccio Collection, box 7, IHRC.

37. John Fiske, *Understanding Popular Culture* (Boston: Unwin Hyman, 1989), 108.

38. Michael M. J. Fischer, "Ethnicity and the Post-Modern Arts of Memory," in *Writing Culture: The Poetics and Politics of Ethnography,* ed. James Clifford and George E. Marcus (Los Angeles and Berkeley: University of California Press, 1986), 218–19.

39. Regarding the changing roles of immigrant women, see, for example, Kathy Peiss, *Cheap Amusements: Working Women and Leisure in Turn-of-the-Century New York* (Philadelphia: Temple University Press, 1986); Elizabeth Ewen, *Immigrant Women in the Land of Dollars: Life and Culture on the Lower East Side, 1890–1925* (New York: Monthly Review Press, 1985).

40. "Come Darling," Migliaccio Collection, box 8, IHRC.

41. "Mi no spicco guddo inglisce," Migliaccio Collection, box 6, IHRC.

42. For nuanced descriptions of the complex balance in the lives of Italian immigrant women between power and subservience, see, for example, Robert A. Orsi, *The Madonna of 115th Street: Faith and Community in Italian Harlem, 1880–1950* (New Haven, Conn.: Yale University Press, 1985); Virginia Yans-McLaughlin, "A Flexible Tradition: Southern Italian Immigrants Confront a New Work Experience," *Journal of Social History* 7, no. 4 (Summer 1974): 429–45. According to Lawrence Mintz, the depiction of men as "the victims of attractive flirts who control, torment or disorient them" in ethnic stage humor was common. See Mintz, "Humor and Ethnic Stereotypes," 21.

43. There is a psychoanalytic interpretation to consider here as well. Ralph R. Greenson has discussed attachment to the mother tongue in terms of attachment to the mother; "words may be experienced as milk; thus, the child's relation to the mother's breast is a decisive influence on his future relation to the mother tongue." Learning a new language then can be perceived by the speaker as initiating a separation from the mother. This idea may have particular relevance for Italian immigrants given the strong symbolic position that the mother occupies in Italian culture. Leon Grinberg and Rebecca Grinberg, *Psychoanalytic Perspectives on Migration and Exile* (New Haven, Conn.: Yale University Press, 1989), 105–6.

44. "Mary," Migliaccio Collection, box 4, IHRC.

45. "A Lengua d' 'a Dummeneca," Migliaccio Collection, box 8, IHRC.

46. The line is a reference to the phrase *risciaquare i panni in Arno* (to rinse one's

clothes in the Arno), which is derived from Manzoni's novel. I am indebted to Alessandro Adorno on this point.

47. "Pasquale Catena," Migliaccio Collection, box 3, IHRC. This type of character also appears in a satire dedicated to Migliaccio. See Pasquale Seneca, *Il Presidente Scopetta* (Philadelphia: Artcraft Printing Co., 1927).

48. There is evidence that Italian immigrant women have been more likely to retain the dialect, the language of the home and family. See Hermann W. Haller, *Una lingua perduta e ritrovata: L'italiano degli italo-americani* (Firenze: La Nuova Italia, 1993), 29; Haller, "Between Standard Italian and Creole: An Interim Report on Language Patterns in an Italian-American Community," *Word* 32, no. 3 (December 1981): 187.

49. "O Cafone c' 'a Sciammeri a," Migliaccio Collection, box 2, IHRC. "Sciammeri" is a reference to an overcoat made of a lightweight material worn by peasants who could not afford any better. It also has the sexual connotation of "a quickie." For a translation of the entire song, see "'Farfariello' Sings About Courting and Marriage in America, 1910," translated by Nancy Carnevale and Maria Galletta, in *Major Problems in the History of American Sexuality*, ed. Kathy Peiss (Boston: Houghton Mifflin Company, 2002), 281–82.

50. "Ammore All'americana," Migliaccio Collection, box 5, IHRC.

51. "Picchetto d'Amore," Migliaccio Collection, box 2, IHRC.

52. "Pasquale Catena," Migliaccio Collection, box 3, IHRC. This piece also goes by the title "L'Italiano al 100%," Migliaccio Collection, box 3, IHRC.

53. "Mastantonio," Migliaccio Collection, box 4, IHRC.

54. "O Sunatore 'e Flauto," Migliaccio Collection, box 5, IHRC.

55. "Il Discorso Del Presidente Cornacchia alla Seduta Della Societa," Migliaccio Collection, box 11, IHRC.

56. This discussion relies on John Lowe, "Theories of Ethnic Humor: How to Enter, Laughing," *American Quarterly* 38, no. 3 (1986): 439–60. See also Joseph Boskin and Joseph Dorinson, "Ethnic Humor: Subversion and Survival," in *American Humor*, special issue, *American Quarterly* 37, no. 1 (Spring 1985): 81–97; Holger Kersten, "Using the Immigrant's Voice: Humor and Pathos in Nineteenth Century 'Dutch' Dialect Texts," *Melus* 21 (Winter 1996): 3–17. For the concept of ethnic boundaries, see Fredrik Barth, ed., *Ethnic Groups and Boundaries: The Social Organization of Culture Difference* (Bergen-Oslo, Norway: Universitets Forlaget, 1969).

57. Lowe, "Theories of Ethnic Humor," 448.

58. Hidden transcripts refer to the ways subordinated peoples communicate with each other outside of the accepted speech forms of the dominant society. See James C. Scott, *Domination and the Arts of Resistance: Hidden Transcripts* (New Haven, Conn.: Yale University Press, 1990). In his study of Jewish song in America, Mark Slobin notes that "ethnic caricature" carries quite different meanings when written and performed by an insider for an "in-group audience." More palatable, "softened self-caricature" replaces "stiff stereotypes" and stock characters. Mark Slobin, *Tenement Songs: The Popular Music of the Jewish Immigrants* (Urbana: University of Illinois Press, 1982), 60–61.

59. "The P & R Variety Show," Migliaccio Collection, box 10, IHRC.

60. "Pastafazoola," by Eddie Clark, Frank Sabini, Gus Van, and Joe Schenck, Migliaccio Collection, box 3, IHRC.

61. Esther Romeyn makes similar observations on the transformation Migliaccio and his work undergo in the move from theater to radio. Romeyn, "Farfariello."

62. On the assimilative function of ethnic theater, see McClean, *American Vaudeville;* Sellers, *Ethnic Theatre in the United States;* Kaufman, *Yiddish Theater.* On the homogenizing affect of popular culture, see, for example, Peiss, *Cheap Amusements.*

63. Bertellini, *Southern Crossings,* xiii.

64. Ibid., 533.

65. Ibid., 525–46. Drawing largely on the anthropological literature on performance, Esther Romeyn sees Farfariello as a clown figure and "comic double" of immigrants who, through exaggeration, allowed the immigrants to reflect on their new in-between identities while helping them to make the transformation from one identity to another: from the world they knew to the upside down world of America. He achieved this by educating his audiences in the new moral codes of their adopted home and, more importantly, by serving as a cultural mediator in his role as a clown. Although she notes Farfariello's use of the mixed language of the immigrants and how he helped to legitimize an Italian American idiom, she does not situate Farfariello's language humor within its southern Italian context and thus misses the importance of the complicated relationship southern Italian immigrants had with language both in Italy and in America. Romeyn, "Farfariello;" Romeyn, "Juggling Italian-American Identities: Farfariello, King of the Character Clowns," *Italian American Review* 9, no. 2 (Fall/Winter 2002): 95–128. My critique of Romeyn is subsumed within Bertellini's broader contention that Romeyn fails to engage with the "southernist character of the *macchiette*" (Bertellini, 534).

Chapter Five: The Identity Politics of Language

Epigraph: Comte George de Buffon, eighteenth-century French naturalist, quoted in an advertisement to parents to enroll children in Italian language classes in New York city high schools. *Corriere d'America,* May 9, 1932.

1. Horace M. Kallen, *Culture and Democracy in the United States: Studies in the Group Psychology of the American Peoples* (New York: Boni and Liveright, 1924). Montalto argues that Covello was not a cultural pluralist, although he did believe in respecting ethnic cultures. Ultimately, he, like other ethnics in the intercultural education movement, was bent on forming one culture out of the diverse nationalities of the United States. Still, Montalto distinguishes between people like Covello in the movement and Rachel DuBois, whom he describes as a "scientific Americanizer." Nicholas V. Montalto, *A History of the Intercultural Education Movement, 1924–1941* (New York: Garland Publishing Co., 1982), 119; Montalto, "The Intercultural Education Movement, 1924–41: The Growth of Tolerance as a Form of Intolerance," *American Education and the European Immigrant: 1840–1940,* ed. Bernard J. Weiss (Urbana: University of Illinois Press, 1982).

2. Covello's interest in creating a unified, but ultimately fictitious Italian American culture through food, is discussed in Simone Cinotto's "Leonard Covello, the Covello Papers and the History of Eating Habits among Italian immigrants in New York," *Journal of American History* 91, no. 2 (September 2004): 497–521.

3. Matteo Pretelli, "Culture or Propaganda? Fascism and Italian Culture in the United States," *Studi Emigrazione/Migration Studies* 43, no. 161 (2006): 171. In a related strategy, Mussolini attempted to influence electoral outcomes in the United States beginning in the early 1930s by pressing Italian immigrants to become naturalized and thus gain the vote. Pretelli, "Culture or Propaganda?" 171–72; Stefano Luconi, *La "Diplomazia Parallela:" Il regime fascista e la mobilitazione politica degli italo-americani* (Milan, Italy: Agnelli, 2000).

4. See, for example, David A. Gerber, "Language Maintenance, Ethnic Group Formation, and Public Schools: Changing Patterns of German Concern, Buffalo, 1837–1874," *Ethnicity, Ethnic Identity, and Language Maintenance*, ed. George E. Pozzetta, American Immigration and Ethnicity 16 (New York: Garland Publishing, Inc., 1991).

5. For the history of the Italian language in the public schools, see Joseph G. Fucilla, *The Teaching of Italian in the United States: A Documentary History* (New Brunswick, N.J.: American Association of Teachers of Italian, 1967). See also Covello, "The Teaching of the Italian Language in the United States;" Leonard Covello Papers, The Balch Institute Collections, Historical Society of Pennsylvania (hereafter, Covello Papers), box 97, folder 1; "Why Study Italian?" Covello Papers, box 98, folder 6; untitled history of the Italian language study in the United States, n.d., box 97, folder 1.

6. Fucilla, *Teaching of Italian*, 263; Leonard Covello, "The Teaching of the Italian Language in the United States: A Glance Backward and a Look Forward, " Covello Papers, box 23, folder 12. Fucilla notes fifty-five schools that taught Italian in 1938 but Covello cites forty-six. Covello offers slightly different figures in the text of a speech. He notes that in New York City in 1939, Italian was offered in a total of forty-three junior high, senior high, and evening high schools. He puts total enrollment in 1939 at 16,572. See his "The Growth of Italian Language as a Cultural Subject in the Public Schools of New York City," Speech to American Association of Teachers of Italian, Massachusetts Division, 9 December 1939, Covello Papers, box 13, folder 7. Regarding 1922 enrollments, Fucilla gives 898 as a figure but Covello notes 1,140. A chart among Covello's papers offers still other figures, including a 1922 enrollment of only 399. See "Enrollment in Italian in New York City and San Francisco High Schools, 1924–1930," Covello Papers, box 97, folder 25.

7. For a 1932 French enrollment figure of 104,091, see Giuseppe Prezzolini, "Per lo studio dell'Italiano negli Stati Uniti d'America," Covello Papers, box 97, folder 10. For lower enrollment numbers for the study of French (72,033), see Dr. Alberto C. Bonaschi, "The Teaching of Italian in the Senior High Schools," Covello Papers, box 97, folder 2.

8. Leonard Covello, "The Role of Foreign Languages in American Citizenship Training," Covello Papers, box 97, folder 15.

9. "Italo-American Educational Society," 1935, Covello Papers, box 89, folder

16; Leonard Covello, "Language as a Factor in Social Adjustment," manuscript of chapter from *Our Racial and National Minorities*, ed. Francis James Brown and Joseph Slabey Roucek (Upper Saddle River, N.J.: Prentice-Hall, Inc., 1937), 18, Covello Papers, box 21, folder 19.

10. Covello, "The Growth of Italian Language as a Cultural Subject," 8.

11. Philip V. Cannistraro, "Fascism and Italian Americans," in *Perspectives in Italian Immigration and Ethnicity*, ed. Silvano M. Tomasi (New York: Center for Migration Studies, 1977), 51–66; Vincent Lombardi, "Italian American Workers and the Response to Fascism," in *Pane e Lavoro: The Italian American Working Class*, ed. George E. Pozzetta (Toronto: Multicultural History Society of Ontario, 1980), 141–57; John P. Diggins, *Mussolini and Fascism: The View from America* (Princeton, N.J.: Princeton University Press, 1972); Stefano Luconi, *From Paesani to White Ethnics: The Italian Experience in Philadelphia* (Albany: State University of New York Press, 2001), chap. 5; Gloria Ricci Lothrop, "A Shadow on the Land: The Impact of Fascism on Los Angeles Italians," *California History* 74, no. 4 (Winter 1996/1997): 338–53; Constantine Panunzio, "Italian Americans, Fascism, and the War," *Yale Review* 31, no. 4 (Summer 1942): 771; Pretelli, "Culture or Propaganda?" 174; Rudolph J. Vecoli, "The Making and Un-Making of the Italian American Working Class," in *The Lost World of Italian American Radicalism: Politics, Labor, and Culture*, ed. Philip Cannistraro and Gerald Meyer (Westport, Conn.: Praeger, 2003), 53; John Morton Blum, *V Was for Victory: Politics and American Culture During World War II* (New York: Harcourt Brace Jovanovich, 1977), 149–51.

12. "Italian-American Publications Defend Their Earlier Faith in Fascism," 27 July 1945, Security-Classified Intelligence Reference Publications ("P" file), 1940–1945, Office of Strategic Services, Foreign Nationalities Branch News Notes, No. N-415, RG 165, NA.

13. Stanislao Pugliese, "The Culture of Nostalgia: Fascism in the Memory of Italian America," *Italian American Review* 5, no. 2 (Autumn/Winter 1996/1997): 14–26.

14. Carol Lynn McKibben, *Beyond Cannery Row: Sicilian Women, Immigration, and Community in Monterey, California 1915–99* (Urbana: University of Illinois Press, 2006), 77.

15. Pretelli, "Culture or Propaganda?" 174; Vecoli, "Making and Un-Making," 53–54; Philip Cannistraro, *Blackshirts in Little Italy: Italian Americans and Fascism 1921–1929* (West Lafayette, Ind.: Bordighera, 1999), 102–9.

16. Diggins, *Mussolini and Fascism*, 255–57; Gaetano Salvemini, *Italian Fascist Activities in the United States*, ed. Philip V. Cannistraro (New York: Jerome S. Ozer Publishers, 1977), chap. 1; Vecoli, "Making and Un-Making," 54; Cannistraro, *Blackshirts in Little Italy*, 18–20.

17. Committee on Education of the Order Sons of Italy, letter to Dr. Clarence E. Meleney, n.d., Covello Papers, box 97, folder 3.

18. "The Italian Language," n.d., Covello Papers, box 82, folder 13 (the folder is labeled "Casa Italiana Educational Bureau Italian Language Campaign Report 1933").

19. Covello is cited three times by Salvemini for involvement with Fascists between 1922 and 1934. He also notes in an aside that Covello was decorated by

Mussolini sometime in the early 1930s. Salvemini, *Italian Fascist Activities*, 130, 175–76, 203.

20. Leonard Covello, *The Heart Is the Teacher* (New York: McGraw-Hill Book Company, Inc, 1958), 3–4, 19.

21. Ibid., 5.

22. Ibid., 20–21.

23. Ibid., 25–27.

24. Ibid., 32, 43.

25. Ibid., 57, 68.

26. Ibid., 68–70.

27. Ibid., 76.

28. Ibid.

29. Ibid., 77.

30. Ibid., 107.

31. Ibid., 121–29. Covello later received a PhD in sociology from New York University. His dissertation was the basis for a landmark work on Italian Americans, *The Social Background of the Italo-American School Child: A Study of the Southern Italian Family Mores and Their Effect on the School Situation in Italy and America*, ed. Francesco Cordasco (Totowa, N.J.: Rowman and Littlefield, 1972).

32. Leonard Covello, "Language Usage in Italian Families," Covello Papers, box 20, folder 30, p. 4.

33. Ibid.

34. Ibid., 4–5.

35. Ibid., 7.

36. Ibid.

37. Montalto, "Intercultural Education Movement." The quote is the subtitle of his article.

38. Montalto notes that most of the exceptions to the intolerant form of intercultural education came from educators who, like Covello, were members of ethnic minorities. Montalto, "Intercultural Education Movement," 143. Paula Fass takes a more critical view of intercultural education, calling the "open-door school policy" advocated by Covello and others that sought to incorporate the community "ambiguous," at once "an expression of democratic aspiration and an intrusion upon the community it was meant to serve." Paula Fass, *Outside In: Minorities and the Transformation of American Education* (New York: Oxford University Press, 1989), 58.

39. On Covello's tenure at Benjamin Franklin, see Michael Johanek and John Puckett, *Leonard Covello and the Making of Benjamin Franklin High School* (Philadelphia: Temple University Press, 2007); T. J. Fontera, "Leonard Covello's Community Centered School: Italian-American Students at the Benjamin Franklin High School in East Harlem, New York, 1934–1944," (PhD diss., Harvard University, 1993); Gerald Meyer, "Leonard Covello (1887–1982): An Italian American's Contribution to the Education of Minority-Culture Students," *Italian American Review* 5, no. 1 (Fall 1996): 36–44; Meyer, "Leonard Covello: A Pioneer in Bilingual Education," *Bilingual Review 12*, nos. 1 and 2 (January-August 1985): 55–61.

40. Alberto C. Bonaschi, "The Teaching of Italian in the Senior High Schools,"

30 March 1936, Covello Papers, box 97, folder 2; Alberto C. Bonaschi, "Teaching Language as a Means of Social Adjustment," 27 June 1938, Covello Papers, box 97, folder 2.

41. Alberto C. Bonaschi, "The Racial Basis of Language Choice," 7 February 1936, Covello Papers, box 97, folder 2.

42. Tommasso Russo, "La lingua e la letteratura dell'Italia nel Massimo Tempio di cultura Americano," *Bolletina della Sera*, 29 February 1932, Thomas Russo Clippings, Collection #007, Center for Migration Studies, Staten Island (hereafter, TRC). All translations from the Italian are mine.

43. Tommasso Russo, "Vogliamo affermare vittoriosamente lo studio della lingua Italiana nelle scuole Americane?" *Bolletino della Sera*, 13 June 1932, TRC.

44. Tomasso Russo, "Cifre e fatti eloquenti sullo studio della lingua Italiana neglie Stati Uniti," *Bolletino della Sera*, 18 January 1932, TRC.

45. Russo, "Cifre e fatti eloquenti."

46. Ibid.

47. See the following articles by Tomasso Russo in the *Bolletino della Sera*, TRC: "La lingua e la letteratura dell'Italia nel Massimo Tempio di cultura Americano," 29 February 1932; "La lingua e la letteratura Italiana sono in Auge nell'Antica Universita del Wisconsin," 9 May 1932; "La South Philadelphia High School for Boys, e' Orgogliosa della sua sezione d'Italiano," 23 May 1932; "La New York University vanta una sezione molto importante per lo studio dell'Italiano," 31 May 1932; "Vogliamo affermare vittoriosamente," 13 June 1932.

48. Giuseppe Prezzolini, "Per lo studio dell'Italiano negli Stati Uniti d'America," *Il Progresso Italo-Americano*, 11 August 1932, Covello Papers, box 97, folder 10.

49. Mary E. Todaro, "Why Study Italian," Covello Papers, box 98, folder 7; Tomasso Russo, "La Brown University vanta un nuovo centro di studio per l'Italiano che promete molto," *Bolletina della Sera*, 2 May 1932, TRC; Leonard Covello, letter, "Ai genitori dei ragazzi del 7B della Edward P. Shallow Junior High School," Covello Papers, box 97, folder 21; "La lingua Italiana nelle high schools," Covello Papers, box 97, folder 1; Prezzolini, "Per lo studio dell'Italiano negli Stati Uniti d'America;" Aurelio Sofia, "La lingua Italiana nelle high schools. Ai genitori Italiani," Covello Papers, box 97, folder 21; "Alle societa di New York per lo studio dell'Italiano," *Il Progresso Italo-Americano*, 19 September 1933, Covello Papers, box 97, folder 21. For similar appeals by Italian elites in other American cities on the subject of Italian language instruction, see John W. Briggs, *An Italian Passage: Immigrants to Three American Cities, 1890–1930* (New Haven, Conn.: Yale University Press, 1978), 129–33.

50. Leone Piatelli, "Un appello ai genitori di origine italiana," Covello Papers, box 97, folder 21.

51. "Ascoltatori Carissimi," Covello Papers, box 8, folder 12.

52. Covello, "The Growth of Italian Language," 18.

53. Ibid.

54. Pretelli, "Culture or Propaganda?" 180; Peter D'Agostino, *Rome in America: Transnational Catholic Ideology from the Risorgimento to Fascism* (Chapel Hill: University of North Carolina Press, 2004): 158–93; 251–57; D'Agostino, "The Scalabrini

Fathers, the Italian Emigrant Church, and Ethnic Nationalism in America," *Religion and American Culture* 7, no. 1 (Winter 1997): 121–59; Vecoli, "Making and Un-Making," 54.

55. Salvemini, *Italian Fascist Activities*, 107–18.

56. Pretelli, "Culture or Propaganda?," 182.

57. Ibid., 179.

58. D'Agostino, "Scalabrini Fathers," 143–44.

59. Ibid.; Pretelli, "Culture or Propaganda?" 181, 183. For more on the Fascist-sponsored Italian language classes in the United States, see Dino Cinel, *From Italy to San Francisco: The Immigrant Experience* (Stanford, Calif.: Stanford University Press, 1982), 252–54; Lothrop, "A Shadow on the Land," 338–53; Diggins, *Mussolini and Fascism*, 80, 99–100.

60. Diplomatico del Ministero degli Esteri, Archvio Scuole, Relazioni Culturali, 1936–1945, box 120, folder "New York." I am indebted to Matteo Pretelli for this information.

61. Diggins, *Mussolini and Fascism*, 80.

62. On American schools as instruments of assimilation, see, for example, Stephan F. Brumberg, *Going to America Going to School: The Jewish Immigrant Public School Encounter in Turn-of-the-Century New York City* (New York: Praeger Publishers, 1986); Fass, *Outside In*. For Italian immigrants' suspicion of American schools, see Selma C. Berrol, "School Days on the Old East Side: The Italian and Jewish Experience," in *Education and the Immigrant*, ed. George E. Pozzetta (New York: Garland Publishing, Inc., 1991) 27–40; Salvatore J. LaGumina, "American Education and the Italian Immigrant Response," in Weiss, ed., *American Education and the European Immigrant*, 61–77; Covello, "The Growth of the Italian Language."

63. Russo, "La lingua e la letteratura Italiana."

64. Beatrice J. Crisonino, "Perche studiare l'Italiano?" Covello Papers, box 98, folder 7.

65. Tomasso Russo, "La Seward Park High School altro germoglio pieno di promesse per lo studio dell'Italiano," *Bolletino della Sera*, 16 May 1932, TRC.

66. Giuseppe Prezzolini, "The Language of the 'Giobba,'" Covello Papers, box 30, folder 12.

67. Franco Ciarlantini, "The Italian Language in the United States," *Atlantica*, March 1930, Covello Papers, box 97, folder 10.

68. Franco Lalli, "La lingua Italo-Americana 'la prima santa di America," Covello Papers, box 97, folder 1.

69. Alberto C. Bonaschi, "The Teaching of Italian in the Senior High Schools," 30 March 1936, Covello Papers, box 97, folder 2; Wesley R. Burnham, principal of Harlem High School, letter to Leonard Covello, 28 January 1937, Covello Papers, box 97, folder 2. Jonathan Zimmerman makes a similar point. Other European ethnics were also funneled into "'industrial' or 'commercial' tracks," thus precluding them from foreign language instruction. See Jonathan Zimmerman, "Ethnics Against Ethnicity: European Immigrants and Foreign-Language Instruction, 1890–1940," *Journal of American History* 88 (March 2002): 1402.

70. Gabriel R. Mason, principal of Abraham Lincoln High, letter to Leonard Covello, 21 April 1936, Covello Papers, box 97, folder 2; Zimmerman, "Ethnics Against Ethnicity," 1402.

71. Riccardo Russo, letter to Generoso Pope, 9 October 1935, Covello Papers, box 97, folder 2. See also the letter from Nicola Trombetta to Pope, 16 September 1935, Covello Papers, box 97, folder 2.

72. Alberto C. Bonaschi, "The Racial Basis of Language Choice," 7 February 1936, Covello Papers, box 97, folder 2.

73. Alberto C. Bonaschi, "The Teaching of Italian in the Senior High Schools," 30 March 1936, Covello Papers, box 97, folder 2.

74. Zimmerman makes this point for European ethnics in general. See "Ethnics Against Ethnicity," 1402.

75. Nino Landrini, letter to Alberto Bonaschi, n.d., Covello Papers, box 97, folder 2; Letter from unidentified student to Alberto Bonaschi, 15 November 1937, Covello Papers, box 97, folder 2.

76. This is suggested by the number of high school teachers who were women that Russo met with as part of his series of articles. See "La sagra d'Italianita' alla Washington I.H.S. e'stata una manifestazione senza precedenzza," 5 July 1932, TRC.

77. Bonaschi, "The Teaching of Italian in the Senior High Schools."

78. Zimmerman, "Ethnics Against Ethnicity."

79. Vecoli, "Making and Un-Making," 54.

80. Covello, *Heart Is the Teacher*, 136.

Chapter Six: Language, Italian American Identity, and the Limits of Cultural Pluralism in the World War II Years

This chapter is a revision of an earlier article: Nancy C. Carnevale, "'No Italian Spoken for the Duration of the War,' Language, Italian-American Identity, and Cultural Pluralism in the World War II Years," *Journal of American Ethnic History* 22, no. 3 (Spring 2003): 3–33.

1. Garry Boulard, *"Just a Gigolo": The Life and Times of Louis Prima* (Lafayette: Center for Louisiana Studies, University of Southwestern Louisiana, 1989), 72.

2. Gary Gerstle, "Interpreting the 'American Way': The Working Class Goes to War," in *The War in American Culture*, ed. Lewis A. Erenberg and Susan E. Hirsch (Chicago: University of Chicago Press, 1996), 114; John M. Blum, *V Was for Victory: Politics and American Culture During World War II* (New York: Harcourt Brace Jovanovich, 1976), 147–81. On ethnics achieving whiteness in the World War II era, see, for example, Gary Gerstle, *American Crucible: Race and Nation in the Twentieth Century* (Princeton, N.J.: Princeton University Press, 2001), chap. 5; Matthew Frye Jacobson, *Whiteness of a Different Color: European Immigrants and the Alchemy of Race* (Cambridge, Mass.: Harvard University Press, 1998), 95, 98–99, 110.

3. For the changes the concept undergoes during the war years, see, for example, Gerstle's *Working-Class Americanism: The Politics of Labor in a Textile City, 1914–1960*

(Cambridge: Cambridge University Press, 1989), 293–95; Philip Gleason, *Speaking of Diversity: Language and Ethnicity in Twentieth Century America* (Baltimore, Md.: Johns Hopkins University Press, 1992), chap. 6; Richard W. Steele, "The War on Intolerance: The Reformulation of American Nationalism, 1939–1941," *Journal of American Ethnic History* 9 (Fall 1989): 9–35.

4. "Il sindaco La Guardia ha proclamato il 17 Maggio 'I am an American Day," *Il Progresso Italo-Americano*, 11 April 1942. Gary R. Mormino and George E. Pozzetta, "Ethnics at War: Italian Americans in California During World War II," in *The Way We Really Were: The Golden State in the Second Great War*, ed. Roger W. Lotchin (Urbana: University of Illinois Press, 2000), 151–52.

5. Reed Ueda, "The Changing Path to Citizenship: Ethnicity and Naturalization During World War II," in *The War in American Culture*, ed. Lewis A. Erenberg and Susan E. Hirsch (Chicago: University of Chicago Press, 1996), 203; Carol Lynn McKibben, *Beyond Cannery Row: Sicilian Women, Immigration, and Community in Monterey, California 1915-99* (Urbana: University of Illinois Press, 2006), 80–85. Gerstle interprets the increase in naturalization rates as evidence of "Euro-American workers' deepening connection to America." Gerstle, "Interpreting the 'American Way,'" 114–15.

6. Werner Sollors, *Beyond Ethnicity: Consent and Descent in American Culture* (New York: Oxford University Press, 1986); Mary C. Waters, *Ethnic Options: Choosing Identities in America* (Berkeley: University of California Press, 1990). For a critical discussion of this approach that also emphasizes the constraints to forming an American ethnic identity, see Gary Gerstle, "Liberty, Coercion, and the Making of Americans," *Journal of American History* 84, no. 2 (September 1997): 524–58. See also Kathleen Neils Conzen, David A. Gerber, Ewa Morawska, George E. Pozzetta, and Rudolph J. Vecoli, "The Invention of Ethnicity: A Perspective From the U.S.A.," *Journal of American Ethnic History* 12, no. 1 (Fall 1992): 1–38.

7. Lawrence Di Stasi, ed., *Una Storia Segreta: The Secret History of Italian American Evacuation and Internment During World War II* (Berkeley, Calif.: Heyday Books, 2001), 307.

8. Stephen Fox, *The Unknown Internment: An Oral History of the Relocation of Italian Americans during World War II* (Boston: Twayne Publishers, 1990), 184–85; Gloria Ricci Lothrop, "The Untold Story: The Effect of the Second World War on California Italians," *Journal of the West* 35, no. 1 (1996): 9; Lothrop, "Unwelcome in Freedom's Land: The Impact of World War II on Italian Aliens in Southern California," in Di Stasi, ed., *Una Storia Segreta*; Mormino and Pozzetta, "Ethnics at War," 144. For further discussion of the difficulties the war years created for Italian Americans, see Lawrence Di Stasi, "How World War II Iced Italian American Culture," in *MultiAmerica: Essays on Cultural Wars and Cultural Peace*, ed. Ishmael Reed (New York: Viking Press, 1997), 169–78; Stefano Luconi, *From Paesani to White Ethnics: The Italian Experience in Philadelphia* (Albany, N.Y.: State University of New York Press, 2001), chap. 5. I am indebted to Lawrence Di Stasi for helping me to refine my discussion in this paragraph.

9. Notice to Aliens of Enemy Nationalities, INS Central Office, E. Johnson 1940–1943, Forms used for Registering Aliens, (RG 85, NA II, Washington, D.C.

10. United States Department of Justice, *Regulations Controlling Travel and Other Conduct of Aliens of Enemy Nationalities* (Washington, D.C.: Government Printing Office, 1942).

11. On Japanese internment, see, for example, Ronald Takaki, *Double Victory: A Multicultural History of America in World War II* (Boston: Little, Brown and Company, 2000), 144–64.

12. Luciano J. Iorizzo and Salvatore Mondello, *The Italian Americans* (New York: Twayne Publishers, Inc., 1971), 208. For a contemporary perspective on the devaluation of all things Italian during the war years, see Leonard Covello, "Italo-American Youth in War Crisis," 28 March 1943, Covello Papers, box 15, folder 3. See also James E. Miller, "A Question of Loyalty: American Liberals, Propaganda, and the Italian American Community, 1939–1943," *Maryland Historian* 9 (1978): 60; Ronald H. Bayor, *Neighbors in Conflict: The Irish, Germans, Jews, and Italians of New York City, 1924–1941* (Baltimore, Md.: Johns Hopkins University Press, 1978), 120; Lorthrop, *The Untold Story*, 12; Luconi, *From Paesani to White Ethnics*, 99–101; Salvatore Lagumina, *The Humble and the Heroic: Wartime Italian Americans* (Calgary, Alberta: Cambria, 2006), 111–17. For opposing views see Philip A. Bean, "Fascism and Italian American Identity, A Case Study: Utica, New York," *Journal of Ethnic Studies* 17, no. 2 (Summer 1989): 101–19; Gleason, *Speaking of Diversity*, 164.

13. The relatively prompt repeal of the enemy alien status of Italian Americans was in recognition of the need to enlist Italians both at home and abroad in the war effort as well as President Roosevelt's concern about alienating such a large portion of his base of ethnic voters. See Lothrop, *The Untold Story*, 13; Luconi, *From Paesani to White Ethnics*, 106; Madeline Goodman, "Ethnicity, Nationality and War: Italian Americans, Fascism and the Construction of Cultural Pluralism during World War II," paper presented at the Rutgers Center for Historical Analysis, New Brunswick, N.J., March 24, 1994. Pozzetta points to "more subtle reasons" for the relatively mild treatment accorded Italian Americans, including the influence of stereotypes about them. Italians may have been considered criminals and lower class, but they were not associated with "treachery, disloyalty, deviousness, or authoritarianism," all qualities that were more readily attributed to the Germans and the Japanese at the time. The national popularity of a few prominent Italian Americans, notably Joe DiMaggio, also helped diffuse more negative views of Italian Americans. George E. Pozzetta, "Alien Enemies or Loyal Americans: The Internment of Italian-Americans," in *Alien Justice: Wartime Internment in Australia and North America*, ed. Kay Saunders and Roger Daniels (Queensland, Australia: University of Queensland Press, 2000), 86.

14. Enemy Alien Minorities in Eastern Cities, 22 June 1942, p. 3. Office of Secret Service (OSS), Foreign Nationalities Branch Files (FNBF), INT 10EU-228, microfiche, NA.

15. Gay Talese, *Unto the Sons* (New York: Alfred A. Knopf, Inc., 1992), 5, 50–51.

16. Diane di Prima, *Recollections of My Life as a Woman: The New York Years* (New York: Viking Press, 2001), 20–21. The fear of encountering relatives on the battleground was not an imagined one. Some Italian American soldiers, among them my grandfather, were asked pointedly if they would be willing to shoot their

relatives if they were sent to fight in Italy. Servicemen were asked to sign waivers that would allow them to be stationed anywhere in Italy despite their misgivings. Lagumina, *Humble and the Heroic*, 239–42.

17. di Prima, *Recollections of My Life as a Woman*, 40.

18. Martin Dies, *The Trojan Horse in America* (New York: Dodd, Mead & Company, 1940), 346.

19. Panunzio, "Italian Americans, Fascism, and the War," 771.

20. Alaska, Italian Activities in, 6 November 1942, Army Intelligence Decimal File (AIDF), 1941–1948, From: 291.2 Germans To: 291.2 Italians, RG 319, NA. Italian Americans living in areas of the country where their numbers were small appear to have been subjected to greater scrutiny, including arrests, than those living in larger Italian communities that had more political and economic clout. Pozzetta, "Alien Enemies or Loyal Americans," 84.

21. General Italian Intelligence Survey in the Buffalo Field Division, 23 September 1943, Federal Bureau of Investigation (FBI) file no. 65–1338 LMC, AIDF 1941–1948, From: 291.2 Germans To: 291.2 Italians, RG 319, NA.

22. General Italian Intelligence Survey Cincinnati Field Division, FBI file no. 65–1061, AIDF 1941–1948, From: 291.2 Italians To: 291.2 Japanese, RG 319, NA.

23. General Italian Intelligence Survey in Houston Field Division, 11 August 1942, FBI file no. 65–130 LTJ, AIDF 1941–1948, From: 291.2 Italians To: 291.2 Japanese, RG 319, NA; General Italian Intelligence Survey Louisville Division, 11 May 1942, FBI file no. 65–522, AIDF 1941–1948, From: 291.2 Italians To: 291.2 Japanese, RG 319, NA; General Italian Intelligence Survey in the Little Rock Field Division, 15 May 1942, FBI, AIDF 1941–1948, From: 291.2 Italians To: 291.2 Japanese, RG 319, NA.

24. General Italian Intelligence Survey in Oklahoma City Field Division, 13 October 1942, FBI file no. 65–585, AIDF 1941–1948, From: 291.2 Italians To: 291.2 Japanese, RG 319, NA.

25. General Italian Intelligence Survey in Oklahoma City Field Division, 13 October 1942.

26. Questions and Answers on Regulations Concerning Aliens of Enemy Nationalities, Forms Used for Registering Aliens, United States Department of Justice, INS Central Office, E. Johnson 1940–1943, RG 85, NA.

27. General Italian Intelligence Survey in the San Antonio Field Division, 22 December 1942, FBI file no. 100–271, AIDF 1941–1948, From: 291.2 Germans To: 291.2 Italians, RG 319, NA.

28. General Italian Intelligence Survey in the San Antonio Field Division, 8 April 1943, FBI file no. 100–271, AIDF 1941–1948, From: 291.2 Germans To: 291.2 Italians, RG 319, NA.

29. General Italian Intelligence Survey in Oklahoma City Field Division, 13 October 1942.

30. Ibid.

31. Ibid.

32. Milton Bracker, "Italian Remains Greek to Yanks," *New York Times*, November 13, 1944.

33. "Interpreters Serve Purpose," editorial, *New York Times*, November 17, 1944.

34. The Italian Language Press in the United States, Security-Classified Intelligence Reference Publications ("P" file), 1940–1945, OSS, FNB News Notes, no. N-176–no. N-182, RG 165, NA.

35. Bayor, *Neighbors in Conflict*. 120. For more on Pope and Italian American Fascism, see Philip V. Cannistraro and Elena Aga Rossi, "La politica etnica e il dilemma dell'antifascismo Italiano negli Stati Uniti: Il caso di Generoso Pope," *Storia Contemporanea* 17, no. 2 (1986): 217–43; Stefano Luconi, "Generoso Pope and Italian American Voters in New York City," *Studi Emigrazione* 38, no. 142 (2001): 399–422.

36. Luigi Antonini, Italian American Labor Council, to Alan Cranston, Chief, Foreign Language Division, 8 April 1942, Office of Facts and Figures, Office of War Information (OWI), RG 208, NA.

37. "Historical Essay," New York Grand Lodge, Inventory, Order Sons of Italy (OSIA) Collection, IHRC.

38. Di Stasi, "How World War II Iced," 172.

39. General Italian Intelligence Survey in the Indianapolis Field Division, 29 October 1942, RG 319, NA.

40. Alan Cranston to Anthony Fiore, 6 November 1942, OWI, RG 208.

41. General Italian Intelligence Survey in Oklahoma City Field Division, 13 October 1942.

42. Ibid.

43. Gerd Horten, "Unity on the Air?: Fifth Columnists and Foreign Language Broadcasting the United States During World War II," *Ethnic Forum* 13, no. 1 (1993): 13–14; Miller, "A Question of Loyalty," 54. See also Horten's *Radio Goes to War: The Cultural Politics of Propaganda During World War II* (Berkeley: University of California Press, 2002).

44. General Italian Intelligence Survey in the Washington Field Division, 26 December 1941, FBI file no. 65–2090, AIDF 1941–1948 From: 291.2 Italians To: 291.2 Japanese, RG 319, NA.

45. Horten, "Unity on the Air?" 14–15, 24–25.

46. Bracker, "Italian Remains Greek to Yanks."

47. Horten, "Unity on the Air?" 14–18; Miller, "A Question of Loyalty," 57; Alan Cranston to Luigi Antonini, 12 March 1942, NC-138, OWI, RG 208; "Foreign Language Press Needed for Victory," *Il Progresso Italo-Americano*, 13 September 1942.

48. General Italian Intelligence Survey in Saint Louis Division, FBI, 1 July 1943, AIDF 1941–1948, From: 291.2 Italians To: 201.2 Japanese, RG 319, NA.

49. Alan Cranston to Editor of *Il Crociato*, Brooklyn, N.Y., 22 September 1942, NC-138, OWI, RG 208, NA.

50. Memorandum to Director of Strategic Services, et al., 1 July 1943, OSS FNB, RG 165.

51. See, for example, Foreign Nationality Groups in the United States, Memorandum to the Director of Strategic Services from the Foreign Nationalities Branch, see issues 18 April 1944, 27 July 1945, 29 September 1945, 24 May 1945,

OSS, FNB, RG 165. The Division of Press Intelligence performed a similar function for English language publications in the United States.

52. Lorraine M. Lees, "National Security and Ethnicity: Contrasting Views During World War II," *Diplomatic History* 11, no. 2 (1987): 113–25.

53. Speech to be delivered by Alan Cranston, Office of Facts and Figures, on Tuesday, 2 June 1942, OWI, RG 208.

54. Paolino Gerli to Alan Cranston, 18 June 1942, OWI, RG 208.

55. Max Corvo, "The OSS and the Italian Campaign," in *The Secrets War: The Office of Strategic Services in World War II*, ed. George C. Chalou (Washington, D.C.: National Archives and Records Administration, 1992), 183–84. For a detailed account of his central role in the OSS, see Max Corvo, *O.S.S. in Italy, 1943–1945* (Westport, Conn.: Praeger, 1990; New York: Enigma, 2005). Citations are to the 2005 edition.

56. Corvo, "The OSS and the Italian Campaign,"183–93; Lagumina, *Humble and the Heroic*, 165–67.

57. For a history of the Italian American OGs, see RG 226, NA, entry 99, box 45, folder 6, file 186.

58. Emilio T. Caruso, "Italian American Operational Groups of the Office of Strategic Services," *Gli Americani e la guerra di liberazione in Italia*. Atti del Convegno internazionale di Sudi Storici, Venezia, 17–18 ottobre 1994 (Presidenza del Consiglio dei Ministri, Dipartimento per l'informazione e l'editoria), 218–24.

59. Caruso, "Italian American Operational Groups," 219.

60. "Operations," 13, NA, RG 226, entry 99, box 45, folder 6, file "Caserta OG-OP-5."

61. Report of the Sardinia Operation, 26, NA, RG 226, entry 99, box 45, folder 6.

62. Conticelli Interview, 1975, p. 212, Oral Histories #7, Records of the International Ladies Garment Worker's Union (ILGWU), 5780/110, box 4, Kheel Center for Labor-Management Documentation and Archives, Martin P. Catherwood Library, Cornell University School of Industrial and Labor Relations. Lagumina notes in his book, which combines historical research with personal recollections, that he believes most were unaware of this history until well after the war. See *Humble and the Heroic*, 161–62.

63. James M. Mead, letter to Luigi Antonini, 23 April 1942, Antonini Papers, Records of the ILGWU, 5780/023, box 1, folder 6, Kheel Center.

64. There is evidence that Italian American women participated in the war effort in limited numbers through the Women's Army Corps, the Army Nurse Corps, and the United Service Organizations. The largest number probably contributed through the manufacture of military clothing. Lagumina, *Humble and the Heroic*, 74–79.

65. "Italo-American Youth in War Crisis" speech to United Nationalities Council, 28 March 1943, Covello Papers, box 15, folder 3.

66. Letter to Lido Belli, 21 September 1943, Covello Papers, box 15, folder 10.

67. Boulard, "*Just a Gigolo*," 74.

68. RKO, Boston, May 11. Louis Prima Orch., The Barretts, The Pitchmen, Jack Powers, Lily Ann Carol; Swing Parade 1946 (RKO), *Variety,* May 15, 1946.

69. Jack Zero, "For Mari-Yootch (I Walka da Pooch)," The Very Best of Louis Prima, Louis Prima, Pair Records Portraits, PDC-2-1354. The song was recorded in 1949.

70. Letter to the editor from Jack Furniss Jr., *Life Magazine*, September 10, 1945.

71. Boulard, *"Just a Gigolo,"* 72–75.

72. Gia Prima, e-mail to the author, 15 November 2007.

73. Boulard, *"Just a Gigolo,"* 34, 40.

74. Ibid., 74–75.

75. Ibid., 76–77.

76. Richard Hayes Jr., et al., letter, *Life Magazine*, September 10, 1945.

77. Boulard, *"Just a Gigolo,"* 28.

78. Gary Boulard, "Blacks, Italians, and the Making of New Orleans Jazz," *Journal of Ethnic Studies* 16, no. 1 (Spring 1988): 53–66; Boulard, *"Just a Gigolo,"* 62–63.

79. Boulard, "Blacks, Italians, and the Making of New Orleans Jazz," 61.

80. This information is based on Boulard's book and article previously cited. For more on the role of Italian Americans in the creation of jazz, see Julia Volpelletto Nakamura, "The Italian American Contribution to Jazz," *Italian Americans Celebrate Life, The Arts and Popular Culture. Selected Essays from the 22nd Annual Conference of the American Italian Historical Association* (Staten Island, N.Y.: American Italian Historical Association, 1990), 141–51. On Italians and blacks in Louisiana, see Vincenza Scarpaci, "Walking the Color Line: Italian Immigrants in Rural Louisiana, 1880–1910," in *Are Italians White? How Race is Made in America*, ed. Jennifer Guglielmo and Salvatore Salerno (New York: Routledge, 2003), 60–78; Scarpaci, "Immigrants in the New South: Italians in Louisiana's Sugar Parishes, 1880-1910," in *Studies in Italian American Social History: Essays in Honor of Leonard Covello*, ed. Francesco Cordasco (Totowa, N.J.: Rowman and Littlefield, 1975), 132–52.

81. "New Band Hit," *Life Magazine*, August 20, 1945.

82. Boulard, *"Just a Gigolo,"* 74.

83. Rosemary Clooney, with Raymond Strait, *This for Remembrance: The Autobiography of Rosemary Clooney, an Irish-American Singer* (Chicago: Playboy Press, 1977), 131.

84. Boulard, *"Just a Gigolo,"* 95.

85. Clooney, *This for Remembrance*, 141 ("Mambo Italiano" is not cited in her autobiography). In his survey of popular music in America, Charles Hamm notes the increasing popularity of humorous novelty songs in the 1950s without providing any context for understanding why. He cites "Come on-a My House" as an example. Charles Hamm, *Yesterdays: Popular Song in America* (New York: Norton, 1979), 388–89.

86. Gary R. Mormino and George E. Pozzetta, "Ethnics at War," 150–51; Richard D. Alba, *Italian Americans: Into the Twilight of Ethnicity* (Englewood Cliffs, N.J.: Prentice Hall, 1985), 77; Mormino and Pozzetta, *The Immigrant World of Ybor City: Italians and their Latin Neighbors in Tampa, 1885–1985* (Urbana: University of Illinois Press, 1987), chap. 10. In his study of Philadelphia's postwar Italian

American community, Stefano Luconi discounts the notion that suburbanization dampened ethnic identification. Luconi, *From Paesani to White Ethnics*, 139.

87. Joshua Fishman, V. Nahifny, J. Hoffman, and R. Hayden, *Language Loyalty in the United States* (The Hague: Mouton, 1966); Alejandro Portes and Rubén G. Rumbaut, *Immigrant America: A Portrait*, 3rd ed. (Berkeley: University of California Press, 2006), 196; Richard D. Alba, *Ethnic Identity: The Transformation of White America* (New Haven: Yale University Press, 1990), 93–101.

88. "Lo studio della lingua Italiana," *Il Progresso Italo-Americano*, April 7, 1942; Fucilla, *Teaching of Italian*, 264–65; Fucilla, "An Historical Commentary on the Italian Teachers Association," *Italian Americana* 2, no. 1 (1975): 105–6; Horten, "Unity on the Air?"; Alba, *Italian Americans*. 77.

89. The quote appears in Lagumina, *Humble and the Heroic*, 195. On Joe DiMaggio's experience as emblematic of how Italian Americans had to mute their cultural distinctiveness in the postwar era in order to enter the American mainstream, see Gerstle, *American Crucible*, 264–66.

Epilogue

1. "Anxiety in the Land of the Anti-Immigration Crusader," *New York Times*, June 24, 2007.

2. "In Language Bill, the Language Counts," editorial, *New York Times*, May 27, 2006.

3. Alejandro Portes and Rubén Rumbaut, *Immigrant America: A Portrait*, 3rd ed. (Berkeley: University of California Press, 2006), 241.

4. Roseann Duenas González with Ildiko Melis, eds., *Language Ideologies: Critical Perspectives on the Official English Movement*, vol. 1 (Mahwah, N.J.: Lawrence Erlbaum Associates, Inc.; Urbana, Ill.: National Council of Teachers of English, 2001), xxviii.

5. "Children of Hispanic Immigrants Continue to Favor English, Study of Census Finds," *New York Times*, December 8, 2004; "Latino Immigrants' Children Found Grasping English," *New York Times*, November 30, 2007.

6. Matthew Frye Jacobson, *Roots Too: White Ethnic Revival in Post-Civil Rights America* (Cambridge, Mass.: Harvard University Press, 2006).

7. "In Queens, Classes In Mandarin Are Also Lessons In Adaption," *New York Times*, May 28, 2007; "Long Scorned In Maine, French has Renaissance," *New York Times*, June 4, 2006; "In U.S. Name Count, Garcias Are Catching Up With Joneses," *New York Times*, November 17, 2007.

8. Portes and Rumbaut, *Immigrant America*, 234.

9. "Vincenzo Ancona, a Poet, Is Dead at 84," by Eric Pace, Obituary, *New York Times*, March 5, 2000. All biographical information comes from his obituary.

10. "Malidittu la lingua!" in Vincenzo Ancona, *Malidittu La Lingua/Damned Language*, ed. Anna L. Chairetakis and Joseph Sciorra (New York: Legas, 1990), 46–47.

Index

Abruzzi, region of, 99
Adams, John, 5, 45, 46
Addams, Jane, 61, 70, 210n110
African American populations, 75, 175
Alaska, 164
Alter, Stephen, 53
America! America! (Margariti), 109, 111–12
American Academy of Arts and Letters, 74
American Eugenics Society, 57
Americanization: adult education courses in English, 67, 72, 73; assimilation model of, 10, 12, 190n31; campaigns of, 16; criticism of, 69, 72–73, 211n118; immigrant knowledge of English, 51–52; Italian language maintenance programs in New York City, 136–57; process and meaning of, 66; programs for immigrant women, 67–68, 209n96; through language, 64–73, 208nn79–80; YMCA program of, 143–44. *See also* assimilation
The American Language (Mencken), 68–69
American Mercury, 115, 117
American Revolution, 45
Ancona, Vincenzo, 182–83
Antonini, Luigi, 166
Apennine Mountains, 1
Apollo Theater, 175
Argentina, Italian immigrant populations in, 14
Armstrong, Louis, 174, 175
Aryan race, 53–54, 55, 56, 58, 60, 205n36
Ascoli, Graziadio Isaia, 24
assimilation: classic model of, 10, 190n31; defining, 10, 190n31; effects on languages, 3; immigrant generational language changes, 10–11; role of American schools in, 152–53, 227n62; through language, 64–73, 208n79;

totalizing narrative, 17, 193n51. *See also* Americanization
Astaire, Fred, 26
Atlantica Magazine, 145
Avigliano, 141, 142

Bakhtin, Mikhail, 189n24, 219n21
Barth, Frederik, 132
Bembo, Pietro, 23
Benedict, Ruth, 57
Benjamin Franklin High School, 136, 147
Bennett Law, 48
Bernagozzi, William, 90
Bertellini, Giorgio, 134–35
bilingualism, 5, 9
Boas, Franz, 57, 58–59
Boccaccio, 23
Boelhower, William, 99, 105, 109, 111–12
Bogardus, Emory S., 70
Bollettino della Sera, 40, 148, 154
Bonano, Sharkey, 175
Bonaparte, Napoleon, 28
Bonaschi, Alberto, 147, 148, 155
Bonfiglio, Thomas Paul, 74
Bossi, Umberto, 30
Bourdieu, Pierre, 8
Brinton, Daniel G., 59
Bruni, Francesco, 34
Burgess, Walton, 47
Burnett, John, 63

Calabria, 29, 31, 36, 111
Calandra, Biaggio, trial of, 94–95
California, Italian immigrant populations, 36, 37
calques, 37, 199n61
Campagnia, region of, 32, 109
Casa Italiana Educational Bureau, 137, 141, 145, 149

NANCY C. CARNEVALE is an assistant professor of history at Montclair State University in New Jersey.

Statue of Liberty–Ellis Island Centennial Series

The Immigrant World of Ybor City: Italians and Their Latin Neighbors
   in Tampa, 1885–1985   *Gary R. Mormino and George E. Pozzetta*
The Butte Irish: Class and Ethnicity in an American Mining Town, 1875–1925
   David M. Emmons
The Making of an American Pluralism: Buffalo, New York, 1825–60
   David A. Gerber
Germans in the New World: Essays in the History of Immigration
   Frederick C. Luebke
A Century of European Migrations, 1830–1930   *Edited by Rudolph J. Vecoli and*
   Suzanne M. Sinke
The Persistence of Ethnicity: Dutch Calvinist Pioneers in Amsterdam,
   Montana   *Rob Kroes*
Family, Church, and Market: A Mennonite Community in the Old and the
   New Worlds, 1850–1930   *Royden K. Loewen*
Between Race and Ethnicity: Cape Verdean American Immigrants, 1860–1965
   Marilyn Halter
Les Icariens: The Utopian Dream in Europe and America   *Robert P. Sutton*
Labor and Community: Mexican Citrus Worker Villages in a Southern
   California County, 1900–1950   *Gilbert G. González*
Contented among Strangers: Rural German-Speaking Women and Their
   Families in the Nineteenth-Century Midwest   *Linda Schelbitzki Pickle*
Dutch Farmer in the Missouri Valley: The Life and Letters of Ulbe Eringa,
   1866–1950   *Brian W. Beltman*
Good-bye, Piccadilly: British War Brides in America   *Jenel Virden*
For Faith and Fortune: The Education of Catholic Immigrants in Detroit,
   1805–1925   *JoEllen McNergney Vinyard*
Britain to America: Mid-Nineteenth-Century Immigrants to the United States
   William E. Van Vugt
Immigrant Minds, American Identities: Making the United States Home,
   1870–1930   *Orm Øverland*
Italian Workers of the World: Labor Migration and the Formation of
   Multiethnic States   *Edited by Donna R. Gabaccia and Fraser M. Ottanelli*
Dutch Immigrant Women in the United States, 1880–1920   *Suzanne M. Sinke*
Beyond Cannery Row: Sicilian Women, Immigration, and Community in
   Monterey, California, 1915–99   *Carol Lynn McKibben*
Merchants, Midwives, and Laboring Women: Italian Migrants in Urban
   America   *Diane C. Vecchio*
American Dreaming, Global Realities: Rethinking U.S. Immigration History
   Edited by Donna R. Gabaccia and Vicki L. Ruiz

The University of Illinois Press
is a founding member of the
Association of American University Presses.

—————————————————————————

Composed in 9/13 ITC Stone Serif
with ITC Stone Sans display
at the University of Illinois Press
Manufactured by Sheridan Books, Inc.

University of Illinois Press
1325 South Oak Street
Champaign, IL 61820-6903
www.press.uillinois.edu